Decade of Denial

Decade of Denial
A Snapshot of America in the 1990s

Herbert London

LEXINGTON BOOKS
Lanham • Boulder • New York • Oxford

LEXINGTON BOOKS

Published in the United States of America
by Lexington Books
4720 Boston Way, Lanham, Maryland 20706

12 Hid's Copse Road
Cumnor Hill, Oxford OX2 9JJ, England

British Library Cataloguing in Publication Information Available

Library of Congress Cataloging-in-Publication Data

London, Herbert Ira.
    Decade of denial / Herbert London.
        p. cm.
    ISBN 0-7391-0278-8 (cloth : alk. paper)—ISBN 0-7391-0279-6 (pbk.: alk. paper)
    1. Social values—United States. 2. Popular culture—United States. 3. United
States—Social conditions—1980– 4. United States—Moral conditions. 5. Nineteen
nineties. I. Title.

HN90.M6 L66 2001
306'.0973—dc21

                                                                    2001032664

Printed in the United States of America

♾™ The paper used in this publication meets the minimum requirements of American
National Standard for Information Sciences—Permanence of Paper for Printed Library
Materials, ANSI/NISO Z39.48–1992.

To the memory of my mother and my dear friend Peter Shaw.

Contents

Preface

One can just imagine young Herb London running his hands over his slicked-back hair and attempting to swivel his hips like Elvis Presley. He offers us that image of his own youth in the '50s to mark a contrast: what passed for rebellion then looks awfully innocent by today's debased standards.

In our time, we have seen not just the diminution of taste, discretion, and self-control; we've witnessed, in the form of postmodernism, the abandonment of the very idea of standards. All judgments, we are told, are illegitimate expressions of class or other biases.

Decade of Denial is not just a chronicle of what actually happened in the '90s to American society—from movies and television to the academy, to sports, and to science—it is a full-throated affirmation that judgment is necessary and good. It matters that sports figures now spit on umpires, throw temper tantrums on the field, and grab their coaches by the throat. Not only does this debase professional sports, it has trickle-down effects on the rest of society. While professional sports figures have been behaving like brutes—some even committing crimes—the conduct of adults at Little League games and other children's activities has also steadily declined, to the point where communities have been forced to make parents sign written agreements requiring sportsmanlike behavior on the sidelines before children are permitted to participate in games. In one case in Massachusetts, a parent actually assaulted and killed the referee at his son's ice hockey game.

Naturally, with parents like these, large numbers of children in American society are not being "raised," they are simply growing, like Mark Twain's Topsy. They curse their teachers, defy authority, carry weapons to school, and in the worst cases, turn schools into killing fields.

It is with more than mere nostalgia that London recalls a man of simple dignity, Joe DiMaggio. Though he dominated baseball in his time and was famously married to the most glamorous movie star of that era or perhaps any time, Marilyn Monroe, DiMaggio kept his own counsel. His movements on the field were undramatic yet smoothly effective. And he kept the secrets of his romantic life secret, giving a hint only by the roses he unfailingly sent to Monroe's gravesite for the remainder of his life.

It is a steep slide from Joe DiMaggio to Latrell Sprewell.

But London's purpose is not just to decry this precipitous slide into vulgarity, greed, and all-around slackness. London's underlying belief in the American experiment is strong and continuing. The decline of American education is bad enough in its own terms, and London provides telling examples—only 11 percent of Ivy League college students know, for example, that Thomas Jefferson wrote the Declaration of Independence—but it is particularly threatening to a nation that relies upon an informed and (dare we wish it?) virtuous citizenry to maintain its freedoms and its greatness.

It is in that spirit that this book examines the failures of the past decade. It isn't that Americans are unaware of their problems; too often it is that they've chosen the wrong solutions. Spending on schools has risen astronomically, but the money has gone to administration, counselors, and special programs more than to classroom teachers or textbooks. New York City alone has more school administrators than all of Western Europe. Nor have schools heeded the call to return to basics, continuing instead to experiment with proven failures like Whole Language and Whole Math. It need hardly be said that the result has not been excellence. American students lag behind all but the most undeveloped nations of the world in math and science. (Without a constant influx of well-educated immigrants, our vaunted high-tech economy would grind nearly to a halt.)

Nor is the "dumbing down" limited to primary and secondary education. As the chapter on the universities demonstrates, faddishness, foolishness, grade inflation, and even anti-intellectualism have taken powerful hold of many of the nation's formerly great institutions of higher learning. "If a university loses sight of its core purpose," London writes, "if faculty members retreat before the 'nonnegotiable demand' for student freedom, then the university as we have known it and on which our society depends will be an institution marginalized by its unwillingness to uphold the best that is known and written."

To which the only proper response is, "Not while Herb London is alive."

Mona Charen

Introduction

The children of affluence, although only a small portion of the baby boomer generation, rocked the foundation of social stability in the late '60s and early '70s by espousing adolescent fantasies of utopia and glibly asserting mankind's potential for sweetness and goodness. To a large extent, the cries were hollow and often hypocritical, but since these were formative years for the baby boomers, the slogans and experiences of the era became deeply etched in the generation's imagination. To a somewhat predictable degree, the '90s represented the full flowering of this utopian mind-set.

Although rarely expressed as Pelagianism (the denial of original sin and mankind's fundamental imperfections), the baby boomers' vanguard for social reform embraced perfectionism—the belief that people are inherently good but are corrupted by evil institutions. This notion brings up an obvious question that its adherents never ask: how can human institutions be so bad if people are fundamentally good? Rather than address their own obvious contradictions, the generation followed existentialists and assumed that in questioning every principle, in challenging their own middle-class status, they could be the handmaidens of a more fair and humane society than their parents had experienced. Thus was born a new search for cosmic justice, the pursuit of a chimera that has intoxicated well-meaning dreamers from the beginning of recorded history.

What separated the dreamers of the '60s and '70s from their predecessors was sanctimony, an attitude embodied most graphically in the Clintons, who expressed the rhetoric of their adolescence as a catechism and assumed self-righteously that all Americans would willingly embrace it.

Yet something went awry. Utopianism ran into the brick wall of unshakable reality, cemented by the maxims that not all people are good and that sanctimonious proclamations are not a substitute for personal virtue. In challenging every standard, the radicals upended admittedly imperfect norms but replaced them with nihilistic relativism. "Anything goes" became the calling card for a generation of malcontents.

It is ironic that the adolescents who said, "You don't know what hell is like until you've lived in Scarsdale," are the '90s Gore disciples fighting against sprawl so that their Scarsdales may remain pristine. The claim was and remains risible, but for a time a portion of the self-conscious middle class took it seriously.

The pre-'60s culture was derided as seriously flawed, "uptight," unimaginative, and wedded to middle-class morality. From the wreckage of '60s nihilism was supposed to emerge an artistic flowering. Instead, the '90s has produced excrement-laden "art" and work designed to shock a now shockproof audience. The "Sensation" exhibit at the Brooklyn Museum in 1999 was not merely shocking, as Mayor Giuliani noted; it demonstrated the virtual end of aesthetics altogether. It showed that cultural relativism had destroyed taste.

For the privileged radicals of yesteryear, there was no more significant symbol of wrongheadedness and personal despair than the bitch goddess Mammon. The children of privilege came to hate the wealth their parents had accumulated by dint of hard and diligent effort. These were third-generation Buddenbrookses who preferred playing guitars to meeting payrolls.

In the '80s, a character was invented who symbolized all they despised: Gordon Gekko, the lead figure in the film *Wall Street*, whose catchphrase was, "Greed is good." Gekko was an enemy because he embodied their view of the "prototypical" businessman who is avaricious and self-absorbed. Presumably, the radicals were natural and real, whereas Gekko was fake and a poseur.

But something happened on the Eden express to Woodstock utopia. The stops along the way were laden with unexpected tragedy. Better living through chemistry led to drug addiction and, sometimes, overdoses. Free love resulted in personal abuse and the dismantling of beneficial romantic rituals. Sweetness turned sour, and Orwellian language inversions insinuated themselves into the lives of soi-disant reformers.

Even the hated Gekko became a different person by the '90s. The children who despised Mammon became Mr. and Mrs. Dot Com, more obsessed with wealth than their parents and more lavish in their spending. Today, Mammon is king as the arrivistes buy $15 million Manhattan brownstones and outdo one another in the design of expensive homes in the Hamptons and Silicon Valley. East Hampton is a million miles from Woodstock metaphorically, but the same people populate and populated these mythic centers of the culture.

The self-indulgent children of the '60s argued in the '70s that students should make professors teach only what they wanted to learn. Astonishingly, it happened. Universities caved in to the radical onslaught. By the '90s, the ivory tower, where the free exchange of opinion was once promoted, had been transmogrified into a propaganda center for a radical orthodoxy. A parent who grew up in the '70s and was on a college tour with his teenage son said to me recently, "We got more than we bargained for." Indeed, that is true. From speech codes to ostracism, mechanisms have been put in place to quash or curtail a variety of viewpoints. "Diversity" actually means the detestation of a Euro-centered, free market, heterosexual, male-dominated culture—the very society that makes these universities possible.

Semioticians have turned the world on its head by denying the existence of truth. If rationality itself holds us in its grip like rigor mortis, there cannot be any truth except by imposition, an artifice accepted without reflection. This is what is sometimes called postmodernism. If truth doesn't exist, if it is merely an artificial construct imposed by a powerful establishment, then that establishment must be excoriated and toppled. For several decades the contemporary revolutionary has argued for power as the replacement for truth. "Our truth will replace your truth," they have said, as if objectivity could be written out of observation.

Remarkably, this too has happened. One person's opinion is now commonly said to be as good as any other. History is now thought of not as a record of the past but merely a nightmare from which we must awaken. For those who believe that the adjudication of rights determines what view of truth will be imposed, power is the only possible goal. Students at all levels of education glibly assert, "Well, you have your view, and I have mine," as if all positions are equally valid.

When so-called postmodernists visit my ninth-floor office, I always ask them to leave by way of the window. If truth doesn't exist, they should certainly be able to defy the laws of gravity. No one, of course, takes me up on this suggestion. They know, as we all know, that there are truths by which we must abide. They know as well that although truth is elusive, the search for it is the essence of academic pursuits.

In perverting the truth itself into a relative soteriology, postmodernists have assumed an edge. For them, deconstruction—taking apart the secrets behind meaning—offers authority and, perhaps more telling, power over others who may not understand the secrets of "encryption." The Rosetta stone for the postmodernist is his ability to interpret—to reveal to the uninitiated the dirty secrets behind previously accepted texts.

Ultimately, then, what counts is power: power over interpretation and power to determine what is truth. They of the innocent love-is-all generation have become the power-obsessed academic moguls of the '90s. It is hardly coincidental that a term such as *postmodern* would flourish today, given that the term is blatantly self-contradictory. How can a theory be beyond new? How much beyond can it be, and who determines that condition? Obviously those who determine, control. Antiwar activists, who condemned the "arrogance of power" during the Vietnam War and berated the government for its "imperial impulse," have arrogated to themselves the role of intellectual power brokers. Even the hated Lyndon Johnson and Robert McNamara weren't so arrogant as to do that. What a difference a couple of decades make!

Yet the turnabout isn't surprising when one considers the sanctimony that accompanies '90s' actions. Surely the routinely challenged superficiality of film and TV production in the overheated decade should have resulted in a more substantive and reflective popular culture. Instead, one is besieged by a celebrity cult—comprising a motley collection of talentless people manufactured by public relations firms.

It wasn't so long ago that civil rights activists (in the interest of full disclosure, I should note that I am firmly in that camp) deplored quotas that excluded blacks and other minority groups from university admission and job opportunities. Ironically, by the '90s, quotas have become ensconced in the misleading affirmative action movement and legislation. Rather than considered a handicap, race is now an advantage. But overlooked in this evolution is that a preoccupation with race is neither lawful nor moral. The evils of the past are merely revised for the present. In what real sense is the segregation of students by race at many American universities—employing the euphemism of "thematic dormitories"— different from the segregation in the South enforced by Bull Connor?

While American society has taken full advantage of technology's miracles to produce a period with more wealth, health, and security than it has ever known, the nation's cultural road is now paved with quicksand. The '60s generation's challenge to every verity of the past has forced even those with enormous wealth to engage in a frantic search for meaning. A theme of "fat wallets, hollow souls" overtook us in the '90s. This is not an issue that falls neatly into public-policy brackets or allows for sensible responses. When every spiritual doctrine is challenged by positivists, when manners are considered anachronistic, when respect is thought of as authoritarianism, when the society's belief structure is torn asunder like a hammer hitting plaster, culture is bereft of answers. Most important, the replacement for reasoned debate is a vacuous image on a television set with lips that move words but words that don't move people. In such a culture, government grows commensurate with national wealth, a condition never anticipated by socialists of the past, but government is powerless to do anything about what ails us. As a consequence, the manifest uneasiness that searches for a political answer finds that government is a questionable repository of solutions (the magical quick fix) or even direction.

The contemporary quest for meaning has ushered in a strange breed of new conditions. Media spokesmen have discovered lifestyles. Whatever happened to lives? Spiritual pursuit ends in cults or causes. Whatever happened to religion? The newly minted wealthy want to make a social contribution. Whatever happened to charity? Aspiring pols are eager to leave an imprint. Whatever happened to limited government?

While revolutionary zealotry has produced negative side effects in the '90s, these conditions, while easily ascertained in statistical measures and narrative insight, have been submerged by the outpouring of creative work and technological marvels. I am often asked: If the culture is so sick, how can the economy be so well?

As I see it, there is enormous malleability in American society, and the new technologies that have inspired economic success do not require communitarian sentiments but rather openness and the free expression of individual initiative. It may well be that in the short term (twenty to fifty years) a debased culture can coexist with a vibrant economic system. But as Daniel Bell and Joseph Schumpeter, among others, have noted, cultural contradictions can undermine capitalism's success.

A free society and a free market must be constrained by virtue. Without it, freedom becomes license and license invariably becomes authoritarian or totalitarian control. The challenge then is to reinstill virtue in a culture that has seemingly lost it. Media presentations are presently the enemy of virtuous goals, but it needn't always be so. Even Hollywood, debased as it is, can undergo vigorous change.

In two decades, the counterculture, composed of the adversaries of every bourgeois belief, has become the culture. Hence a new counterculture has the ability, or at least the promise, of capturing the culture again. First must come the realization of the monumental cultural shift that has occurred. We need to understand how completely the radical agenda has conquered every aspect of cultural life. Then, from the recognition of defeat, a guerrilla strategy for reclamation can be drafted.

Second, in ways that are strikingly Orwellian, the slogans, shibboleths, and mantras that once attracted armies of discontented explorers have been turned on their head. The '90s was a period of utter denial, a time when openness became stealth, diversity became homogeneity, affirmative meant negative, and honesty signified deceit. Mirabile dictu, the radicals looked in the mirror as adults and saw caricatures of their parents. Their radical view of society was far more successful than they could have ever imagined, but now they were no longer confident that it was worth all the fury.

In the pages that follow are illustrations that bolster my hypothesis. This is not a history of the '90s, nor is that decade chronologically precise. In my judgment, the cultural change of decade began with Clinton's election in 1992; where it will end is anyone's guess. As in Frederick Lewis Allen's books *Only Yesterday* and *Since Yesterday*, the accounts included in this volume are intended to provide a sense of where we are today and from where we have recently come.

If I am guilty of any infraction, it comes from an earnest effort to understand what I have experienced. Unfortunately, my experiences cannot possibly tell the national tale. I hope that even though admittedly flawed, this anecdotal, critical record will help to inform the historical one to come.

Chapter 1

Media

People often ask how, in the world of narrowband frequencies when five hundred channels can exist, all of that airtime will be filled. Are there enough productions for all the space? Are there enough program ideas under consideration?

Although these questions cannot be answered just yet, theorists considering this matter need not fret. The future has been observed, and the Decade of Denial set the tone. What will fill the airwaves is talk—Talk Television. America is talking. Everyone has an opinion, and every opinion will be expressed—on the air.

This condition boggles the imagination. But it is already here in condensed form with cable channels devoted exclusively to talk. Most of the conversation is barren, some of it pathetic. Yet audiences keep coming back for more, hoping, I would guess, for five minutes under the klieg lights.

This talk can be lethal. After a twenty-four-year-old Michigan man was embraced on *The Jenny Jones Show* by a homosexual admirer in an unexpected encounter, the former went to the man's apartment and killed him. This violence cannot be countenanced, but the episode (certainly disquieting for any heterosexual) shows that television producers do not fathom the explosive power at their disposal.

Talk shows emphasize the pathological. Normal behavior translates into low ratings. As a result, dark secrets, personal revelations, and tastelessness are laid out for all to see. Jerry Springer and Oprah Winfrey argue that their shows promote self-expression, but they really provide titillation. Imbecility is now a national pastime. Venting is good, repression bad.

I'm reminded of a meeting between Wittgenstein and Freud. The philosopher of language turned to the would-be-master of the mind and asked about psychoanalysis. Freud argued that through protracted and undirected talk, the trained psychologist can ultimately decipher the mystery of the unconscious. Wittgenstein remained unpersuaded. "Sigmund," he reportedly said, "the reason I believe you are wrong is that talk without limit or purpose is usually foolish." It seems to me that Wittgenstein was making a valid point not only about psychotherapy but about the future of television.

There was a time when ignorance was an impediment to discussion. People who knew very little were fearful of displaying just how little they knew. That is no longer the case. Now everyone is preening in front of a camera, saying, in effect, I too want to be heard. With five hundred stations, they will be heard. Amid the dissonance, to be sure, there is an occasional voice of reason. Most often, however, what one hears is bizarre, the vocal expression of the unconscious.

Talk television is driven by the god that public opinion has become, the failure of people to distinguish the worthwhile from detritus, and the desire for Americans to be famous, not for fifteen minutes but for an hour-long freak show.

The Rise of "Public Opinion"

Talk TV taps the same national impulse for expression that Ross Perot discovered when he advocated the application of television and computers to democratic decision-making. Advanced technology allows for real-time referendums on every national issue. That, in many instances, is what talk television is engaged in at this very moment. Hosts ask, "How do *you* feel about welfare?" or, "What is your opinion of homosexuals in the military?" All opinions are valid, all feelings are sought. There aren't any distinctions among opinions. As a matter of fact, hosts usually contend that all opinions are useful in illuminating an issue.

That some opinions may be more valid than others is an idea far outside the television-land sensibility. This was evident, in spades, during the impeachment saga of President Clinton. Many, if not most, politicians failed to be "a majority of one." Unlike, say, Eugene McCarthy who (rightly or wrongly) stood for principle, pols during the constitutional process were captives of pollsters who suggested what the public was likely to embrace.

Media attitudes have changed too. Instead of asking whether the leadership in the House of Representatives stood by principle, the press asked how the leadership could "defy" the will of the American people. That the chief legal officer of the country might have engaged in perjury was rationalized by editorialists who contended that the president should be allowed to complete his term whatever the infraction because, among other things, "the American people are overwhelmingly opposed to removal."

This attitude that opinion polls make right does grave damage to the rule of law and moral health of the nation. It also changes a basic precept of our democratic republic—that we elect representatives to interpret the will of the people or, as the case may be, defy the will of the people when such action is necessary. If the public's will constituted the basis for all acts, then it would be appropriate to dispense with Congress altogether and let the polls determine policy. But this idea—while consistent with democracy—is not appropriate to a republic, nor is it consistent with the view of the Founding Fathers, who were suspicious of direct democratic participation and believed deeply in the need to sustain policies without erratic swings in judgment.

There is no room for these fears of Madison and Jefferson, however, in the new five-hundred-channel universe of television. John and Mary Q. Public are instead upheld as the standard-bearers of good sense. In the race for a good sound bite, conscience and the rule of law are too often trampled.

One may disagree with the impeachment decision, but reliance on polls and television to justify that position is deceitful, inappropriate, and inconsistent with the traditions of this republic. I fear that many other constitutional decisions will turn into decisions by plebiscite.

Babbling Crudity

Talk TV calls to mind sociologist Pitirim Sorokin's argument of fifty years ago (in *Crisis of Our Age*) that the West had entered an "advanced sensate age," a period in which sensual pleasures are superordinate to other values. One can only wonder what Sorokin would say about Western culture today, a culture so degraded and so well disseminated that the average person acquiesces in his own degradation.

Talk TV has opened a Pandora's box of strange fantasies. It's hard to know if the talker experienced, wants to experience, or will experience some event. The past, present, and future all converge in television space. Audiences are shock-proof. They often don't know whether to be aghast, angry, fearful, or amused.

Do the odd characters on talk TV really exist, or are they actors rehearsing responses with a director? It is hard to imagine, yet nonetheless plausible, that freaks or freaks in training will eventually dominate the airwaves, talking themselves and the rest of America into a state of bewilderment. "Did she really mean to say something so silly?" audiences ask. Perhaps not, but live television doesn't have an eraser. Standards continue to fall.

Evidence provided by television researchers suggested that network shows became racier in the '90s to attract larger audiences. A study by the Parents' Television Council found that vulgar language on television programming had increased by 4 percent on a per-hour basis in two years. This nastiness also pervaded the plots. On the 1998 season finale of *Dharma and Greg*, for instance, the stars engaged in sexual activity in public places. This tasteless story line occurred in an alleged comedy airing at 8:30 p.m. (7:30 in the more socially conservative states in the central time zone) even though the program was obviously unsuitable viewing for any family other than the Borgias. MTV cheerfully explores the boundaries of acceptable viewing, with partial nudity and simulated scenes of fornication now the norm.

This crudity rapidly seeps out into other media and public mores. In the film *The Wedding Singer*, one of the female characters, employing crude language once reserved for sailors on furlough, tells the lead actor that if he enters her home, bedroom delights await him. That is hardly an unusual scene in films today, but what is particularly dismaying is that major newspapers described this film as "sweet and uplifting."

Riding on a public conveyance in any American city will quickly confirm that civility has been interred. Young people almost never give elderly people a seat, and people rarely cover their mouths when coughing.

The language heard on the streets is yet another symptom of degradation. Even middle-class children employ the "f" word as an adjective for any activity, whether pleasant or unpleasant. Of course, the models for this contamination of language can be found in pseudo-sophisticated adults such as those in Joe Klein's roman à clef, *Primary Colors*, and the Julia Roberts comedy *My Best Friend's Wedding*, where the continual use of obscenities is presented as a sign of toughness and sophistication.

At the 1998 Academy Awards ceremony, Ben Affleck, receiving an Oscar for the screenplay of *Good Will Hunting*, told a billion viewers, "I thought this night would either suck or be great." This from a person winning an award for best screenplay!

It was recently reported that at least 65 percent of American students cheat on exams and see nothing wrong with it. And the local news on major stations is invariably a litany of lurid murders and rapes with the most grisly details graphically elaborated. Such nightmarish scenes comprise the presleep fare for millions of Americans.

For producers of any popular cultural vehicle, there is only one test that counts: audience share. Taste always seems to take a backseat to popularity—or perhaps we had best call it notoriety—and ratings and the V-chip merely provide the cover for increasingly irresponsible programming.

Programmers know that the effect of culture is osmotic; there is no way that parents can effectively insulate their children from the vulgar and titillating nonsense that surrounds us. Popular culture has become almost uniformly vulgar, and we have slid through the trapdoor as Sorokin predicted. We are beyond outrage, beyond the sensate. Perhaps we are even beyond hope—but the seeds of cultural regeneration may reside in the muck of popular culture. The only problem is knowing where to find it and how to recognize it.

Fame and Infamy

Our search for regeneration is not made easy by all the talk-show guests who never stop talking. All their jabbering makes it impossible to think—which may be the idea in the first place. The talkers don't want to elucidate the issues; they want to become the issue. The desire for fame (and, hopefully, fortune) drives the modern talk television culture.

Some time ago—one cannot discern precisely when the balance tilted—*infamy* and *fame* had clear, discernible meanings. Infamy clearly designated a reputation derived from an evil, brutal, or criminal act, and fame was related to positive public estimation. The current edition of *Webster's Collegiate Dictionary* uses *renown* as a synonym for fame. But one could easily apply words such as *celebrated, eminent, distinguished,* and *illustrious* as well. In short, *infamous* and *famous* were opposite poles separated by a divide of social deeds, those disavowed and those approved.

Today, however, attention or recognition is the main standard by which celebrities are judged, and any act that draws newsprint or television space, however questionable, attains considerable acceptability. Engaging in the bizarre has great benefits if in the end it enhances one's celebrity status. Hence the comedienne Whoopi Goldberg is admired for her irreverence, even though it takes the form of using obscenities (or perhaps precisely because it does).

Basketball player Dennis Rodman became a national figure in the '90s, despite his one-dimensional basketball talent, because he dyed his hair a variety of unattractive colors, adorned his body with tattoos, sometimes wore lipstick and eye makeup, and wore a wedding dress to a book signing. Richard Morris, formerly an adviser to President Clinton, was discovered to have had regular liaisons with a prostitute whom he allowed to listen in on his telephone conversations with the president. For this indiscretion and others he was rewarded with a seven-figure book contract, a newspaper column, and pundit status on television.

What is going on here is that as standards for public approbation have dissolved like soap bubbles, only recognition counts. It is less important that a celebrity be admired than that he or she simply be recognized. As a consequence, a popular figure like Madonna, who has a limited singing range and even more limited acting ability, is universally admired for her ability to market herself as a celebrity. Never mind that this marketing takes the form of public nudity, blasphemy, depicting herself in degrading sexual acts, and the rest of her unique brand of immorality. She is, as they say in the business, recognizable, and that means marketable.

Marketing undergirds the manufacture of celebrities, and getting people to notice you is all that counts, so handlers push the envelope of attention, forcing the culture to new extremes. What was avant-garde yesterday is passé today. Recently a young man who engaged in a brutal murder said, unrepentantly, "Well, at least now I'll be noticed." Alas, he was correct.

Fame must be reserved for those whose behavior is praiseworthy, and must be denied to the desecraters of culture. Tupac Shakur was infamous, not famous. Donald Trump is infamous, not famous. Don King is infamous, not famous. It may be in the interest of the *National Enquirer* or *Star Magazine* to confuse these words, but to those of us who realize that civilization rests on a gossamer-thin foundation of norms and traditions, it is clear that such tears at the fabric of society are not easily repaired. Those who heal our social wounds deserve fame; those who inflict those wounds deserve infamy.

There was a time, not so long ago, when the pictures on the front page of the *New York Times* or *Washington Post* were of popes, presidents, and other influential leaders. Celebrities of the movie-star variety or from the publishing world were restricted to the back pages, where one was accustomed to reading about their latest exploits only after perusing more important stories. That condition has now changed.

Gossip drives today's journalistic muckraking. If it weren't for the insatiable curiosity about celebrities among a large segment of the population, the paparazzi wouldn't exist. And maybe Princess Diana would still be alive.

Having been victimized by irresponsible journalistic practices during a run for public office, I realize how dastardly members of the press can be. But I can only imagine the torturous shadowing Princess Diana was obliged to suffer at the hands of the paparazzi.

There is certainly much that the public should know and much that it shouldn't. That distinction is critical. Unfortunately, in this era of "anything goes," tabloid journalists respond only to Mammon, not to the dictates of ethical and tasteful standards. And the public, inured to television journalism that pushes the envelope of appropriate behavior to new levels of tastelessness, often wants sensational and lurid reporting that satisfies their curiosity about those in the news.

When the editors of the *New York Times* placed Tina Brown's picture on the front page accompanying a story of her resignation as editor of the *New Yorker* magazine, and many other papers followed suit, the era of celebrity journalism was clearly in its ascendancy. After all, Ms. Brown, whatever her talents, is certainly not a world leader; one might even regard her influence as narrowly circumscribed within the magazine industry, a very small slice of the domestic economy. How, then, did she qualify for a front-page photo?

The answer is more obvious than it might have been twenty years ago. We live in a celebrity age. What is deemed important now may be related more to connections and media hype than any objective reality. Ms. Brown is a creation of her own carefully manipulated personal and professional relationships.

The nation is caught up in the celebrity trap. People who appear on television are, ipso facto, stars worthy of national attention. When Jerry Seinfeld brought his television program to an end, the nation shed tears of remorse, and editors devoted front-page stories to the occasion even though it had been anticipated for months. One might think that something truly terrible had occurred.

Most significant, the truly important issues are thus relegated to the back pages. Whatever happened to the story about the Loral Corporation and its sale of a missile-guidance system to the Chinese military? What is the current state of so-called peace negotiations in the Middle East? And what are the implications of all these events for our future peace and prosperity?

There is so much I would like to know. Instead, I am told that Tina Brown is moving from the *New Yorker* to take a job for Disney's Miramax film subsidiary, editing a magazine explicitly designed to provide public relations for the company's films. Should I really care? Only insofar as it shows a further decline in the independence of journalists from the people they cover.

Current journalistic practices seem to appeal to the superficial and banal. "Tell it like it is" is a cliché employed by people who never tell it like it is. Once-serious newspapers, purportedly presenting all the news that is fit to print, now publish little more than the news that celebrity hounds want to read, and it becomes increasingly difficult to distinguish them from papers of the explicitly disposable variety sold at supermarket checkout lines. In the past, journalists could be counted on to distinguish between promotion and accomplishment. That is a distinction blurred today by bad judgment, television notoriety, and the tabloidization of once-serious newspapers.

Saving the Media from Themselves

As I see it, there are few more important objectives in American life today than redeeming the media. If the American people are continually deceived, what chance does democracy have against such powerful forces of deception? The march of the "adversary culture" through the press, the schools, Hollywood, the philanthropic community, academia, and the arts has been so complete a victory that what was once the adversary is now the culture. If redemption is to occur, traditionalists must begin a long march of their own.

There must be three essential characteristics in this effort to save the media from itself. Because traditionalists accept the importance of free markets, they should take the lead in promoting diversity in the media. For every Phil Donahue or Oprah Winfrey, there should be the call for a Rush Limbaugh. Surely there isn't any lack of critics who understand the spin doctors in the media. Traditionalists should demand that the media give them a voice.

Second, traditionalists should call for "truth in advertising"; just as critics on the Left have demanded this reform for products, traditionalists should demand it for presumptive experts. For example, Ralph Nader should be introduced as someone other than a defender of consumer interests. After all, I'm a consumer, and he doesn't represent my interests. It's important that full disclosure of one's background, affiliations, and interests is mentioned on-air or at the bottom of opinion pieces instead of the usual benign two-sentence description that conceals more than it reveals.

Third, traditionalists should demand historic context in all news stories. When it is reported that the atrocities in El Salvador, including the murder of women, children, and nuns, was promoted by government forces trained by the U.S. military, it should also be noted in the same story that the FMLN revolutionary forces started the war in this beleaguered nation and, therefore, deserve much of the responsibility for these harrowing acts. It is not necessary to be an unthinking apologist for American actions or the acts of our allies, but it is necessary to place these matters in a context that allows for disinterested judgment.

Diversification of opinion, "truth in advertising," and establishing the historic context won't, in themselves, bring us back from the long, dark night of media manipulation that was the '90s. But it would be a good start, and it is a start that relies on previously established journalistic standards. We should hoist the journalists by their own petard. Use the standards in this profession to keep journalists honest. At a minimum, the application of these three conditions would do more to revolutionize the media industry than all the animadversions of bias and unfairness. As long as the press believes that the present orchestrated criticism is the carping of right-wing zealots, they will do nothing to correct the problem. In fact, press resistance will be entrenched.

Instead, I contend that the journalists should be called on to meet the standards they presumably advocate. Force them to apply what they preach. Let Jennings, Brokaw, and Rather stand by their sanctimonious positions as the public holds them to account by the long-accepted standards of their own profession. The way back to sensible media presentations is the path of accepted journalistic principles.

Chapter Two

Hollywood, TV, and Cultural Icons

Entertainment, '90s-style, took its tone early in the decade, during the very first summer, when the managing director of a new magazine—*Entertainment Weekly*—resigned because Time-Warner executives objected to his plan to feature tough reviews and offbeat subjects in the then four-month-old publication. The final straw apparently came when the magazine published a review panning the box-office smash *Pretty Woman* as hopelessly naive.

To be sure, personnel changes occur frequently in the world of popular magazines, but the case of Jeff Jarvis and *Entertainment Weekly* suggested something about the cultural struggle in the United States that existed in 1990 and increased over the next ten years.

Arrayed on one side was a generational view challenging the status quo, from those eager to debunk bourgeois myths and serve as avatars of cultural forms for the expression of cultural change. On the other side were average Americans whose taste was not refined but who basically distrusted the radical sensibility and the notion that the nation must be altered.

Pretty Woman captured the conflict. Adversary cultists saw the film as a tribute to capitalism in which the wealthy man influences his Galatea and the prince finds Cinderella. They found it crass, apocryphal, misleading, and a glorification of the values they deplore. This view that the film promotes America's banality overlooked the simple fact that average filmgoers found it entertaining, liking its happy ending, joyful emotion, and ability to promote a simple engagement with the screen.

9

The cultural struggle continued for ten long years. The result? The three primary forms of modern entertainment—movies, television, and music—were thoroughly debased. By decade's end, America was celebrating "gangsta" rap while mourning the death of Superman.

Hollywood Horrors

Films

What is Hollywood all about? An answer can be found by examining the five films nominated in a typical year—1997—for the Best Picture Oscar. Presumably each film represents the best of film fare.

- *The Full Monty*, widely admired for its "charm," is the story of a group of unemployed factory workers who become male strippers in an effort to earn a quid. At no point does anyone suggest that this behavior is morally wrong. Rather, in the Hollywood context, it is cute, like a walk in the park with one's children. The lead character, in fact, brings his child to rehearsals. After observing the trials and tribulations of the prospective strippers, the youngster comes to admire his father's pluck in pulling off the public exhibition.
- *L.A. Confidential* is a dark story in the "Chinatown" tradition of greed, corruption, and despair. No one can be trusted, except, of course, the prostitutes who display the only innocence on screen. Violence is rampant, and the one cop who seemingly wants to apply the rules is ultimately beaten by "the system." A gratuitous beating of innocent Mexicans in a jail cell captures the mood of human degradation.
- *Good Will Hunting* tells of a brilliant youngster who reads everything and can solve math problems that defy MIT professors, but is accustomed to speaking in monosyllabic obscenities. Of course, he is emotionally flawed, having been raised by an abusive father. When he meets a psychologist played by Robin Williams, his life is turned around. The moment of psychological discovery occurs when Williams chants, four times, "It's not your fault." With this epiphany, the hero breaks down, and the road to recovery is within his grasp.
- *As Good As It Gets* is the tale of a misogynistic man in his middle years who has fallen into obsessive and compulsive patterns of behavior he cannot shake. The warm side of his personality is finally revealed when he falls for a waitress and comes to understand the plight of his homosexual neighbor. In the key moment of the film, the waitress asks, "Why can't I have a normal boyfriend?" and her mother responds, "Darling, there is no such thing."
- *Titanic* was the Best Picture winner in 1997, of course, and was film of the decade (and century) if the number of Oscars it garnered is any indication of its artistic merit. (In my judgment, the Oscars are more accurately related to box office success, a condition Hollywood moguls always confuse with

merit.) Here is a tale of grandeur and romance, or so we are supposed to assume. At its core, *Titanic* is a film about puerile class conflict. As one might assume, the rich are joyless and insensitive, the poor joyful and life-affirming. The heroine, caught in an arranged marriage, finds fulfillment in the steerage, where people sing and dance amid woeful conditions. Groucho Marx may be long gone from Hollywood minds, but Karl Marx is alive and well in the imagination of James Cameron, the director and scriptwriter of *Titanic*.

What conclusion can one draw from the Oscar-nominated films? For one thing, degradation is in vogue; corruption of the spirit afflicts heroes and rogues alike. There is virtually nothing uplifting about the human experience, except for those infrequent redemptive moments designed as a respite from despair. It can also be argued that the heroes in these films are uniformly flawed. They might be saved by another flawed personality or the psychiatrist (who is to Hollywood today what a priest or a nun was in Hollywood's yesteryear), but in Hollywood logic to be flawed is to be heroic.

And remember, these are the "best" films Hollywood has to offer, the ones the Academy wants to recommend to the world. Many non-nominated films—the vast majority—are even more enthralled with perversity. Consider 1993's *Three of Hearts,* which tells the story of a lesbian spurned by her bisexual girlfriend who becomes best friends with the male gigolo she hires to restore a relationship with her former mate. As this film shows, the idea that boy meets girl, falls in love, and marries girl is almost a prelapsarian notion. Now boy meets girl and sells his mate to another boy (*Indecent Proposal*).

Hollywood does not simply promote certain attitudes; it believes it should be on the cutting edge—"out there" is the phrase in the current vernacular. Clark Gable and Claudette Colbert would not be able to understand, much less appreciate, the current sensibility. And Hollywood is winning the war. Surely there has been no great outcry against its campaign.

For Hollywood, Marxism hasn't been defeated; it lives as a shorthand device to characterize wealthy people as avaricious and poor people as the saviors of social order. One can only wonder what these wealthy Hollywood producers actually think of themselves. If their films are any indication, that should be easy to deduce.

Directors

Three directors, three generations of Hollywood: Elia Kazan, Stanley Kubrick, and Steven Spielberg. Disgraced, dead, and deified—in that order. Their movies, as well as their lives, shed much light on Hollywood and America.

Elia Kazan
Kazan was arguably the most important director of a generation. With *On the*

Waterfront, *Baby Doll*, *Viva Zapata*, and *America, America*, he made four of the most memorable films of the last fifty years. He was also the brilliant director of plays by Arthur Miller and Tennessee Williams and a figure of such looming genius that he cast a spell over actors as diverse as Marilyn Monroe, Marlon Brando, and Paul Newman through his Actors' Studio affiliation.

Acting out of idealism and dismay with America's class hierarchy, Kazan joined the Communist Party in the 1930s. Like many idealists of his generation—including Paul Robeson—he believed that communism could be channeled into salutary social activism.

When Communist Party members prevailed on Kazan to alter his scripts to satisfy their ideological order, he refused. After several overtures and refusals, Kazan left the party. But what Hollywood could never forget or forgive was that Mr. Kazan testified before the House Un-American Activities Committee and, in a phrase attributed to Victor Navasky, publisher of *The Nation*, "named names."

Kazan, influenced by Sidney Hook, New York University professor of philosophy, among others, arrived at the conclusion that loyalty to artistic freedom was more important than loyalty to former colleagues in the Communist Party. For this act, he has been branded. A metaphorical "scarlet letter" has been put on his chest. His accomplishments have been treated like items in the Soviet encyclopedia. He is an invisible man.

Yet for film historians, he is hard to ignore. Kazan is the equivalent of yesteryear's Steven Spielberg. Not everyone liked his films, but his influence on the medium cannot be overlooked.

It seems to me that if Hollywood and the *New York Times* can sanitize the reputation of Paul Robeson, they should do the same for Elia Kazan. In fact, if one relies on actual achievement instead of sentimentality, it's no contest. Kazan wins hands down.

When the Motion Picture Academy honored Kazan at its 1999 ceremony, some Academy members pointedly refused to applaud. The event might have cleansed the past; it might even have generated some balance in the overheated rhetoric associated with the Hollywood blacklist. Instead, it was marred by politics, as Hollywood usually was during the Decade of Denial.

As awful as the blacklist was, it was not "the American gulag," as Carl Bernstein, the journalist, once asserted. Joseph McCarthy surely had a chastening effect on artistic freedom, but so too did the American Communist Party. Unfortunately, few people—with the obvious exception of Elia Kazan—were willing to say so. That remains true today.

Stanley Kubrick

Stanley Kubrick, a man fascinated by the dark shadows of life, died in his sleep in 1999. At the height of the Cold War, Kubrick made *Dr. Strangelove*, subtitled *How I Learned to Stop Worrying and Love the Bomb*, a satire that paraded his antiwar sentiments and his distaste for the strategists of deterrence. The lead character, played by Peter Sellers, is a composite of Henry Kissinger and Herman Kahn, with Herman's words from *On Thermonuclear War* and *Thinking the Unthinkable* borrowed generously without attribution and out of context. What Kubrick wanted to depict were jingoistic yahoos itching for a chance to unleash nuclear weapons. In the film, Slim Pickens actually rides a nuclear bomb to its target. The truth, of course, was far more complicated than Kubrick's visual depiction. Kahn was interested, first, in how to prevent the use of nuclear weapons, and second, in how to survive if by some chance they ever were deployed.

Kubrick was obsessed with military culture, as his films *Paths of Glory* and *Full Metal Jacket* suggest. His interpretation, however, was one-dimensional. Military leaders, for him, are pathological and hypocritical, and battle brings out the worst in human behavior.

The absurdity of violence is embodied in *Dr. Strangelove* when the sweet music of *We'll Meet Again* is employed as a backdrop for images of nuclear catastrophe. Similarly, Malcolm McDowell, the cruel gang leader in *A Clockwork Orange*, crows *Singin' in the Rain* while delivering savage blows to one of his many victims.

Kubrick's reputation as a filmmaker was established with *Paths of Glory*, a World War I drama starring Kirk Douglas, which delivers a devastating indictment of military duplicity and puts on display his unalloyed misanthropy.

While his prejudices were inserted into films over which he demanded full control, his brilliance was also evident. *Barry Lyndon*, a film based on the Thackeray novel, is from my perspective among the most visually interesting films I've ever seen. His science fiction film, *2001: A Space Odyssey*, has psychedelic images and innovative special effects that paved the way for George Lucas's *Star Wars* films.

Spartacus, *Lolita*, and *The Shining* are other groundbreaking films that confirmed the macabre and subconscious dimensions of Kubrick's oeuvre. More than any contemporary filmmaker, Kubrick loved to penetrate his audiences' emotional and normative barriers. He aimed to shock, to force reconsideration of surface assumptions. His scripts were derivative, their originality found in the work of their literary sources: Arthur Clarke, Vladimir Nabokov, Anthony Burgess, and Stephen King, among others. However, he gave the literature visual texture with imagery that was sui generis.

Film is unquestionably the art form of the twentieth century, and Kubrick is unquestionably among its most talented artists. But artists have a responsibility to the society in which their work is nurtured. Kubrick seems never to have understood that.

When critics claimed that the savagery in *A Clockwork Orange* was romanticized, he dismissed the charge as the blind ravings of misguided moralists. Ultimately, he was forced to withdraw the film from distribution in the United Kingdom after the film inspired a number of copycat crimes.

Kubrick was cold and distant, a perfectionist and a deeply opinionated man, an avatar of the absurd with a taste for the bizarre. The young man born in the Bronx left his homeland to find artistic freedom in Great Britain. But he was never able to free himself from the demons in his soul. To his credit, he sublimated that angst into some of filmdom's most memorable visual experiences.

In 1999, as the decade came to a close, Kubrick completed his final film, *Eyes Wide Shut*, with Tom Cruise and Nicole Kidman. This psychosexual thriller based on an Arthur Schnitzler novel deals with the dark side of human experience. On that point, there were no surprises.

Steven Spielberg

For reviewers and pundits who have commented on Steven Spielberg's remarkable film *Saving Private Ryan* there is ostensibly only one issue: why young men in the prime of life put themselves in harm's way only to see their bodies dismembered and the lucky survivors shaken to the core of their existence.

While many, including Spielberg himself, describe *Saving Private Ryan* as an antiwar movie, one is obliged to ask why so many willingly gave their lives so that future generations could survive.

Although I cannot offer empirical evidence, I believe that the World War II generation recognized that its world was at stake in a life-and-death struggle. This wasn't merely a just war; it was a war against tyrants in order to preserve what is right and just about our system.

Tokyo Rose and her German counterpart made few converts during the war. American soldiers generally knew what they were fighting for. They were no more willing to give up their lives than soldiers today, but they knew the risks of their D-Day mission. The beaches at Normandy would lead inexorably to Berlin.

Three years earlier, those men who exited landing barges at Omaha Beach were skating at Venice Beach, making out at lakefront locations, and sweating through final exams in school. They did what teenagers ordinarily do, then and now.

When duty called, these young men responded. Their blood drenched the sand on the beaches of northern France as Nazi machine gunners mowed them down. But still they came. When bullets penetrated their bodies, they called out for Mom or a girlfriend. They prayed for recovery. Some never knew what hit them.

In the end they displayed the bravery essential for national survival. None wanted the mantle of heroism, yet so many earned that honor. One cannot remain free of emotion in the cemeteries of Normandy, where row after row of dead American adolescents were buried so that our future could be secured.

But there is a nagging question that emerges from watching this film, one that none of the pundits, to my knowledge, has asked: Would the contemporary generation of Americans be capable of responding to the demands of bloody war as did the adolescents of World War II?

Of course, this question begs speculation and a little more. Would young people in the age of Bill Clinton rally to battle? Have we grown skeptical of all government-inspired activity? Has narcissism diminished a concern for anything but the self? Is there a residual patriotism dormant in the body politic that can be awakened by a just cause? Are there any wars young people would consider just? Do we consider modern warfare, in which missiles are exchanged, to be bereft of bloodshed and gore?

In my judgment, *Saving Private Ryan* is a period piece, a moment from our past not easily recaptured. One hopes that we will never actually witness the horror and brutality of that kind of war again, and one hopes that if, God forbid, we are obliged to fight, there will be Americans in the fields of Iowa and on the sidewalks of New York who will have the courage to offer up their lives for their country.

Nations depend not only on the rule of law, the promise of opportunity, and the expression of compassion but also on a citizenry that appreciates responsibility for themselves and those generations who follow.

As hard as it was to watch this film and even harder to imagine the chaos and violence on the beaches of Normandy, I am privileged to say I am an American, a mere dwarf who fully appreciates the giants who gave their lives so that people like me could survive.

If Spielberg simply wanted to say that war is hell, he accomplished his goal. But if he is asking why, despite the hell, some continue to fight and prevail, he is raising a different question, one that we would be wise to think about and digest. It is good for this nation to be aroused from her complacency, even if it takes Hollywood to do it and even if the director is somewhat confused about his purpose.

Television Trash

Television in the '90s, of course, was a long way from the days of *Leave It to Beaver*. Forget the standards of '50s program editors. The popular '90s show *Murphy Brown* proved one point: Ward Cleaver is dead.

In 1992, in one of the seminal cultural events of the decade, Vice President Dan Quayle called national attention to the *Murphy Brown* segment in which the lead character, played by Candice Bergen, has a child out of wedlock. He noted, rightly, that it was yet another case of television mocking the importance of fathers and traditional families. And unlike many critics of today's entertainment industry, Quayle did an unusual thing—he stuck to his guns by saying, "Hollywood thinks it's cute to glamorize illegitimacy."

Time is proving Quayle right. To argue, as Hollywood did in defense of Bergen's plot line, that the society is unaffected by television programs is to be myopic to the way culture molds normative attitudes and behavior. Culture is a composite of those attitudes deemed acceptable through instruments of popular culture such as television. *Murphy Brown* was a critical cultural step toward creating the illusion that it is not wrong or unusual for a single woman to give birth to a child.

At least Murphy never shot anyone during the show's run. In that regard, she was something of an anomaly. Doubt it? Then consider the findings of the National Television Violence Study, a four-year, $3.5 million research project commissioned by the cable industry. Begun in 1994, the study monitored ten thousand programs on 23 different channels. Among its findings: Television violence is glamorized and sanitized; nearly three-quarters of the violence involves no remorse, criticism, or penalty; evil characters go unpunished on 40 percent of the programs; the number of violent programs has risen 14 percent on the networks and 10 percent on the cable stations; and children under age seven are watching violent programs at an increasing rate.

Television programming, in short, is designed to titillate. Every year the envelope of acceptable behavior (such as Murphy's illegitimate child and Ellen DeGeneres's "coming out" as a lesbian on her slumping sitcom) is pushed to new extremes in an effort to generate high ratings. Nonviolent programming of the *Touched by an Angel* variety infrequently attracts a sizable audience. It's no wonder, then, that the airwaves are increasingly cluttered with violent shows.

Let's return for a moment to *Murphy Brown*, perhaps the decade's defining television program. Not only did the lead character's private life mirror (and help create) broader social problems, but the show's setting—a television news program—reflected the continuing collapse of television standards even among news divisions. Sometimes during the '90s it was hard to tell if we were watching the news or entertainment.

News came to be defined as a litany of horror stories and grotesqueries: A cop allegedly sodomizes an arrested man in his custody; two brothers kill their parents; a professional basketball player wears a wedding dress to a book signing; a television sports announcer pleads guilty to assault and battery for viciously biting a woman. When the bizarre qualifies as newsworthy, the list goes on endlessly.

In what is unquestionably the most graphic and bizarre event to unfold on a Los Angeles freeway, or for that matter on any highway, a man with a gripe against HMOs parked his pickup truck at a busy intersection, set it ablaze, and then committed suicide as television cameras captured every detail of this grisly incident.

David Jones, a maintenance employee in Long Beach, stopped his truck in plain view of police cars, helicopters, and television newspeople, unfurled a banner with hand-lettering that read "HMOs are in it for the money! Live free, love safe, or die," returned to his truck, ignited a Molotov cocktail, and set the vehicle on fire. Engulfed in flames, his hair and clothing on fire, he managed to peel off his pants. Dazed and disoriented, he walked back to the smoking truck, picked up his shotgun, braced its butt against the low freeway median wall, bent down to it, and pulled the trigger.

Once the magnitude of what had occurred set in, Channel 4 News in Los Angeles apologized for broadcasting the suicide. Yet this was little more than an extension of the horror live coverage has often promoted. There was no editing in this case, and no control either. Just turn on the camera and shoot whatever passes.

The news, or what passes for news, is driven by a cameraman who turns a switch. "Journalistic responsibility" are mere words pegged into the lexicon of a less sanguine era.

An insatiable need for the sensational has conspired with off-center and exhibitionist types to make Russian roulette into nightly news fare. How can news directors resist? After all, if one does restrain himself from filming these lurid scenes, another will be offered encomiums for beating the competition.

Ken Walters, a journalism professor at Pepperdine University, said the urge to broadcast live reflects the profit-driven incentive to present news as drama— and thus entertainment. If anything, the Jones episode is another example of television desensitizing audiences to violence. The real and the staged are no longer easily distinguishable. For many, Michael Douglas in *Falling Down* and David Jones on the Los Angeles freeway are one and the same.

That television news producers want sizzle, not illumination, was brought home in 1998 when CNN inaccurately charged the U.S. government with dropping sarin gas on American defectors during the Vietnam War. Not only did the "report" besmirch the reputation of everyone associated with the war effort, but CNN's subsequent stonewalling—after the story was proven to be an utter fabrication—was even worse. Instead of apologizing to every serviceman who served in Vietnam, CNN chose to engage in evasion. What do these actions tell you?

Television news is to news what rap is to music. And that is saying something. . . .

Musical Mayhem

In the mid-'50s I spent hours in front of a mirror imitating Elvis Presley's hip-swivel and singing style. I combed my hair like Presley and even spoke with a southern drawl, despite residing with my parents in Queens, New York.

This paid off. By 1959 I had a modest hit record of my own titled "We're Not Going Steady." Yet whenever I listen to this record I hear Elvis Presley as much as myself. He was my idol, and clearly imitation is and was the highest form of flattery.

The Presley that I imitated was not a rebel, despite all the claims to the contrary. Although he was linked in the public mind to James Dean and Marlon Brando and condemned for rotating his hips, his music was benign by contemporary standards. Presley loved this nation, was devoted to his mom, and sang, "Don't be cruel to a heart that's true."

Surely Presley's style offended some people suckled on the saccharine sounds of Perry Como, but Presley wasn't a social revolutionary trying to undermine conventions.

In fact, Elvis's courtship of Priscilla (later to become his wife) was the essence of bourgeois rectitude. He asked her parents for permission to date, and when she was a mere teenager he hired a chaperon whenever they were together.

Of course, there is the dark side of Presley, the side filled with barbiturates, diapers worn because of incontinence, and the women who came and went without a trace. Yes, Elvis became a caricature of himself. But he was never a card-carrying member of the counterculture.

Presley sang "I Want You, I Need You, I Love You" as opposed to Meatloaf, a generation later, who sang "Ain't No Way I'm Ever Gonna Love You" but "Two out of Three Ain't Bad." Dusty Springfield embodied the sexual revolution with her song "You Don't Have to Say You Love Me." Presley, on the other hand, titillated innocent females by singing "Love Me Tender."

And Presley was a choirboy compared to Madonna, whose 1992 opus *Sex* vividly portrays acts of pedophilia, rape, sadomasochism, bestiality, homosexuality, orgies, and just about every sexual act that might shock a bourgeois sensibility. What *Sex* did was to try to break down the boundary between art and smut. The distinction, which has never had to be spelled out ("I know it when I see it"), has been blurred by Madonna and her fellow travelers. Madonna believes that crass commercialism is all that counts.

Presley, on the other hand, if one turns from the hype, from the sideburns and the pelvic gyrations on stage, reasserted bourgeois principles—courtship, love, and marriage. While this point is routinely overlooked by critics who contend that Presley was the catalyst for the social upheaval of the late '60s, the evidence supports it fully.

To be sure, the overweight and deeply drug-addicted Presley who spent his last days singing on the Las Vegas stage was a shell of his former self. Wracked by demons, Presley had to be propped up by associates to perform. But the Presley at the top of his game, the one who had a record number of hit records from 1954 through 1959, the one who launched a Hollywood film career—admittedly in second-rate films—was an inadvertent representative of the so-called Silent Majority—the Americans who loved their country, accepted moral norms, and admired free enterprise.

This is the Presley that I, and so many of my generation, admired. It does not serve his memory to convert him into a supporter of countercultural views he never embraced and certainly did not advocate.

To see how far we—and our youth—have fallen, simply compare Elvis Presley with today's rap music. A latitudinarian interpretation of free speech has brought the nation to the point where common decency need not be respected by the numerous popular avatars of the profane. Gang rape, murder, and abuse of prostitutes and homosexuals are merely some of the activities promoted by contemporary rap music. In fact, it could be called rape music.

While rap music has been advertised as music of the ghetto, it is really the music of violence, depravity, and barbarism. Yes, the music does represent a dimension of ghetto life, but it ignores those people in the same setting who maintain traditional standards of morality and intact families. The reality is that many thugs performing on the rap scene present thuggery as an acceptable "lifestyle." The music is a manifestation of these attitudes.

Audiences see rap artists as musical heroes and even models, sources of emulation. As absurd as I consider Snoop Doggy Dogg, for example, he is admired by many youngsters. Mr. Dogg and other such so-called performers are nihilists; their game isn't entertainment, and it certainly isn't uplifting. Where in the Western world can one find a profession with the arrest and violence record found among rap performers?

In N.W.A.'s (one of the nation's most popular rap groups) second album, *Niggaz4life*—which became the country's number one pop album, according to *Billboard*—tales of murder and sex sprees are limned in startlingly profane fashion. According to lead rapper Easy-E, an erstwhile drug pusher, "We wanted to tell it like it is." Apparently "telling it like it is" pays. N.W.A. sold more than 900,000 copies of their new album within a week after release.

What this "gangsta" group sells is shock value, a glimpse at the forbidden. Its sentiment is unadulterated pornography that relies on contempt for women and bourgeois taste. Easy-E denies such charges, noting, in his inimitable style, "We don't dis women. My mother is a woman. We dis bitches. They know who they are." "To Kill a Hooker" is but one shocking song on the current album, defended by group member Ren. "That's been going on from the beginning of time, girls getting killed. People take it too seriously. It's all in fun."

N.W.A. member and producer Dr. Dre assaulted a female television host who criticized the group on air. Dr. Dre hit her in the face and pursued her after she fled. Ren said, "She shouldn't have did what she did. She knew the consequences before she did it. Why dis us? We were doing her a favor going on the show." He added that beating a woman is appropriate if "they get out of line." The host, Dee Barnes, was hospitalized after the attack.

It is hard to imagine a level of cultural depravity more base than what N.W.A. has produced. Even Jean Genet never reached the depths of these thugs masquerading as new-age artists. Of course, new-age art is a form of thuggery. The only mission of this rap group and many others, including the Beastie Boys, Tone Loc, and Vanilla Ice is to shock those already numb by the continual cultural assault. This isn't music of even the banal variety; it is war.

What apologists for this so-called music do not realize is that the lyrics are recognizable to the very young, those most vulnerable to suggestion. What these words represent, would, if decency prevailed, remain ineffable. This language is beneath contempt. It is a language of murder, theft, rape, and humiliation. It takes the perverse and brutal and sanitizes them as a cultural expression. Alas, so far down the perversity slope have we gone that decency and respect need not be balanced against the great contemporary god, self-expression.

Where this will lead is clear. The cultural road we are on takes us to a deracinated society of violence and decadence. Anything goes for record moguls who count their tainted money behind a barrier of First Amendment rights. Never willing to admit that culture affects attitudes, the record producers demand an unfettered market for their music, one that they often deny in their politics.

Admittedly the young aren't obliged to buy these perverse records, but they are largely without guidance. Perhaps the best that can be done is a sunlight provision in which lyrics are printed in a family newspaper each day. Mom and Dad generally don't know how sinister these rap groups are. If this art is fun, as Ren contends, then cutting a leg off an animal is fun and rape with a broomstick is fun.

I am not calling for a censorship campaign—not because I am philosophically opposed to censorship, but because I don't think it would work. What I am suggesting is a campaign to inform, so that a respectable public and sensible parents will be aroused. It's time to realize how the word *fun* has been redefined among rap musicians.

Art for Elite's Sake

Whatever solutions may exist to the coarsening of American culture, certainly government, particularly the National Endowment for the Arts (NEA), is not the solution. Indeed, it is a major part of the problem.

Since its inception in 1965 when President Lyndon Johnson decreed that a Great Society needs great art, the NEA has been mired in controversy. Adherents assert that the NEA makes cultural programs available to those who can least afford them and protects the nation's cultural heritage. Despite these claims, the agency is obviously a direct subsidy to the cultured upper-middle class. And rather than promote the best in art, it offers federal funds for "art" that most Americans find offensive.

The Alec Baldwins and other Hollywood types contend that any attempt to engage in retrenchment or elimination will lead to artistic disaster. But as Larry Jarvik, an expert on the endowment, points out, the contentions are exaggerated, misplaced, or inaccurate. NEA subsidies represent a drop in the proverbial artistic ocean. For example, in 1996, the Metropolitan Opera of New York received $390,000 from the endowment, a federal subsidy equivalent to the ticket revenue of one performance. More than 20 percent of NEA grants go to multimillion-dollar arts organizations that do not cater to the poor and middle class to which NEA brochures make repeated reference.

NEA funding has created a mini-industry for a small group of artists increasingly dependent on this funding source. Such favoritism imperils artistic freedom by encouraging dependency, and it endangers funding for otherwise worthy arts organizations not in the cultural loop.

Most of the recent history of the NEA is replete with examples of art that intentionally reject general standards of decency and respect, with some grants promoting incest, child sex, and sadomasochism. In addition, to satisfy acolytes of multiculturalism the agency promotes art by race, ethnicity, gender, and sexual orientation, often excluding aesthetics and artistic merit from its grant considerations.

In an era when Republicans and Democrats were speaking about the need for budget constraint, when the need to reduce the federal deficit was forcing fundamental choices about vital needs, such boondoggles as the NEA served as symbols of profligate spending.

With all of the ballyhoo surrounding NEA funding, there is almost no evidence that the agency has produced or helped produce great art. Maybe even a Great Society cannot produce great art by willing it or subsidizing it, particularly when the "it" is so elusive.

After more than three decades, the NEA has failed in its mission to enhance the nation's cultural life. Isn't this the overarching reason for its elimination? Or must Americans continue to pay for agencies that have outlived their usefulness?

To ordinary Americans observing tax dollars converted into so-called art that intentionally offends their sensibility, the NEA is an outrage. It is yet another example of Washington panjandrums who ignore the will of the people. In fact, the NEA is an unwarranted extension of the federal government into the voluntary sector. If people want to subsidize the arts, they can attend the local symphony orchestra or a rock concert; they do not need federal bureaucrats to tell them which artists to patronize or what kind of art to promote.

If I could wave a magic wand and eliminate NEA funding this instant, it wouldn't have the slightest effect on the arts generally, and it would most certainly go unnoticed by the large majority of Americans. Why, then, has this matter generated so much controversy? Any time a sacred cow of the elite is gored, passions rise to the surface. Hollywood actors speaking in high dudgeon try to convince Americans that the elimination of NEA funding is a First Amendment attack. Of course, no one points out that the First Amendment does not provide a sacred right for artists to receive federal funds. Nor do defenders of the NEA note that, by and large, funding is offered for those arts ordinary Americans do not embrace. The elite wants the NEA for its own elitist agenda. It is time the taxpayers understood that, and it is time the Congress responded accordingly.

Death of an Ideal

Perhaps nothing better symbolizes the past decade than the news, in 1992, that the Man of Steel, after long years of selflessly saving the nation from the ravages of evil invaders, was no more. Superman, dead at age fifty-four.

He was born in 1938 and raised in an era when supermen were needed to defeat the likes of Hitler, Mussolini, and Hirohito. He penetrated the Iron Curtain with his heroic defense of the American way against Soviet adventurism. With the exception of his vulnerability to Kryptonite, Superman was invulnerable to physical assault. That is what made him so appealing in the past—and so unappealing during the Decade of Denial.

Superman did not die because Hollywood created a lumbering and exhausted facsimile, as the *New York Times* alleged; he died because the country no longer admired real heroes. After years in which heroes have been derided and mocked, when physical strength has been subordinated to sensitivity—the highest virtue in the New Age—it is understandable that Superman would have to go. His assets were inconsistent with an era of moral ambiguity and androgynous sexuality.

Clark Kent used his perch on the top floor of the *Daily Planet* to survey the scene in Metropolis. He responded to any crime by changing into his Superman cape and flying off to rescue someone in distress. But the *Daily News*, often thought to be a model for the *Planet*, is in financial trouble from which it may not recover. Superman would not have recognized the chaotic New York City of the '90s. And old-fashioned innocents like Lois Lane and Clark Kent couldn't hope to survive in such an urban quagmire.

There are no telephone booths for Clark Kent's wardrobe change. The skies over most urban centers are filled with aircraft circling to land—the Federal Aviation Administration would declare Superman a hazard to airplane traffic. Clark's interest in Lois Lane would most likely be interpreted as sexual harassment. Superman didn't suffer from angst; he went about his business of rounding up the bad guys without any concession to the Miranda decision.

Superman doesn't fit with the antiheroes of this age. Now we want heroes tortured by psychological dilemmas. We expect failure and occasional apostasy, but people of deep conviction, unwavering in their belief and successful to boot, are virtually unrecognizable in the present cultural environment.

Superman went the way of many other comic strip characters of his generation. Joe Palooka has been interred, as has Captain Marvel. Yet Superman was different. He was more bold than the others; he was a national icon crafted from Nietzchean visions of a super race. He found legislative gridlock and bureaucratic police activity a source of derision. Superman made decisions on the spot.

He was also unusual in that he defied gravity. When he was first created, there wasn't much commercial air traffic. Now everyone flies, rockets have taken men to the moon, and jets can be installed in one's boots so that individuals can take off. Technology has caught up with Superman. Superman could stop a bullet in flight; he could fly faster than a jet airplane, and he could penetrate steel with infrared eye rays. These feats of derring-do, however, are not particularly awe-inspiring for youngsters brought up on television's magic. Superman has been made bland in his middle years by the rush of modernity.

There is a rumor that Superman will be resurrected, but I'm not convinced that it will happen, nor that such an event would engender much interest. Superman is not a hero for this time. He is an anachronism, a model of a bygone era when virtue mattered, morality wasn't relative, and the distinction between good and evil didn't require an arcane, hour-long lecture. Clark Kent was a simple man with a basic middle-American sense of justice. In his Kent persona, Superman seemed a lot like Tom Sawyer, a kind of American Adam.

There will be new comic book heroes, but they are likely to resemble their television counterparts—technical wizards and moral dwarfs. Superman was indeed a figure of his time, towering above the others, a hero to emulate. Like the heroes of yesteryear, however, he is gone, and with his interment we have buried popular heroism and the belief in individuals' sacrifice for the public good. Superman will be missed, but more important, the virtues he embodied will be missed even more sorely.

Chapter Three

Sports

For most of my life, sports have been a joy. I often root for the home team, applaud the efforts of great players, and daydream about feats of athletic heroism. I still read the sports page before turning to the news because I, like former Chief Justice Earl Warren, prefer to read about human accomplishments before reading about human failures.

I love to recall Babe Ruth's affable smile, Lou Gehrig's "luckiest man alive" speech, and Jackie Robinson's ability to turn the other cheek when confronted with on-the-field racism. These moments are etched into my imagination, and they inspire my present interest in sports. I keep hoping to see the next generation of Ruths, Gehrigs, and Robinsons.

Alas, realism suggests that my hope is in vain. Other than rare exceptions such as Michael Jordan and Karl Malone, athletes today are products of the "me" generation. Few seem to care about the fans or the game itself. They want expensive contracts based on personal performance, which incites a notice-me-first attitude. Jordan's retirement and the National Basketball Association (NBA) lockout illustrate this transition vividly.

There was a time when a player who hit a home run would trot quickly around the bases—head down—to avoid embarrassing the pitcher (and keep from getting "beaned" next time up). Now, sluggers routinely stand at home plate and watch the ball soar into the stands. Elsewhere, Dennis Rodman pierced every orifice and Anthony Mason had messages sculpted on the side of his head just to be noticed.

Many call these harmless diversions, but such behavior reflects a fundamental change in the athletic code of conduct—the team now comes *after* the individual. A contemporary baseball player doesn't sacrifice himself by moving a runner into scoring position; he swings for the fences. Players who refused to follow the rules used to be thrown out of the game regardless of batting average or point production, but Dennis Rodman insulted the Mormons, received a fine, and returned immediately to the playoffs. Fights are common on professional basketball courts and endemic to hockey, and players in all sports berate coaches with impunity.

Super Bowl, Super Hype

If one is looking for a sign that American sports have lost their way, the Super Bowl provides an insight. There was a time not so long ago when the country, in a moment of reflection, celebrated two national events, the Fourth of July and Labor Day. The former was the unofficial beginning of summer and the latter its end. Now, however, there is one national event, a day in which party frenzy reaches fever pitch and almost all Americans pay obeisance. It is Super Bowl Sunday.

Having attended the 1999 game in Miami between the Denver Broncos and Atlanta Falcons, I can attest to the newly recognized national celebration. Clearly the pyrotechnics, the jets overhead, Cher's rendition of the "Star Spangled Banner" were impressive. But the halftime show of thousands jumping around is starting to wear thin.

Most of the people in the stands weren't football aficionados. They wanted to be part of the national celebration, to say they were at the Super Bowl, to be seen and to see the celebrities in the stands. The fellow seated behind me called every person he knew to tell them he was at *the* game. Well-endowed females pranced up and down the aisles as if this were a fashion show, with the obligatory catcalls and obscene gestures from beer-soused males in the stands.

The game itself is anticlimactic. What counts is what precedes it: Parties, parties, and more parties. South Beach was converted into Partytown, U.S.A. There wasn't any way to drive through, since it seemed every twenty-year-old in America could be found on this patch of beach. Exhibitionists are drawn to this weekend like metal scrapings to a magnet. Some paint their bodies, others dance to the music on their CD players, and still others shout to be recognized. Hard bodies wear clothes sufficiently revealing so that observers know they have hard bodies.

At the parties, drinks flow like a Niagara. There are enough shrimp to feed an ocean full of whales for a decade. And many people I saw were either inebriated or acting as if they were. If you could stay awake during the day, there were golf tournaments, but most people slept the day away in anticipation of the night's activity. The National Football League (NFL) commissioner had his own party, as did designers like Tommy Hilfiger. And the glitterati came.

This was the national tribute to excess: too much food, too much drink, too much showing off, too much noise. It was a synthetic spectacle whose lasting effect is comparable to an Alka-Selzer. Yet the hype goes on.

It doesn't require great imagination to realize that Super Bowl weekend is a tribute to a nation searching for meaning and confusing that meaning with "more." There were more fancy cars, more flamboyant women, more money tossed around than ever before. I only wish I could interview Vince Lombardi, former Green Bay Packers coach, now watching from the heavens with bemusement. I suspect he would say, "What the hell does all that stuff have to do with football?"

Well, it doesn't have much to do with football, just as Christmas doesn't have much to do with Christ nowadays. Every event is an outgrowth of commercial interest. P. T. Barnum was right: Anything can be sold. In fact, everything is sold.

Clearly, affluence is better than poverty, and as a nation we should take pride in the fact that so many have so much. But we would be wise to flaunt it less, conduct ourselves with dignity, restrain our excesses, and show the world an America that can have a good time without converting it into a hedonistic holiday. Sports are supposed to be about achievement, not anarchy, and a healthy society shows respect for the real meanings behind its rituals.

Trading Jackie Robinson for Latrell Sprewell

Overlooked among the Super Bowl excesses is an important question: Whatever happened to dignity in sports? Alas, who even asks the question? Dignity and sports are now rarely found together. When Latrell Sprewell, a star player of the San Francisco Warriors (and now New York Knicks), choked and then punched his coach, P. J. Carlesimo, it became a headline story in every newspaper in the land. As a result of the incident, Sprewell was banned from the NBA for a year.

Yet even before the ink on that story dried, rationalizations for Sprewell's behavior came rushing in. Chet Walker, a former NBA star, argued "that a lack of respect for authority in sports can be derived from social and economic conditions afflicting black Americans." Others maintained that the coach's belligerent and mocking manner invited the attack. Still others contended that the passion in the game leads to situations where players lose control.

Sprewell, to be sure, is a gentleman compared to Mike Tyson. Tyson has been convicted of rape, was banned from boxing for biting Evander Holyfield's ear in a title fight (a ban since lifted), allegedly pummeled two motorists in Maryland, threatened to kill a Brooklyn photographer, ran his motorcycle into a retaining wall, and has been in a series of bar and street altercations.

Before society was psychologized, people would have said that Tyson was one of the bad guys. Now, of course, everyone is misunderstood—and Tyson's crimes are written off as the product of low self-esteem. The team of psychologists who argued in favor of allowing Tyson to fight again described "a constellation of neurobehavioral deficits" and claimed that their client was a misunderstood victim incapable of self-control. The shrinks say that what Tyson needs is a big shoulder to cry on—one that I hope he will not bite.

I can recall a time when coaches once told their players that gentlemanly behavior was required on the court. Trash talking, braggadocio, displays of arrogance, and showboating were taboo. In fact, the last thing you wanted to do was show up your opponent. Now, of course, winning is almost everything, except for the extracurricular activities that show up on highlight films.

Dignity is a notion alien from sports as felons, gang members, and street thugs have become multimillion-dollar athletes. Unfortunately, you can take the athlete from the streets, but in the absence of guidance and genuine penalties, you can't so easily take the streets out of the athlete.

It is rare to find a team anywhere in big-time sports that doesn't have players with arrest records. It is also a barely concealed secret that almost every team has produced at least twice its number in illegitimate children.

Two Heroes

It wasn't always that way. The '90s denial of personal responsibility has created this situation. Simon and Garfunkel once asked plaintively, "Where have you gone, Joe DiMaggio?" Where indeed? DiMaggio was the Fred Astaire of baseball. He moved with grace and effortless agility. DiMaggio's first seven years in major league baseball are among the most productive in the history of the game. DiMaggio didn't strut after a home run or pump his fist in the air after a game-winning hit. He simply went about his business without fanfare, without any of the flamboyant rituals that now accompany modest accomplishments. One might say that Joe was a reluctant hero who understood the virtue of humility.

In the interest of full disclosure, I was not a DiMaggio fan. That was largely because Joe's talent was used against my beloved Brooklyn Dodgers in the 1941, 1947, and 1949 World Series. Joe may have grimaced when Al Gionfriddo robbed him of a home run with two outs, two runners on, and the score 8 to 5 in the sixth game of the '47 Series, but the Yankees still won it all.

Willie Mays is arguably the most exciting center fielder who ever played the game, but even Willie didn't possess Joe's graceful manner. DiMaggio didn't dive for balls or catch them at his shoe tops or lose his hat chasing a fly ball. He simply got to every ball without a stir; dignity was his middle name.

DiMaggio's exploits on the diamond were duplicated by his demeanor out of baseball. When his storybook marriage to Marilyn Monroe came to an end, he didn't write a kiss-and-tell book. He guarded his memories to the end. The tabloids couldn't buy his story for any price.

Moreover, when Robert Kennedy visited the Yankee dugout during a 1960s Old Timers game, DiMaggio refused to shake his hand. He could not forgive Kennedy for his exploitive treatment of Marilyn and refused to be hypocritical about it. Joe didn't forgive, and he didn't forget. Until shortly before his own death, Joe sent a half-dozen roses each week to Marilyn's gravesite in Hollywood. Impeccably tailored, DiMaggio walked through the Yankee dugout in his later years as if beatified. He was a model to the young players, an icon for the older players. It is inconceivable that DiMaggio would wear a baseball cap backward or throw his bat in anger after a weak showing at the plate.

He was a model of rectitude; he wrote the book on decorum at the stadium. Play hard with determination, but don't show up your opponent. Run out every hit ball. Don't upbraid your teammates in public. Don't show off. Don't demean yourself with degrading public appearances. And always respect the game.

Baseball and the rest of sports could benefit from a healthy dose of DiMaggio's dignity. Unfortunately, most players today seem unable to respect an athlete who refuses to engage in degrading behavior on and off the field.

Where have you gone, Jackie Robinson? When the major leagues celebrated the fiftieth anniversary of Jackie Robinson's entry into baseball, breaking the color barrier, and integrating the sport, my mind flashed back to 1948, the year I met him. It was Jackie's second year with the Brooklyn Dodgers. He had already been named rookie of the year the previous season. On a day off, Jackie came to my elementary school on Oceanview Avenue in Brighton Beach, Brooklyn.

I was in the fourth grade and a fanatical Brooklyn Dodger fan. Seeing Robinson was a dream come true; it wasn't only because Robinson displayed courage in standing up to racial taunts, it was because he was the single most exciting player of his generation. He wasn't as smooth as Joe DiMaggio. He didn't have Ted Williams's batting eye or Stan Musial's graceful swing. But when Robinson was on base, he brought drama to the game. He could unnerve a pitcher more than anyone else I have ever seen on the diamond; his mere presence could change the complexion of a game.

When Robinson entered the school auditorium, my heart beat so quickly I could barely breathe. My fourth-grade teacher introduced me as an aspiring major league baseballer. My knees shaking, I asked Jackie to sign his baseball card, which was one of my prize possessions. (As happened to a lot of other collectors, my cards were all eventually discarded by my mother.) He did so without hesitation, inquiring what position I liked to play. "Shortstop," I blurted out. "Well, I used to be a shortstop with the Kansas City Monarchs," he replied.

Having read every book on Robinson, I was well aware of his minor league history, including his very successful year in Montreal before Branch Rickey called him up to the majors. For a moment I felt as if Robinson and I were the only people in the room. "Kid, do you ever get to the games at Ebbets Field?" Jackie inquired. "When my dad can take me," I answered. "Well, here are two tickets for a game against the Pirates; if you want to play in the big leagues, you should become acquainted with the field."

I flew home from school that day. I couldn't wait to tell my friends and parents about my good fortune. From that day in 1948 until Robinson's retirement when he was sold to the hated New York Giants, I imitated Jackie's pigeon-toed gait. I held my bat high in the batter's box as Robinson did, and I followed every statistic that applied to him. In 1949 I used a slide rule for the first time, to determine whether he, Ted Williams, or George Kell led the majors in batting, since they all ended the season with .342 averages. (By the way, Kell won and Jackie led the National League in hitting.)

When my dad and I used the tickets Robinson gave us, we arrived at Ebbets Field early—very early—and waited at the players' entrance until Robinson came. When Jackie saw me, he borrowed a stickball bat and a "spaldeen" from a youngster playing nearby and said, "show me what you've got." His pitch was moderately fast, batting-practice speed. I got around on it well and hit the ball about three sewers away. As I ran to retrieve the ball, Jackie said to my dad, "Your son is quite a hitter." My father glowed.

I never made it to the big leagues, although I did play college basketball. But Robinson was and remains my hero. In an era of greedy, self-indulgent athletes, I like to remind myself that Robinson never earned more than $35,000 a season and didn't complain about his salary. He signed autographs without a fee. And he influenced a life unknowingly; a press agent didn't have to tell him how to treat admirers.

Robinson was a towering figure on the diamond, but he was an even more imposing figure off the field—he was a gentleman. He didn't have to pitch to me. He didn't have to tell my dad I was special. He did those things because he was a gracious man who understood his place in history.

Jackie Robinson will be remembered for changing the game of baseball. Turning his cheek when players on his own team refused to play with him or opponents intentionally spiked him has become part of baseball lore. But I remember Robinson because he touched me, a poor kid from Brooklyn who idolized the Dodgers.

When Robinson died in 1972, I went to his funeral with thousands of other admirers. My suspicion is that more than a few people in that long line of mourners were touched by Jackie as I had been. In those moments when I daydream about the past, I can see Jackie dancing off third, running halfway home, and forcing the opposing pitcher into a balk. I see him throwing that spaldeen to me, and I see my dad with a big smile on his face as Jackie's fastball exploded off my stick.

The Blame Game

Mahmoud Abdul-Rauf is no Jackie Robinson. Abdul-Rauf, a former Denver Nuggets guard, firmly refused to stand for the national anthem prior to a game. The commissioner's office suspended him indefinitely, a suspension that translated into a $31,707 loss per game. Abdul-Rauf claimed that his "religious principles" were more important than his job. He contended that the "Star Spangled Banner" was a symbol of tyranny and oppression and that his adopted religion

(Islam) forbids nationalistic rituals.

Several days after this story broke, Abdul-Rauf and NBA officials reached a compromise: He would stand for the national anthem but "pray for those who are suffering." Why this couldn't have been done in the first place isn't clear. After all, no one tells those standing for the "Star Spangled Banner" what to think. As I see it, this so-called resolution did not bring this matter to an end.

Ironically, Abdul-Rauf maintained, "My intentions were not in any way to be disrespectful to those who regard the national anthem as a sacred ceremony." Presumably as an African-American who believes in the Koran, he is merely exercising his religious liberty and free speech—conditions, he neglects to point out, that "this nation of tyranny and oppression" guarantee, unlike most others.

According to Muslim scholars, nothing in the Koran militates against showing respect for the national anthem. Moreover, if Abdul-Rauf was dissatisfied with NBA rules that require players to "stand and line up in a dignified posture" during the national anthem, he could resign from the league, join another league without this requirement, play for a Muslim nation in Africa, or create his own league with his own rules.

If Abdul-Rauf did not wish to make his sentiments public or engage in this flamboyant act of national repudiation, he might have remained in the locker room until the anthem was over. Obviously, however, he wanted to make a statement in front of a captive audience. To describe this as a juvenile act doesn't quite do it justice. It was an act of political preening based on the same propagandistic assumptions about the United States that the multiculturalists propound as gospel.

To make matters worse, a number of NBA players stood behind Abdul-Rauf's symbolic act, suggesting that he "should be allowed to voice his opinion" and "it takes courage to stand up for your beliefs." Yes, free speech is a First Amendment prerogative and courage is an admirable trait, but if a Denver guard wants to make a political statement he should run for office or write an article or get on the lecture circuit. One doesn't have to be a patriot to realize that a basketball court is not the place for the exercise of political discourse. Fans pay a portion of their hard-earned wages to see Abdul-Rauf launch three-pointers, not vacuous political prescriptions.

While the American record is certainly not flawless and African-Americans and others have indeed suffered in this nation, it is also worth asking why Abdul-Rauf had a multimillion-dollar contract in this "land of oppression"? How many people, white or black, can afford to engage in symbolic acts that result in a loss of more than $30,000 per event? I certainly don't know how this young man from Denver sees himself, but most Americans would describe him as one of the nation's privileged.

As I see it, this issue is yet another manifestation of multiculturalism. Reading American history through the prism of categorical injustice, the freedoms and privileges unique to this nation are ignored. Without a global perspective, the United States is seen as the nation of venality. Even worse than historical revisionism is the attempt to create racial and ethnic enclaves, to have groups say which parts of the social compact suit them and which do not. If a school of jurisprudence promoted by several black law professors can contend that black juries should acquit black defendants regardless of the evidence against them, then indeed equality before the law is a sham.

The Disappearing Student-Athlete

The "blame society" culture buffs contend that black student-athletes face formidable challenges in obtaining degrees from predominantly white colleges. These rationalizers contend that blacks are isolated from white society and that they are obliged to live in a fishbowl usually reserved for celebrities.

Richard Lapchick, director of the Center for Study of Sport in Society, says, "For any black student athlete, the mission to get a degree in these kinds of circumstances takes on almost heroic proportions." Former Iowa State football player Dennis Ross notes: "It isn't so much that black student-athletes can't do the work. It's that many don't know how to overcome the difficulties they confront or don't have someone to work with."

That there is a low graduation rate among black student-athletes is undeniable. But the reasons for it are far more complicated than Lapchick and Ross suggest. Even a cursory examination of the evidence would lead to conclusions very different from the stigmatization-of-race argument.

For one thing, the graduation rate of black athletes at predominantly black colleges is not significantly different from the rate at predominantly white colleges. Surely the contention that blacks are isolated won't wash at black colleges. It is also the case that every Division I team travels with a tutor who is there to assist students with their studies during extended road trips. It is simply incorrect to argue that students don't have someone to work with. At Georgetown, the basketball team tutor even sits on the bench, although there isn't much tutoring she can offer during a game.

The real problem with student-athletes is that most are athletes and very few are students. Most enter college with the assumption that they are there to play basketball. Despite lip-service coaches give to academic opportunity, they expect to find their recruits in the gym, not the classroom. Coaches aren't paid for high graduation rates among their players.

Any gifted athlete who wants to study is afforded extraordinary privileges. The fact is, few take advantage of them. Most athletes at Division I schools gravitate to "gut courses" that allow them to maintain their eligibility. At many institutions, courses are labeled for athletes, e.g., sociology for football players.

It is the height of hypocrisy to contend that an athlete must be heroic to graduate. All an athlete has to do is attend classes when his sport is not in season and fulfill minimum requirements. In most instances, instructors will go out of their way to assist such athletes. What remains unsaid in most big-time athletic programs is that athletes are coddled. They are given freedoms denied to other students. They are indeed celebrities, but celebrities without responsibility.

Rather than provide a support system as Dennis Ross argues, most schools should simply insist on a reasonable standard of attendance and performance. If athletes can't meet the standard, they should be denied eligibility. Of course, the introduction of such a reform would eliminate most Division I programs and, as a consequence, will not be considered. But I would argue that if the charade is going to continue, we should give up the pretentious student-athlete tag. Call these athletes semi-professionals and be done with it.

Those desirous of attending a college program should be free to do so, but as students, not as student-athletes with their own modified standards. Should they choose not to attend classes, they would be semi-professional athletes in the employ of colleges, there for the sustenance of the institution.

Reforms at the periphery that deny the essential quality I've described cannot come to grips with the contradiction between big-time athletics and serious study. The Bill Bradleys of college sports are a rarity, but even if they weren't, support programs and heroic efforts to assist with their graduation would be superfluous. Many college athletes don't belong in a college. Were it not for their ability to hit a jump shot at twenty feet, they wouldn't be considered for higher education. That point won't be addressed by NCAA officials or big-time coaches. Those people would prefer to rely on racial prejudice as an explanation for their views, even when any disinterested analysis denies their conclusions with vehemence.

Money and Television

How have we come to this state of affairs? Well, for one thing, television contracts are bigger and better than ever. Colleges have come to expect the autumn financial fix. Those dollars are handy when faculty members demand higher salaries and computer services want to upgrade their hardware. Then there is the national obsession with college athletes. From the time they are in junior high school and their athletic potential is established, these young men live by a set of rules unrelated to those the rest of us follow. For most athletes, their emotional development is arrested at fifteen. Then there is the letting-off-steam quotient, the belief that these boys are under enormous pressure and should be allowed to engage in pranks and pratfalls. When they go beyond the bounds of propriety, cowardly administrators are inclined to avert their gaze or rationalize the behavior.

While college athletes were always idealized and often given the benefit of the doubt, their behavior was constrained by coaches who demanded gentlemanly behavior. When I played college basketball, I was obliged to wear a tie and jacket to every game. Violation of this rule meant you didn't play. Coaches could institute rules because it was assumed they were parental surrogates first and coaches second. Now, of course, coaches get paid three and four times what is paid to university presidents if they produce winning teams. Winning is therefore everything; there isn't any compromise that won't be considered in the effort to create a successful team, despite all the empty claims to the contrary.

Pro teams conceive of Division I football teams as their minor league, except that in the case of football the professional teams are not obliged to bear a financial tab for the cultivation of their future prospects. Hence from bottom—high school football—to the top—professional football—no one has a stake in establishing rules. At every level, officials ignore or cover up until, of course, the cover-up won't work. Players may occasionally be reminded of their public role, but when they get in trouble, some assistant coach is usually there to bail them out. Most players quickly understand the double message.

In high-powered college basketball and football programs, it is not uncommon for star players to be indicted for rape, assault, robbery, and other felony offenses. Fresno State University basketball coach Jerry "Tark" Tarkanian rationalized the criminal records of some of his players by noting, "Someone has to give them a chance." One might well be forgiven for doubting that Tark would give these young jocks a chance if they couldn't hit a three-point shot or dunk the ball.

As long as Americans are willing to tolerate a separate standard of appropriate behavior for college football players, the well-advertised atrocities on campus will continue unabated. There isn't any real disciplinary procedure that can be applied by university officials who are complicit in the deception. Only when a felony occurs, forcing the criminal justice system to intervene, will any action be taken. And even then, the university's legal counsel usually defends the athlete.

As early as junior high school, studs are identified, tracked, and elevated to a plateau for Division I material. These kids are then flattered, nurtured, and coddled. They receive scholarships to attend summer camp, where their training for prime time continues. When you aren't on the court, you had better be in the weight room, toughening your body for the grueling activity in the game. There isn't any time for anything else.

The coaches are partly to blame. They contend that their schools give every young man an opportunity to graduate. Technically, that is true; practically, it's a lie. How does one attend twice-a-day, three-hour practices while attending classes and studying?

Money is unquestionably a powerful influence in every phase of a coach's decisions. It isn't simply the contract, it is the local radio and television programs, the sneaker royalty, the summer clinic, and more. Coach John Thompson of Georgetown was invited to join the Nike board of directors.

Players, often caught up in the grandeur of the moment, contemplate future pro careers. Air Jordan isn't just a nickname for a great pro from the Chicago Bulls, it is a metaphor for college players who start to think seriously about ways to cash in on their present celebrity status.

Occasionally someone will point out the mathematical probability of making it to the NBA or even hooking up with a pro team in Europe. But after years of being flattered, it's hard for reality to penetrate the athlete's barrier of illusions. Basketball egos are bigger than life.

The parasites of the game know that building up egos is their job. Agents invariably tell athletes they are better than they really are. Assistant coaches on recruitment missions make promises that cannot be realized. Fraternity brothers and alumni leaders searching for reflected glory always bolster adolescents in need of reassurance. Many girls prefer basketball heroes, and local kids invariably tell the stars they want to emulate them.

I love the game as much as anyone else and admit to being transfixed during NCAA mania, but I believe it's necessary to expose the hypocrisy. I marvel at what these twenty-year-olds can do with a basketball. I also lament the fate of most of them. When the cheering stops, when the cheerleaders go home, when the NBA doesn't beckon, where do these boys of March go?

It is time to look inside this corrupt system, to examine and bring to light present coaching and recruitment practices and the antisocial behavior of some athletes. It is time as well to excoriate the NCAA, which refuses to acknowledge the problem. Unless this happens, there will be many more embarrassing incidents, silly explanations by political and university officials, and coaches self-consciously shaking their heads asking why this is happening to them. They know, of course, and so do the rest of us. Perhaps it is time to blow the whistle on this national travesty.

The Princeton Miracle

For this old member of the Columbia basketball team, the NCAA tournament still embodies all the hoopla, excitement, and spirit associated with March Madness. Sixty-four college teams are selected to participate in a basketball free-for-all until only one team is left standing—the national champion.

A small miracle occurred in round one of the 1996 tournament that bears examination. UCLA, 1995's national champion, with several returning players and three potential All-Americans on the starting team, was matched against Princeton in the tournament solely because the latter won the Ivy League competition. So heavily favored was UCLA that there wasn't a betting line on the game.

Keep in mind that Princeton does not offer athletic scholarships. None of its players will make the All-American team, and none will be on any regional All-Star team. The high scorer averages about ten points a game, and there aren't any special dispensations for basketball players in this center of learning. They take final exams in subjects like math, chemistry, and philosophy just like anybody else. There isn't one communications major on the team. Looking at the two teams also provides insight. UCLA is big and muscular; the Princeton team has height, but the players are bony and awkward.

In order to remain competitive with more athletic teams, Princeton coach Pete Carril orders his players "to take the air out of the ball"—to avoid taking a shot until twenty-five of the forty seconds on the shot clock have elapsed. Carril has his players engage in a cerebral game. They look for seams in a zone; they play tenacious defense—determination is more important than athletic ability on defense—and they run plays, such as "back-door" plays, when almost every other team relies on sheer athletic talent.

For teams that "run and gun," playing Princeton is a nightmare. Instead of scoring seventy-five a game, rivals will score about fifty against Princeton. There are simply fewer opportunities to score. Playing Princeton for big-time college teams is like enduring root canal surgery, not because Princeton is good but because Princeton is different.

Yes, Princeton has had its NBA stars such as Bill Bradley, Billy Campbell, and John Hummer. But in recent years, players of this caliber usually go to the basketball factories in the Big East, Southeast Conference, and Atlantic Coast Conference. Princeton gets a few bright kids who like to play the game, and then Carril teaches them *how* to play his game.

In the contest pitting the David of Princeton versus the Goliath of UCLA, David won by two points. It was a win very few expected, although Princeton had come close to upsetting other national powerhouses in the first round before. As I watched the game, I sympathized with UCLA; they couldn't solve the complicated Princeton zone defenses and they didn't have the patience to cope with the Princeton offense.

When it was all over, Pete Carril, who had already announced his retirement, was a national celebrity. The Princeton Tiger had defanged the perennial basketball power in the nation. It was a moment of triumph for genuine student-athletes, of which there are actually very few, and it demonstrated that intelligence can sometimes overcome physical talent.

The Princeton miracle did come to an end in the second round, when Mississippi State defeated the Tigers handily. But the memory of the first-round victory has not yet faded. Wherever there are gawky but determined players, those who use smarts to compensate for size or skill deficiency, those who can't dunk but can pass and play "d," there is hope.

There may not be many coaches with the intelligence and inspiration Pete Carril brings to the game. But in the 1996 NCAA tournament, Princeton proved that great coaching with marginal athletes can beat marginal coaching with great athletes. It is an important lesson for the NCAA and for the nation.

But too often the NCAA tournament has made college basketball into a big-time business in which the phrase "student-athlete" takes on a unique and perverse meaning. So vast is the scope of the NCAA undertaking that sixty-four teams from every corner of the nation are represented in a near non-stop basketball bonanza. Future pro careers are made, coaching jobs are determined, and a lot of money changes hands. By any dispassionate analysis, the event does not deserve to be called amateur athletics. The NCAA playground is the screen through which future National Basketball Association talent is evaluated.

On occasion, one finds a mathematics or civil engineering major playing on a big-time college team, but this is now so rarely the case as elicit comment. The point is stuffing a basketball, blocking a shot, and developing a forty-four-inch vertical leap. Rarely do the TV commentators ask how a student-athlete can suspend his studies for a four-week period to play in conference tournaments and then the "Road to the Final Four." That too is beside the point.

America's Game

It may be hard for youngsters to believe, but a generation ago baseball was America's favorite game. I grew up memorizing baseball statistics and taking the baseball encyclopedia to the bathroom as a ritual.

Compared to basketball and football, baseball is in the doldrums. The frisson that accompanies a Michael Jordan dunk and the rock-'em-sock-'em features of football appeals to young people weaned on televised excitement.

The opening of the baseball season on the heels of March Madness is like a "cooling down" period, a moment for reflection rather than exhilaration. For baseball, as opposed to basketball, is a hot, lazy day in the sun when the rhythms of life slow down. For the thrill-seeking Generation Next, baseball seems comatose, a game that inspires soporific yearning. Long ago, baseball lost its status as the national game because Americans want instant gratification and the latest thrills at their athletic contests.

Baseball gives its fans a different kind of experience, one in which discussion at the game is encouraged. During the lapses in activity between pitches and every half inning, people in the stands talk. Rarely do the fans talk at a basketball game; there isn't an opportunity to do so.

Recently I went to a spring training game in Fort Myers, Florida, home of the Minnesota Twins. The game was played in a Double A stadium with stands on top of the field. Octogenarians, who have fond memories of baseball's glory days and have retired to Florida, sell tickets and flip hamburgers.

It is charming to see these retirees wait eagerly for an autograph of Paul Molitor, a future Hall of Famer. At the beginning of the game, local retirement centers are honored. I overheard heated arguments about players of yesteryear: "Was Eddie Matthews a better third baseman than Harmon Killebrew?"

Baseball is a game for those with a memory. In the twilight of one's life, it is a sport easy to digest. One's memory for bank accounts and investments may fade, but baseball leaves an indelible mark.

Unfortunately, the modern baseball game is not what it once was. It doesn't help that stadiums are mammoth and largely homogeneous. The friendly environs of Ebbets Field have not been duplicated, even at Jacobs Field (the much-acclaimed Cleveland Indians' stadium). Players today—even when exceptional—don't have the personalities of the game's earlier heroes, such as Willie Mays, the Say Hey Kid; Ted Williams, the Splendid Splinter; and Joltin' Joe DiMaggio. And baseball has adopted its own version of trash talking once monopolized by basketball players. And some baseball players, like Ruben Sierra, do a dance around home plate when they hit a home run. These recent practices detract from the game and undermine the gentility once uniquely associated with baseball.

Baseball owners are often foolish and greedy and can surely learn lessons from the owners of National Football League teams. Big-market teams tend to dominate small-market teams because they can pay more for the best players. Baseball has sought gimmicks like Bat Day to sell the game. Kids don't see much baseball on television because of the dominance of night games and, as a consequence, usually do not share the enthusiasm for baseball I enjoyed as a child.

Yet with all these caveats, with all the flaws that accompany the game, when April arrives and umpires shout "Play ball," I still get a rush of anticipation. The ball is probably juiced up, and pitching talent is diluted through expansion, but the thought that Sammy Sosa of the Chicago Cubs or Ken Griffey of the Cincinnati Reds or Mark McGuire of the St. Louis Cardinals might break the new single-season home-run record is enough to give any season special meaning.

The Pete Rose Tragedy

The fall of baseball can be seen in the fate of one of its greatest players, Pete Rose. Once the majestic hustler and most prolific singles hitter baseball has ever known, Rose has been relegated to a blacklist as baseball's panjandrums made it perfectly clear that he is ineligible for the Hall of Fame. The outcry from baseball's cognoscenti is understandable. On the record, Rose deserves to be enshrined at Cooperstown. Charlie Hustle gave enough to the American pastime to be memorialized.

But what these critics ignore is that the Hall of Fame is not the Hall of Best Performance. It is a pantheon of heroes who performed well and also did well. The Hall not only honors statistical measures, it values people and accomplishments, notwithstanding the inherent ambiguity in these contentions.

Jackie Robinson, for example, played for the Brooklyn Dodgers for one grand decade starting in 1947. His base-stealing ability, Most Valuable Player award in 1949, and his leadership skills are unquestioned. However, if it were statistics alone on which the Hall of Fame decision were made, Robinson would not have gained entry his first year of eligibility. In fact, of course, Robinson was not simply a good baseball player; he was a symbol. When he tore down the color barrier, he changed the national game. Robinson deserved admission even if his cumulative batting average was not over .300.

On the other hand, Ferguson Jenkins, a former pitcher for the Chicago Cubs, was admitted into the Hall of Fame even though he was arrested for buying cocaine. Admittedly, Jenkins broke the law, as did Rose, and on the face of it neither should be accorded the game's highest honor. The reason Jenkins was honored, however, is because his infraction may have damaged his reputation but it was not a direct assault on the integrity of the game. Rose, on the other hand, did what is unequivocally taboo: He bet on baseball games.

For Americans the Hall of Fame has an emotional dimension as significant as the Medal of Honor. This Cooperstown shrine has taken on mythological quality. It is instructive that public malevolence is invariably relegated to a Hall of Shame as if to suggest the difference between nadir and apogee. After all, in the Hall of Fame is Babe Ruth's gigantic bat and Lou Gehrig's glove and Willie Mays's "Say Hey!" picture. The sounds of glorious bygone days come to life as the best on the diamond offer memories for aging baseball aficionados.

It is the fear of tarnishing this exalted image that resulted in the Pete Rose expulsion. That decision was correct, I believe. Perhaps one day when the cynical and self-possessed act of slighting the game is forgotten, the rules may be bent to allow Rose into the Hall of Fame. But the time is not right, and the memory is too well etched in the public imagination. Certainly not everyone in the Hall of Fame was a choirboy. There are drunks and drug users; there are womanizers and adulterers; there are dissimulators and manipulators. Yet each in his way made the game special without tearing down the basic pillars on which it was built.

When Shoeless Joe Jackson was barred from baseball after the 1919 World Series for having allegedly been paid to dump games, there was one moment every fan will remember: A young man, with tears streaming down his cheeks saying, "Say it ain't so, Joe, say it ain't so." Like many baseball fans, I want to believe in Pete Rose. I want to believe that someone with his contributions to the game, someone who broke Ty Cobb's base hit record, wouldn't tarnish *my* game. Yet the evidence is incontrovertible; and worse yet, Rose lied to cover up his infractions.

A Slow Death?

Each year baseball aficionados consider the possibility of someone breaking Joe DiMaggio's fifty-six consecutive games hitting streak or Hack Wilson's runs batted in mark (190) or someone hitting over .400 (Ted Williams was the last to do it in 1941). And who can forget the recent seasons of Mark McGuire and Sammy Sosa?

We should recognize, applaud, and admire the heroes in our midst who are engaged in such record-breaking quests. At times like these, we need heroes, even if they can only be found on the baseball diamond.

Yet something is deeply wrong with America's game.

On July 26, 1993, at Dodger Stadium in Los Angeles, players Vince Coleman and Bobby Bonilla of the New York Mets and Eric Davis of the Dodgers left the parking lot amid throngs of autograph seekers and well-wishers. As they were driving past these fans, Coleman threw a large firecracker out of his window as Davis and Bonilla laughed approvingly. A two-year-old girl suffered facial and eye injuries from the explosion.

There isn't any explanation for this egregious act. To make matters worse, it took baseball and the Mets too long to issue a denunciation. Of course, baseball is still without a commissioner. It is virtually inconceivable that Judge Kenesaw Mountain Landis would have ignored such a destructive adolescent act. Moreover, it is inconceivable that anyone but an immature rascal would risk his $2 million annual salary with such behavior.

However, it is increasingly clear that a lot of spoiled kids with retarded emotional development have entered the game. These are players very different from their predecessors.

Ted Williams neglected to doff his cap after hitting a home run, and was routinely criticized in the Boston newspapers. Babe Ruth's high jinks often made the front page across the nation. And the Black Sox scandal of 1919 almost destroyed the game. But at no point has baseball had as many spoiled, overpaid ballplayers as it does now.

The self-indulgent athletes of the Coleman variety have done more to hurt the game than all the clowns who committed silly acts on the field of dreams in this century.

As a youngster I took my mom's mop handle to the players' entrance at Ebbets Field. Jackie Robinson or Duke Snider or Roy Campanella or Pee Wee Reese would try to hit my fastball thrown at a box drawn on the stadium wall. Rarely did they refuse my overtures. As a kid I came to love baseball because I loved the guys who played the game. I'm sure some of them were lusty drinkers and a few were womanizers, and Carl Furillo—to cite one player—could get pretty surly on occasion. But no one of my generation could imagine one of the old Brooklyn Dodgers throwing a firecracker at their fans. After all, these were men, not grown-up babies, and if they acted like infants, the management, led by Branch Rickey, would have come down on them like a ton of bricks.

Baseball has lost its way because it refuses to exercise its moral prerogatives. Players are indulged if they can hit home runs or bat .300. For years the Oakland Athletics averted their eyes to José Canseco's antics because on the field he appeared to be the second coming of Hank Aaron. When his home run production dropped he was traded, but at no point did management suggest that there was something inappropriate about his behavior. The coddling of high-priced players has become a characteristic of the game.

Some people contend that youthful exuberance for baseball has declined because the game is so often played at night when youngsters are sleeping. Others contend that in the television age baseball is comparatively slow-moving. I find neither argument compelling.

Baseball is dying in large part because relatively few people care about the performance of spoiled adolescents who are allowed to get away with murder by pusillanimous owners and managers. Contract disputes and off-the-field behavior yield as many stories as actual performance on the diamond. Until baseball cleans up its act and gets its players in line, interest in the game is bound to diminish. There must be people of the Branch Rickey and Kenesaw Mountain Landis variety who can save the game. I just don't know where they are at the moment.

I suppose you are wondering why I still watch, when genuine heroes are all but gone and laudable behavior is so rare. I guess hope springs eternal.

Chapter Four

"Lower" Education

Money spent on education does not guarantee success.

William Bennett

Since 1965, when Congress passed the Elementary and Secondary Education Act, the federal government has poured enormous sums of money into public education. Of that, there isn't the slightest doubt. Yet disclosures that appear in an edition of *The Blumenfeld Education Letter* suggest that spending went beyond even my normally jaded expectations. Listed in this publication are yearly appropriations for hundreds of programs as well as aggregates over the decade of the '80s.

As expected, programs are rarely terminated even when their validity is questionable. In fact, despite all the discussions of cuts during the Reagan years, the only accomplishment of his administration in this regard was to slow the rate of increase in spending. This condition hasn't inhibited educators from clamoring for more money. In fact, the NEA continues to suggest that if more federal funds for education were forthcoming, performance would improve—a point belied by almost three decades in which an inverse correlation between spending and academic performance exists.

Perhaps the most egregious example pointed out was the $49 billion spent on Education of Disadvantaged Children (Title I—Chapter I programs) between 1966 and 1986. It would appear that, despite this enormous outlay, there is almost nothing to show for it. This money earmarked for the "culturally deprived" inner-city student was deemed to be an equalization fund. However, even with some improvement on basic-skills tests among black inner-city students, they still lag well behind their white and even Hispanic counterparts.

43

Similarly the Right-to-Read program was a ten-year effort to eliminate national illiteracy. From 1971 to 1981, more than $220 million was spent on this program. Yet the number of illiterates has not declined and is arguably higher than when this program began.

From 1968 to 1986, the federal government spent $1.6 billion on bilingual education programs, even though many educators contend bilingual programs retard the learning of English.

From 1966 to 1986, the Education of Handicapped Children program spent $1.8 billion, excluding such programs as the Handicapped Migrant Workers programs that spent $12 million from 1974 to 1986. Assuming that care for the handicapped is necessary, it is appropriate to ask why expenditures increased by more than 100 percent from 1977 to 1986. As the categories for handicapped status were liberalized to include learning disabilities and those with emotional problems, the number of children covered by this legislation went up exponentially. In 1976, there were 796,000 children classified as disabled; in 1986, the number grew to 1.8 million.

At a time when ideologically motivated instructors clamor for a multicultural curriculum, which they claim has been ignored in public education, evidence shows that from 1974 to 1981 alone almost $18 million was spent designing and encouraging Ethnic Heritage Studies with the presumptive goal of helping students learn about their own heritage as well as those of other cultures.

The financial burden extends beyond special programs. Since the end of World War II there has been a dramatic increase in the number of school employees. The rise in administrators, for example, has been geometric even as the rise in students has been arithmetic. Schools went through an emphasis on specialization which, in large part, was due to a desire for legitimacy. Once in place these administrators created an infrastructure of staff, paperwork, and unions that made it almost impossible to alter the administrative structure.

It should be noted that in the New York City school system—admittedly an egregious example—there are more school administrators than in all of Western Europe. Rather than improve the education system, these administrators tie it down and force all decisions through a bureaucratic maze. The reason why a little red schoolhouse at the turn of the century was generally a better educational institution than the modern suburban structures we call schools, is that education in the past was stripped of entrenched bureaucracy and reduced to educational fundamentals.

Compounding the rise in administrators is the widely held belief that the social pathologies the larger society cannot solve should be addressed in the schools. The consequences of this attitude have been a proliferation of new courses and experiences under the rubric of education. Schools now consider drug abuse, AIDS, illegitimacy, and drunk driving, among other new subjects.

It is obvious in even a cursory review of these spending statistics that the taxpayer is being taken to the proverbial cleaners. The Congress, in an effort to demonstrate its compassionate instincts, has been throwing money at problems neither it nor the professional education establishment knows how to solve. However, the expenditure of funds has created the illusion that something is being done. Bearing the brunt of this profligacy is the taxpayer who has no recourse.

A tax-paying public isn't organized to tackle the powerful NEA lobby. And most citizens, unaware of the patently foolish expenditures, assume that money spent on education must be doing some good.

Reading Failure Continues Because of Ineffective Pedagogy

Despite the ongoing expenditure of millions of dollars on remedial reading programs, reading failure continues to characterize the landscape of American education. Increasingly larger numbers of children are being classified as learning-disabled in reading, and ineffective teaching methods contribute to the trend.

Although *dyslexia* is a word associated with learning disability and some would argue has a biological cause, several reading experts contend that it is induced by a method of reading instruction prevalent in the United States. If true, that means we are spending billions of tax-levied funds to force our children into acquiring, at worst, a learning disability and, at best, dysfunctional reading skills.

In the nineteenth century, the Reverend Thomas Gallaudet invented a sight or whole word method to teach deaf children. He placed a word such as *dog* next to a picture of a dog and found that many deaf children learned to read in this way. Although this method of teaching gained acceptance in mid-century for all children, it lost favor when its flaws became apparent to schoolmasters. By eliminating the sense of sound from reading, the link between the alphabetically written word and its spoken equivalent is broken. Ideographic symbols can confuse youngsters. By the twentieth century, the "look-say" method had lost its following to the phonics approach to reading.

However, in a field where fashions change from one generation to the next, the look-say approach made a comeback. In fact, the Dr. Seuss books were designed to develop a sight and picture vocabulary of 223 words in accordance with John Dewey's progressive method of learning. Presumably the linear sound of phonics was deemed to be the enforcement of undemocratic laws—the autocracy of sound. What Dewey and Dr. Seuss didn't accept is that students taught by their method cannot know how to deal with new words beyond those in their memorized reading vocabulary. Edward Miller, a reading specialist and researcher, tested children using both approaches to reading. He found that in North Carolina, 44 percent of students were becoming dyslexic because of reading instruction that relied on a look-say method, while only 8 percent were becoming dyslexic at a private school in Florida that employed a phonics method.

Miller contends that the millions of tax dollars being spent to ascertain a genetic cause for dyslexia are wasted. Although the reading establishment with a vested interest in the look-say approach has dismissed these data, the Miller view is confirmed by others. In 1965, Louise Gurren at New York University reviewed 36 studies and concluded that "rigorous controlled research clearly favors teaching all the main sound-symbol relationships, both vowel and consonant, from the start of formal reading instruction." In 1973, Professor Robert Dykstra repeated Gurren's analysis and reaffirmed her conclusion. In 1985, a blue-ribbon panel of educators, including James Coleman (University of Chicago), Kenneth Clark (City University of New York), and Jeanne Chall (Harvard University), contended that "a national reading effort should bypass the existing education macrostructure," namely, the look-say method of instruction.

Why, then, hasn't this happened? Why, indeed, are children put at risk to functional illiteracy? The answer to those questions involves an ideological commitment to an approach that goes beyond evidence and rationality. Some educators insist on demonstrating the "effectiveness" of the sight and say method even if children are harmed in the process. The investment in sight-method textbooks is enormous. When these workbooks are obliged to compete with phonics texts, they soon become superfluous. Needless to say, some publishers resist the idea that their method of instruction is ineffective. As a layman examining the evidence, it seems to me that learning the sound of words will allow a youngster to learn 85 percent of the language, as opposed to a sight method in which only several hundred words can be memorized.

American Education Promotes Self-Esteem at the Expense of Academic Achievement

While educators look for new ways to promote self-esteem, the educational achievement of American school children continues to decline. The level of ignorance among contemporary schoolchildren is abysmal, even among students attending prestigious Ivy League colleges. SAT scores, long viewed as yardsticks of academic achievement and excellence, have steadily declined. Yet although the achievement of American students does not hold up well against their European and Japanese counterparts, American students feel better about themselves and remain oblivious to their academic shortcomings. There is little doubt that schools do not teach and students do not learn. The cause is uncertain, but factors to consider include excessive television viewing, lack of parental monitoring, vitiated educational standards, and a "dumbing down" of the society as high and low culture are homogenized.

What Do American Students Know?

When Diane Ravitch and Chester Finn surveyed high school student knowledge and incorporated their findings into a book titled *What Do Seventeen-Year-Olds Know?*, the nation was appalled to learn that the answer is "not much." Many students didn't know the century Columbus set out for the New World or when the American Civil War was fought or whether the American or French Revolution came first.

Since then it has been argued that reforms are underway, that standards have been reintroduced into high school programs, and that steps have been taken to prevent the ritual passage of cohorts from one grade to the next. Well, this is what has been said, but recent evidence would refute the claims of success.

Frank Luntz, an adjunct assistant professor at the University of Pennsylvania conducted a survey of 3,119 undergraduates at seven Ivy League colleges, presumably among the brightest students in the nation if SAT scores and grade point averages are any guide. What Professor Luntz found, however, is the "best" don't make the grade when it comes to general knowledge:

- Forty-four percent did not know that Thomas Foley at the time was the Speaker of the House of Representatives.
- Thirty-five percent did not know that Alan Greenspan is the chairman of the Federal Reserve Board.
- Twenty-three percent did not know that the Supreme Court has nine justices and eighteen percent could not name a single justice.
- Eleven percent did not know that Thomas Jefferson wrote the Declaration of Independence.

This poll was originally published in the *U.S. News and World Report*, where it was described as "the most comprehensive survey" ever conducted. Its results square with my own experience. Several years ago I gave incoming college students at NYU the Western Civilization section of the Kobe University entrance exam. To my astonishment at the time, not one student could pass the exam even though the questions relied on a general familiarity with European history. Japanese students, however, routinely pass that section of the test.

How, indeed, can democracy flourish when students do not understand the culture on which it depends? How can valid public policy decisions be made when ignorance is so widespread? And to what degree can we retain order when so little about our world is understood?

Confusing Mental Health for Education

It is clear that factual knowledge and critical-thinking skills of American students have been subordinated to self-esteem and mental-health issues. Some local educators substitute psychobehavioral goals for academic objectives, as illustrated in a handbook of federal education guidelines. Educators are focusing on nonacademic issues in the name of "restructuring education" without involving parents in their decisions. It should come as no surprise that Johnny can't read or add when he is spending a substantial portion of each day on psychological assessments.

So distracted are educationists by social issues from AIDS to drug abuse that they have assaulted the curriculum with programs dealing with personal beliefs, habits, traits, and feelings about friends and family. Erica Kenney, in a memo detailing educational activity in Pennsylvania, points out that a psychological test called the Educational Quality Assessment (EQA) is routinely used in the schools. While the EQA is labeled a basic-skills test, most of the questions are devoted to a personality profile. In most instances the test is administered without parental knowledge and those students who do not do well are asked to attend an interactive therapy meeting twice a week. Furthermore, parents are refused permission to see the test, with the excuse given that "the validity of the tests would be compromised."

In the first version of the EQA, used extensively in the '80s and still used in some districts today, students are asked to respond to "The prospect of working most of my adult life depresses me. Check yes, or no or sometimes."

And

"I am in a large crowd on a street corner. They are protesting about something. Some people pick up rocks and start throwing them at windows. In this situation, I would also throw rocks when I know: (a) there was no chance of getting caught, (b) I agreed with what they were protesting about, or (c) my closest friend decided to throw rocks."

And

"I wanted contact lenses to replace my glasses. I hate wearing glasses. My parents said I could have them if I kept my room clean for a month. I did it. Then my parents said they couldn't afford the lenses. So I didn't get my contacts. If this happened to you, how much time—none, very little, some, or a great deal—would you spend on each thing listed below? (a) Being upset. (b) Fighting and arguing with my parents. (c) Trying to understand why my parents couldn't get me the contacts. (d) Learning to like my glasses more. (e) Trying to get back at my parents."

Supposedly, student responses offer insight into personality or self-esteem problems. But since the scores are general and the teachers don't examine specific responses, a careful assessment—of what is a dubious test to begin with—isn't possible.

This emphasis on psychobehavioral goals scraps grades and hours as graduation requirements and institutes instead abstract learning outcomes, which in the main are nonacademic. Schoolchildren have become mere cannon fodder for radicals intent on promoting an agenda for social change. On the face of it, the "student learning outcomes" directive is hardly a casus belli. However, the proposed reforms are not benign.

Pennsylvania has established Quality Goals of Education: self-worth, higher-order thought, learning independently and collaboratively, adaptability to change, ethical judgment, citizenship, and wellness and fitness. Notably, most of these goals do not relate to hard subject matter. In the era of psychodynamic education, ideals like self-esteem are more important than knowing how to solve quadratic equations. When Pennsylvania tried out its new "achievement" test—designed by the Educational Testing Service—a personality profile based on answers to certain questions was determined. Those questions included the following:

- "Morton has been playing hard all afternoon with his friends. He comes home a few minutes before supper. If I were Morton, I would not take a shower or bath before supper when I knew: (a) I had already taken a shower that morning, (b) I did smell too bad (sic) or (c) I would miss my favorite TV show."
- "I was elected class president. I came home to tell my parents the good news. They told me that my dad had taken a job out of the state and we were going to move in two weeks. So I had to withdraw from school and move. If this happened to you, how much time would you spend on each thing below? (1) Being upset. (2) Trying to find someone to stay with so I could remain in school. (3) Planning a going away party. (4) Fighting with my parents. (5) Reading about the place we were going to move to."

If students do not answer these questions according to some predetermined personality index, "remedial" measures are prescribed. Presumably this exercise is designed to develop "personal skills" and "understanding others."

In Pennsylvania the three R's are in retreat before the onslaught of "learning outcomes," which now includes the following:

- "All students [K-12] develop interpersonal communication, decision-making, coping and evaluation skills and apply them to personal, family, and community living."
- "All students understand and appreciate their worth as unique and capable individuals and exhibit self-esteem."

What the curriculum does not indicate is the method for measuring these outcomes. For example, how much self-esteem must you exhibit to graduate? In the new age, goals are emphasized instead of weakness, and capability instead of deficiency. The problem is that this is will-o'-the-wisp education. The presumption behind these goals is that parents are neglecting their kids, and teachers are obliged to be surrogate parents. While that may be true for some parents, it is certainly not true for the large majority.

Moreover, in replacing educational fundamentals with empty psychological platitudes, education is becoming a dumbing-down process. Teachers have arrogated the role of parenting for themselves and have disavowed teaching. And students are pawns to be manipulated by New Age instructors with a clear radical agenda about what the schools should accomplish.

Some educators maintain that it doesn't matter how students perform on an admissions test; it is far more important how they do once in college. For the New

Age instructor who views SATs with skepticism and whose classes are the antithesis of rigorous, this argument holds water. For traditionalists, on the other hand, who are obliged to modify their courses and standards in order to accommodate students incapable of reading a serious or complex book, falling verbal scores is a matter to be addressed with utmost seriousness. Unfortunately traditionalists are in decline as are the standards they once upheld. Interestingly, as scores at the top of the academic pyramid continue to tumble, government officials exhibit much hand-wringing about the inability of Americans to compete with students abroad.

Declining SAT Scores and Inflated Grades Tell the Story

The effect of an educational system that places the promotion of self-esteem over academic achievement is reflected in recent College Board reports. The numbers show that while American students' grades are rising steadily, their SAT scores are on a decline. The SAT has, in fact, been renormed so that the 490 of yesteryear is the 510 of today, and the 780 has become a "perfect" 800 score.

The College Board, which sponsors the SAT, contends that test takers with A averages increased from 28 percent of the total to 38 percent in the last ten years, but the mean SAT scores of those students declined. During the period from 1972 to 1992, the number of students scoring above 600 on the verbal section of the SAT had dropped by about one-third (800 is the highest possible score). In 1972, 116,630 of the one million students who took the test scored over 600. By 1992, the number of students who scored above this mark declined to 75,200, even though the number taking the exam increased by 1 percent. Twenty years ago the average verbal score was 453; ten years ago it was 426; today it is 423.

What is of greater concern is that the drop in scores is especially evident among the highest achieving students. The students toward the bottom have received the benefit of most educational resources during the past twenty years, and this is reflected in a nominal rise in their SAT scores. Overall, the average drop is less dramatic than the decline in the highest scores. Some analysts contend that top students have been penalized so those at the bottom can improve. What one can observe in the tests is a compression at the mean, a form of institutionalized mediocrity. The statistics indicate that those affected by the downturn are as likely to be middle class in the suburbs as anyone else. Mediocrity is ubiquitous. Grade inflation is occurring across the board, and many, including the president of the College Board, report not knowing why grades are on the rise. I have my suspicions, however.

First, it should be noted that in an era of radical egalitarianism that cannot accept stratification, the Lake Woebegon influence is quite evident. Everyone is above average. As a student of mine once noted, in today's school environment, a C is tantamount to an F. So widespread is grade inflation that when I was a dean

I suspended the Dean's List because it was so lacking in discrimination. It was like reading the student roster.

Second, since the psychological well-being of students has been superordinated over a display of knowledge, grades are designed to make students feel good about themselves. This is the self-esteem hoax. In the last international exam students were asked to evaluate their prowess in math and other disciplines. American students claimed to be proficient in math, even though their aggregate score was next to last among test-takers from many nations. Americans are now routinely taught to feel good about themselves, even when their performance belies the truth.

Last is the fungibility of standards. As a legislator pointed out to me, "High, inflexible standards will result in more drop-outs and failing students. We can't tolerate that, the voters will kill us." The evidence of continuing grade inflation comes at a time when many states are supposedly requiring schools to adopt higher standards. Teachers, however, have responded to this requirement by arguing that high grades are consistent with high standards since students are performing better than heretofore.

Unfortunately for those who make this claim is the harsh reality of SAT scores. Just as confidence in one's performance is out of step with actual performance, student career aspirations are inconsistent with demand in the labor market and aptitude. U.S. Labor Department projections indicate that the top three growth occupations between now and 2006 are computer-related. Yet relatively few students (5 percent) expressed an interest in computing and information sciences and, if declining math scores on the SAT are suggestive, many students may not have the aptitude for this field. It should also be noted that students taking the SAT may bring calculators with them when taking the test. Presumably this concession was designed to avoid sloppy mistakes. Yet, here again, the math SAT score is declining, despite this gesture.

The dumbing down of America is in full pace as rationalizations are sought for this phenomenon from every quarter. When an objective test, despite its flaws, is used to examine student performance, the resultant picture isn't pretty. Developing a strategy for lifting performance to the level of appearance is the great challenge ahead.

Egalitarianism on the Playing Field

Egalitarianism flourishes in an atmosphere where competition is often derided and when qualitative judgments are deemed psychologically disadvantageous. Radical egalitarians in our midst are relentless in their pursuit of a new national agenda, both in and out of the classroom. Physical education reforms have reduced the competitive atmosphere that once characterized such activity. Gym classes and sports are not considered to "prepare children for lifetime health." Classes are now organized so that kids become aware of their bodies. Skills development is coordinated with each child's size, weight, and aptitude. The Plainfield Community Middle School in Indiana has introduced a policy in which any student may join its teams, regardless of ability.

The once common scene of team captains choosing their players and embarrassing marginal athletes is a relic of the past. Teams now include everyone in a display of random cooperation. Stopwatches that timed performance have been relegated to desk drawers. Judy Young, executive director of the National Association for Sports and Physical Education, said, "The primary shift in focus is toward health-related fitness, and the two major goals of modern physical education are toward physical competence and health for everyone." What Ms. Young and others in this movement are suggesting is that no one need be a klutz.

There is also a backdrop of escalating medical expenses and the need to reduce them by making playtime preventive medicine. Many school systems desire to prepare students for a personal physical program that will ensure healthy attitudes throughout their lives.

There are also vocal feminists in this reform movement who contend boys aren't giving girls a fair chance on the athletic field. And they say boys have a physical endowment that leaves many girls at a disadvantage. Therefore the exercises now preferred apply equally to both sexes: hiking, exploring, dancing, nutrition, and aerobics. The new physical education is personalized, but obviously genderless.

Not everyone embraces this reform movement and I am one of the qualified critics. Yes, it is desirable to encourage lifetime fitness, albeit telling people to walk instead of drive might be a simple way to achieve this goal. And yes, encouraging preventive medical methods is sensible. However, this new physical education curriculum is yet another manifestation of a societal trend away from excellence to mediocrity. The diminution of standards by substituting cooperation for competition undermines the gifted athlete as it rewards the average or marginal athlete. Clearly sports aficionados don't watch their local professional teams because they want to feel involved. Life is based on performance, even if the proponents of radical egalitarianism choose not to believe so.

A compression at the mean may make some teachers, parents, and students feel good, but it generates a deleterious effect on the society. Matthew Guidry, acting director of the President's Council, said, "Some people get upset because they say not everybody can be an outstanding basketball player, but I don't agree with that. We try to encourage outstanding performance, not just average." Alas, not everyone can be an outstanding athlete and no matter how hard gym teachers may try, the number of Michael Jordans emerging from gym classes will be limited. The point, however, is that gifted athletes should have the opportunity to shine. Homogenization of performance—the evolving standard in academic grades, job evaluation, and now athletics—is inconsistent with the meritocracy on which this nation was founded.

I see klutzes every day of the week jogging, or should I say slogging, in their neighborhoods, and I admire them. A sound mind in a sound body is as desirable now as when Aristotle prescribed it more than two millennia ago. However, if the schools promote the belief that what is average is right or that excellence cannot rise to the surface, all Americans will be adversely affected. Sports provide a metaphor for the nation. We don't want average performances from athletes. We ask them to dig down and do more, to pursue excellence even when the goal is elusive.

The reform movement in physical education has some desirable aims, but to the extent that it promotes mediocrity it should be opposed. The Plainfield Community Middle School, fearful that students excluded from a school team might suffer humiliation, instituted a "no-cut" policy for all school clubs and teams. One result of this policy is that there are 72 girls on the cheerleading squad with "a definite sacrifice in synchronization." While Plainfield is not the first school to adopt a nondiscriminatory team and club policy, it has extended this policy to stunning levels, in large part because it is believed a no-cut arrangement will enhance school spirit and participation.

I would contend, however, that this nondiscrimination does not shield students from the emotional scars of failure, but rather exaggerates them. Any effort by school administrators to suppress qualitative differences is ignored by the reality of performance. It is also noteworthy that those students now on a squad by dint of nonselectivity will face the humiliation of public scorn when they can't throw a football or shoot a foul shot. Is it really better to let all students participate even if some are the butt of criticism, or will criticism itself be banned in this new era of egalitarianism? On the other side of the equation are those excellent athletes who will not derive any of the benefits of superior skill. They will never enjoy the exhilaration of knowing that on the basis of talent they made the cut. They may stand out on the field, but they can never take satisfaction from "making the team."

That a school would consider such a policy is hardly surprising in an atmosphere where competition is often derided and when qualitative judgments are deemed psychologically disadvantageous. Yet I wonder how the overweight cheerleader feels when fans from a rival school take wagers on how high she jumps off the ground. In an effort to avoid the painful process of selection, faculty members at Plainfield may have exposed students to an even more painful experience of public humiliation.

Plainfield may be congratulating itself over its no-cut policy. But after all is said and done, what lessons will students derive from their extracurricular experiences? It seems to me that at this middle school in Indiana a nondifferential standard will be engendered in which the illusion of inexorable egalitarianism will be etched in student minds. The school band will still play, but no one will care if the music is discordant. In fact, the school is likely to be a laughingstock among Indiana junior high schools. In short order, the good athletes will transfer, and Plainfield will be known as the center of the nerds. Thus a policy wrought by egalitarians with the best of intentions will most assuredly fall flat on its face.

Curriculum Reforms Used to Promote Multiculturalism

The Rainbow Curriculum

When the controversial "Children of the Rainbow" curriculum was introduced in School District 24 in Queens, New York, some parents were whipped into a frenzy. The curriculum for Grades 1-6 was based on the supposition that children should be taught tolerance for different kinds of home environments, including single-parent families, homosexual families, and foster families. Many parents were outraged because of both the content of the curriculum and the way it had been imposed on their children without parental input. Parents believed it was inappropriate to explain the homosexual lifestyle to six- and seven-year-olds, even though homosexuality was not specifically included in the curriculum.

Joseph Fernandez, chancellor of the city's school system, entered the fray, contending that the District 24 school board acted inappropriately in rejecting the curriculum. He was so incensed that he suspended the board—a decision later rescinded by the city Board of Education. The objective of the controversial curriculum, Fernandez said, was to acknowledge the positive aspects of varied family structures, "including two parent or single parent households, gay or lesbian parents, divorced parents, adoptive parents and guardians or foster parents." Fernandez contended that the curriculum was designed to nurture an understanding and tolerance for "diverse family structures"—"nothing more; nothing less."

"Sadly," he added, "the malicious campaign attacking a curriculum designed, in part, to promote tolerance and improved inter-group relations has succeeded in whipping some people into a venomous frenzy. The curriculum is not about homosexuality. It is about ending discrimination and hate."

To describe Fernandez's view as naive does not do it justice. While it is appropriate to acknowledge the love that may be engendered in various family structures, it is not appropriate to describe different family structures as equally valid. Homosexual couples may raise normal children, but it is more difficult for them to do so.

The Multicultural Curriculum

For at least a decade multiculturalism has been a byword in American education. As an idea it presupposes an emphasis on the ethnic and racial background of students in order to bolster their pride and preserve their cultural identities. The notion that ethnic and cultural groups in the United States should preserve their identities instead of fusing them into the proverbial melting pot is in the ascendancy, as a belief in a distinctive American ethos has lost ground.

For the last several years, the so-called multiculturalists have promoted a raft of reforms designed to improve the self-regard of black students. The focus of their efforts has been the establishment of an African-centered curriculum. While that, in itself, is hardly a matter over which hackles should be raised, in the hands of enthusiastic radicals the net result has been nothing short of calamitous. It is presently estimated that hundreds of schools nationwide, in an effort to create a sense of pride, intentionally or inadvertently mislead their students, teaching in effect what is either untrue, unproven, or patently absurd.

Several bewildering claims have been culled from these African-centered curriculum guides as evidence of the systematic absurdities taught in the public schools:

1. According to an African-Caribbean magazine, *Pride*, distributed in many public schools, Ludwig von Beethoven was not a white European, but a black African;
2. Greek gods, the Ten Commandments, and Aztec and Mayan civilizations are derivations of African culture;
3. Ramses, King Tut, Aesop, and Cleopatra were black;
4. Africa was the center of culture and learning in the ancient world—Greece and Rome were derived from African civilization;
5. Africa's literary, mathematical, and scientific achievements were stolen by white Europeans;
6. From the controversial Leonard Jeffries comes the oft-repeated claim that whites are "ice people" whose colonialism and "savagery" are due to a lack of melanin, the chemical that turns blacks into benign "sun people" with distinct intellectual advantages;
7. African studies of electric eels led to the invention of the battery;
8. Blacks face a conspiracy organized by Jews and the Mafia to foster negative images in the media;
9. Plato and Aristotle plagiarized their work from African philosophers;
10. European history is based on cruelty to blacks and exploitation of all minorities.

Not one of these claims is presented with evidence that can be critically examined. Moreover, most serious scholars of African history deny the veracity of any of these factoids, which by now are recurring themes in predominantly black schools. Although a refutation of these claims appears in a recent book by Arthur Schlesinger Jr., his reasoning has been dismissed by the architects of African-centered studies as the rantings of a "white honkie."

Where this is leading has been clear for some time. Postmodernists have shattered the bonds of rational judgment. History is not a discipline for the pursuit of truth, but a servant of present politics. Literature does not offer insight into the human experience; it is a tribal ritual affirming the official categories of victimhood. News reports are not designed to offer the facts or even the news but rather to reveal the sentiments of the reporter. Education is not an exercise in unveiling the truth but an attempt at self-appreciation. Debate is not engaged in to open the portals of knowledge but a game of one-upmanship in which any rhetorical device, however specious, is permitted.

Recognizing Chauvinism in Ethnic-Studies Courses

Many educators at elementary, secondary, and higher education levels have argued for separate ethnic studies courses, such as Black Studies, Chicano Studies, and Native American Studies, and to a great extent they have achieved their goal. Schools and colleges across the country routinely offer these programs. But now, mirabile dictu, educators at various levels are rethinking the multicultural curriculum, worrying that past efforts to teach separate ethnic studies have widened the divisions many believed such courses would close.

In an early '90s' edition of the *Los Angeles Times*, an article reported that the recognition of special holidays, narrowly sectarian events, and obscure heroes had isolated students from each other and led teachers to question the way in which multicultural study is taught. Ronald Tanaki, ethnic studies professor at the University of California at Berkeley, said, "I think many people, especially in the post-Rodney King era, are beginning to realize that we can't just study ourselves as separate groups. We've gone beyond the need to recover identity and roots, and now we're realizing that our paths as members of different groups are crisscrossing each other."

Clearly Professor Tanaki has his allies and detractors. Multiculturalism has not disappeared, nor will it. However, the important point is that it is being challenged by some of the very same people who were its most ardent proponents. It is now widely agreed that instead of promoting ethnic pride, multiculturalism has promoted ethnic chauvinism; instead of promoting understanding, it has promoted suspicion and isolation.

Even students recognize the baneful effects of most ethnic programs. Instead of simply teaching about one's background, there is a tendency to create barriers that separate instead of bridges that unite. Students critical of the present multicultural approach often contend that courses under this rubric do not offer cultural connections to the nation and its past. They cite the narrowly parochial methods and reluctance to weave the treatment of ethnic groups into the history of the nation. Even in courses that highlight several ethnic groups, there is a tendency to discuss each group separately, such as African Americans one week and Korean Americans the next.

The catalyst for such courses is the belief that the United States discounts the ethnic experience. In order to compensate for this perceived injustice, many educators organized a united front to rewrite the social studies curriculum. However it is increasingly clear—as it should have been from the outset—that the price of ethnic and racial pride is isolation and hostility. Human experience indicates that those who physically separate, refuse to understand the society in which they reside, and learn only about their own culture, are ultimately inhibited from social and economic advancement. The very goal of equal opportunity is being undermined by multiculturalists who, in isolating ethnic groups and shielding them from the larger culture, often restrict a chance for student success. Ethnic pride is not inconsistent with national loyalty, but ethnic chauvinism is. What some multiculturalists are coming to understand is that the approaches in our schools are blocking disadvantaged students from the advantages this society can and often does provide.

The Deception of Multiculturalism

Multiculturalism, according to its proponents, is merely an effort to help students appreciate cultures other than their own. Presumably, the embrace of different cultures is good, a kind of universal brotherhood. On one level, this is a pedagogically sound approach. There are indeed universal characteristics to culture, such as in the relationship between a man and a woman and a husband and a wife.

But the fact is that there are many parts of other cultures that we in the United States should abhor. For example, a recent United Nations report indicates that slavery in many parts of the world endures. The Sudanese government-backed militia sells members of the Dinka tribe as slaves for thirty to sixty dollars each. Child slavery has been reported in Sri Lanka, Thailand, and Haiti. In Brazil, contractors known as *gatos* roam rural areas, hiring people for jobs in distant regions, and then enslaving them. An International Labor Organization report indicated that there are at least fifteen million indentured servants in India and twenty million in Pakistan. It has also been reported that in parts of Africa and Asia, clitoridectomies are routinely imposed on young women as a religious rite. Other forms of mutilation are also common. In the Arab nations, thieves' limbs routinely are severed as punishment.

All over the world, a host of barbaric practices continue unabated. Do the promoters of universalism in our schools say a word about these practices? Do they note that tolerance of evil is not a virtue? It is one thing to be tolerant of people who are different but quite another to confuse a tolerance of difference with a universal acceptance of all that is different. So far down this track has the curriculum gone that the United States is condemned for having once had slavery, but not a word in any curriculum guide can be found on the thriving slave trade in Mauritania.

Clearly a balanced curriculum isn't easy to achieve. However, American educators have erred on the side of an absurd acceptance of all things non-Western and an irrational criticism of all things Western. Freedom of speech, civil rights, respect for women, and other ideas that have emerged from the West should be admired and noted with pride. Instead, multiculturalists exaggerate the warts in Western culture while praising Third World cultures. It would be difficult to conceive of a better plan to undermine the West than this one. But it isn't a conceived plot; it is the expression of good intentions gone awry. It is a fine example of misguided energy.

National Standards for History in Schools

The standards codify what students should know about the nation's past and the globe's history. The revised edition responded to criticism that the first had been too "propagandistic." The revised standard deleted "teaching examples" that accompanied the standards and identified omissions, errors, and examples of bias. Most recommendations were included in the second edition of *National Standards for History*, which were then embraced by Diane Ravitch and Arthur Schlesinger Jr. in the *Wall Street Journal.*

While the standards have unquestionably been improved in this latest edition, I'm convinced there are valid reasons to demur from the Ravitch-Schlesinger ringing endorsement. Although the boilerplate in the document refers to the purposes for studying history that are incontrovertible, the devil is in the curriculum details.

Every unit is infused with the bonding material of race, class, and gender. Conflict, while an obvious theme in American life, is apotheosized to *the* theme in our history. Even in the third and fourth grades' study of one's local region, it is argued that students should "describe the problems, including prejudices and intolerance, as well as the opportunities that various groups who have lived in their state or region have experienced." But suppose prejudice and intolerance don't exist?

The two most often mentioned issues in the U.S. history standards section are race-related matters, including Indian affairs and gender. Industrialization is seen through the lens of slavery's expansion and federal Indian policy, and the Age of Discovery is appraised in changing gender roles. Surely the spread of slavery and industrialization were related, albeit free labor characterized the industrial North as opposed to the feudal South. And assuredly the European voyages to the New World changed the physical and social landscape of America, including the role of women. I would therefore not argue for the deletion of these themes. But I would also argue against the disproportionate emphasis they receive in almost every unit on U.S. and world history. Even the Revolutionary War comes in for this politically correct interpretation, diminishing, in effect, the central reason for and the enduring consequence of the war against Great Britain for independence. On page 87 it is noted: "Compare and explain the different roles and perspectives in the war of men and women, including white settlers, free and enslaved African-Americans, and Native-Americans."

Another theme that permeates the standards report is the implicit immorality in denying women the right to vote, promotion of the slave system, and the relocation of the Indians. While the authors note that students should consider multiple perspectives, there is a penchant for presentist standards of evaluation. For example, most sensible people today would consider it laughable to oppose women's suffrage, but that wasn't true a century ago. Is it therefore appropriate to engage in blanket condemnation?

In addition to the historical error of presentism there are several illustrations of ipse dixit, assertions without proof. For example, on page 99 the authors contend that "Northerners, like Southerners, believed in the social inferiority of blacks." Was that all Northerners? And if so, how does one account for the abolitionist movement? On page 103 the authors maintain "the advent of big business brought about a concentration of the nation's productive capacities in many fewer hands." That may be true, but one could have easily pointed out in the same paragraph that the rise of big business also produced an unprecedented increase of per-capita income. On page 123 students are asked to "evaluate the *effectiveness* of the United Nations in reducing international tensions and conflicts" (my emphasis). And on page 127 it is asserted that "civil-rights agendas . . . lost steam in the '70s." This is a rather curious contention based on the Supreme Court decisions in the '70s that extended the landmark civil rights legislation of the '60s.

When government is not culpable of abuse to the poor or minorities the standards statement would have you believe it is capricious about the nation's bounty. On page 105 the authors argue that students should "Explain how rapid industrialization, extractive mining techniques and the gridiron pattern of urban growth affected the scenic beauty and health of city and countryside." Clearly the explanation is that city and countryside were affected adversely. The fact that the automobile might allow people to reach the countryside easily so that one can breathe fresh air should be put into this historical calculus as well.

If there is one overarching theme in this document, it is internal strife. In a section on modern America, the authors point out (p. 111) the "continuing tension among Protestants, Catholics, and Jews, most dramatically exemplified in the resurgence of Protestant fundamentalism." In a section on the Great Depression and World War II, the authors contend that students should learn about "the irony of racial minorities fighting for democratic principles overseas that they were still denied at home . . ." (p. 116). In the section on postwar America, the authors argue that students should be able to "analyze the continued gap between poverty and the rising influence of the middle class" (p. 122). In a section devoted to the Vietnam War, it is argued that students should be able to "Explain the composition of the American forces recruited to fight the war." In a section on the American Labor Movement, it is argued students should be able to "Explain the response of management and government at different levels to labor strife in different regions of the country" (p. 107). And in contemporary United States history, there is the expectation that students can evaluate "continuing grievances of racial and ethnic minorities . . ." (p. 131).

The curriculum on world history has, in modified form, the same emphasis on conflict, although it should be noted that it appears with ample justification. Similarly, the emphasis on race, class, and gender is as apparent in this global curriculum section as it is in the American history segment. For example, on page 166 it is argued that students should be able to "Assess the importance of women of gentry families in preserving and transmitting Chinese cultural values" and analyze "common women in the context of feudal society."

What distinguishes the world history curriculum from American history is the emphasis given to obscure civilizations and the relatively underweighted attention given to Europe. Zapotec, Moche, Teotihuacan, Anasazi, Mughal, and Songhay societies are given almost equal weight to the emerging European societies. Moreover, Europe is often discussed in a disparaging fashion: "Analyze why the introduction of new disease microorganisms in the Americas after 1492 had such devastating demographic and social effects on American Indian populations" (p. 177).

Even European accomplishments are not evaluated on their own terms; rather, they are applied to the context of imperialism. On page 195 it is noted that students should be able to "Describe advances in transportation, medicine, and weapons technology in Europe in the later nineteenth century and assess the importance of these factors in the success of imperial expansion." Similarly, the effects of colonialism are drawn out with phrases such as "dogged imperial regimes," but a comparison of conditions in Africa during colonialism and afterward is not included. On page 210 there is the expectation that students will be able to "Analyze why economic disparities between industrialized and developing countries have persisted or increased and how both neo-colonialism and authoritarian political leadership have affected development in African and Asian countries." The implication in this statement is clear: A failure to bring about development in Africa and parts of Asia is the fault of the West.

Also insinuating itself into the curriculum is the panoply of limits to growth issues, such as "world population explosion, persistent poverty, environmental degradation, and epidemic disease" (p. 207). Notwithstanding is the fact that the rate of world population increase has been declining since 1955, that this century has seen the rise of a middle class in much of the world that had only known poverty, that environmental degradation has improved in some areas and worsened in others, and that the present ability to control many diseases such as polio and influenza is unprecedented in human history.

Overlooked in the American history standards may be what is most essential to an understanding of the exceptional characteristics in this nation's past. The conflicts so deeply rooted in other nation-states that they can only be resolved by war have been mercifully avoided in this country, with the exception of the Civil War. Labor struggles in this country did not lead to the assumption of Marxist suppositions. On the contrary, the Knights of Labor sought conciliation with management. Various religions have developed a modus vivendi, if not amicable, relations. Even the well-advertised ethnic and racial tensions belie areas of cooperation and mutual support.

In the world history standards, the origins of individual liberty and prosperity rights that are embodied in the U.S. Constitution are beclouded by emphasis on societies with different traditions. That is not to suggest other cultures shouldn't be studied, but the emphasis on cultural relativism has subordinated the importance of those ideas that make the West unique.

As I see it, the revised standards will not undermine the study of history in our schools. But it will certainly not enhance it either. In reading this document I'm reminded of Jean Kirkpatrick's witty remark that we have an obligation to tell the truth no matter how good the news may be. I would second that claim. We should tell our human story fairly and honestly with all the warts exposed, but we should also not avoid our unique accomplishments or assume that through the prism of ideological judgment resides the truth. The United States is not a paragon of virtue, but it has much to be proud of in its past. World history is often sanguinary and barbaric, but strides have been made in improving human welfare for a considerable portion of the globe. That balance is what these history standards should embody. Unfortunately, that is not the case, even in the "new and improved" second edition.

Dumbed Down and Distorted Textbooks

The dumbing down of American education is reflected in the poor quality of many contemporary textbooks. The dumbed down texts are geared to the lowest common denominator, and these books were once accurately described as pabulum for adolescents. Many postmodernist texts ignore facts to promote a historical view intended to develop cultural self-esteem. The resulting political orthodoxy produced silly and banal judgments.

In *The Voyages of Columbus: A Turning Point in World History*, a text published by Alfred Crosby and Helen Nader at the beginning of the '90s, there is an astonishing statement that demonstrates my point. It reads: "In summation, Christopher Columbus crossed the Atlantic in 1492 and opened a period of massive exchanges between the Old and New Worlds. The influence of his voyages on the history of commerce, religion, the nation-state, war, and literature has been immense. But his greatest impact has been the one to which we have paid least attention: his biological impact. Its victims have been many—passenger pigeons, Carolina parakeets, Wampanoags, Omahas, Modocs, Comanches, and so on."

If this claim were made by the producers of *Saturday Night Live* it might be considered laughable, but to entertain this view seriously in a book that purports to be educational is nothing less than criminal. Perhaps Columbus should also be criticized for not calling indigenous women "Ms." or perhaps he committed the environmental injustice of cutting down a tree. So far down Alice's tunnel have we fallen that the truth is merely the handmaiden of contemporary ideology.

It is apparently far more important for youngsters to know the secular catechism than to read an honest portrait of the past. If one were to rely on Crosby and Nader, Magellan would be known not for his circumnavigation of the globe but rather the dumping of garbage at sea. Captain Cook would be known not for his adventures in the South Seas but for spreading disease. Perhaps this ideological brainwashing explains why so many students neither care about nor know history. History has become a politicized discipline, less a concern with the past and more an interpretation of the present. Serious historians decry the efforts to rewrite the past based on present attitudes, but very often serious historians are not engaged in the writing of textbooks, and when on occasion they are, there is the irresistible urge to write what is popular and acceptable.

That Columbus should be remembered as a biological plunderer is patently absurd. Education in the service of ideology is a dicey game, since sophisticated students can easily recognize and reject it and even unsophisticated students will regard such propaganda as unimportant. The real tragedy is that school time is wasted on this nonsense and that the young do not possess the requisite analytical tools to assess their past.

Of course my critique won't deter the true believers eager to shape a new world out of their idiosyncratic interpretation of the old world. If the "excellence in education" movement has any success, the litmus test for it will be whether the ideologists are in retreat. Their kind has already done much that is damaging to our schools. Columbus may have sailed the ocean blue in 1492, but he didn't know much about conservation and, frankly, he didn't care.

Private Schools Have Not Dodged the Next Wave of Political Correctness

It is routinely accepted that public schools have lost their way and have become mired in political correctness, multicultural studies, condom distribution, and teaching homosexuality. Yet, public schools are not alone. Political correctness afflicts private schools as much as its public counterparts and invades all facets of the curriculum.

My six-year-old is in a private school that charges the equivalent of a Mazda each year. For this sum I am privileged to have my daughter indoctrinated with the most fashionable political ideas this side of Greenwich Village. As part of her orientation she was exposed to the plight of the Brazilian rain forest. I was urged to invest in a plot of land in the Amazon basin so that trees won't be cut and exotic animal species won't be rendered extinct. When I balked, my daughter said, "Daddy, don't you want to save the earth?" This was only the beginning.

On AIDS awareness day my daughter went with her class to the Hudson River where they sang "Lean on Me" to a group of people afflicted with the dread disease. How AIDS victims benefited from this song, I do not know. But then, there's a lot about this school I do not understand.

In order to be sure that my daughter is sufficiently sensitive to our neighbors to the south, she and her classmates were obliged to learn "La Bandeira," the Puerto Rican anthem, in Spanish. Since she had not been obliged either to learn or lip-synch the "Star Spangled Banner," I naively regarded this exercise as somewhat curious. When I politely suggested that the national anthem should be sung,

I was told, in no uncertain terms, that "chauvinism" is not countenanced in the school—unless it is for Latin America. Unfortunately I didn't learn my lesson. Since school authorities didn't believe it appropriate to sing the national anthem, I decided to ask if the Pledge of Allegiance could be recited. That was a big mistake. I was soundly criticized for asking children to repeat a pledge they didn't understand. As one parent put it, "Do these kids know to what they are giving their allegiance?" At that moment, I was tempted to bring up "La Bandeira," but civility prevented me from doing so.

Having retreated on this issue, I turned my attention to the flag. Surely the Stars and Stripes would not be offensive to these boosters of cultural diversity. If students can honor the Puerto Rican flag I reasoned, there could be no valid reason for opposing an American flag—especially if I bought it. What I didn't count on was that my logical exegesis was flat-out wrong. American flags are offensive to those who don't care about America.

Defeated yet again, I turned my attention to the three Rs. Who could possibly oppose reading, 'riting, and 'rithmetic? I would soon find out. Since my daughter spells words as she hears them, I suggested at a parents' meeting that the class learn to spell. This proposal was greeted with horror. "Spelling," I was told, "is a middle-class hang-up. At some point all kids learn to spell." Since I meet students in the university who are products of "creative spelling," I wasn't persuaded by that argument. But neither were other parents persuaded by mine. "Creative spelling" remains in the curriculum. The flag, Pledge of Allegiance, and the national anthem remain out.

Occasionally, I remind myself that my daughter is only in the first grade. Conditions are likely to worsen. So far, she doesn't celebrate Malcolm X's birthday and hasn't told me I can't eat meat. Those things will assuredly occur. There is virtually no way to avoid them, unless, of course, I take our daughter out of this private school. But where can she go that would be different from this experience? Perhaps the only way to avoid the imposition of a radical agenda is to keep our daughter at home. At least we can pledge allegiance to the flag and sing the "Star Spangled Banner."

The Ignorance of Many Teachers and the Power of the NEA Contribute to the Decline of American Education

Many Teachers Know As Little As Their Students

According to details in this case, Long Island administrators at the Connetoquot Central School District in Suffolk County found themselves with a surfeit of aspiring teachers. In order to determine who was eligible for teaching positions, they cobbled together a test from eleventh-grade State Regents exams in English, assuming that prospective teachers should be able to communicate at the eleventh-grade level. Every one of the applicants had passed state certification tests and many held master's degrees. Nonetheless, of the 758 who took the test, only 202, or 26 percent, could answer forty of the fifty questions correctly.

While the assistant superintendent in the school district was surprised at the result, it was consistent with evidence accumulated elsewhere. The dumbing down of college requirements, especially in schools of education, has continued unabated. James Madison University, for example, recently decided not to require American history of its students. Presumably students will be able to graduate from James Madison University without knowing who James Madison was.

A survey founded by the National Endowment for the Humanities demonstrated that it is possible to graduate from 78 percent of the nation's colleges and universities without ever taking a course in the history of Western civilization. Moreover, in an era when grammar is rarely required of students and "creative" spelling is accepted, is it any wonder prospective teachers who are products of this education system cannot communicate at the eleventh-grade level?

Schools of education have shifted from a pedagogy of knowledge to one of psychological well-being. Teachers are more likely to be concerned with Johnny's state of mind than what he knows. In a sense well understood by educators, the schools have been Freudianized. If a student cannot meet school standards, it is often determined that holding him back will engender emotional scarring. Skills and knowledge usually take a backseat to psychological health. So what if a student can't add, at least he's happy.

Similarly, in many states the qualification of teachers is less important than the representation of protected ethnic and racial groups in the teaching ranks. As a consequence, "credentialing" has a special meaning in the present context. As the Connetoquot exam pointed out, "credentialed" teachers may not know very much. In some states, the SAT scores for prospective teachers are in the bottom quartile. Should the issue of teacher background knowledge be explored seriously, it would turn out to be a national scandal. For years the public has been told that Johnny can't read and Mary can't add, but very few asked if Mr. Chips can read and add. Perhaps the public didn't want to know very much about the state of the teaching profession.

However, if education is on the political front burner and citizens are concerned about student attainment and national competitiveness, it is also appropriate to ask about the level of instruction and what teachers know. Based on an eleventh-grade exam given to certified teachers in Suffolk County, Long Island, the evidence should make all Americans take notice.

Teachers Often Can't Teach Because They Are Poorly Prepared in Teachers Colleges

The report *Different Drummers: How Teachers of Teachers View Public Education* (1997) published by the Public Agenda, an organization founded by public opinion analyst Daniel Yankelovich and former secretary of state Cyrus Vance, revealed that schools often don't work because those who teach the teachers are so removed from the daily concerns in schools.

This report asserted that though professors of education are not totally indifferent to content, it is the process of learning that most engages them. As a consequence, professors of education tend to see teachers as facilitators, not as transmitters of knowledge. From this position flows the premise that school assumptions about decorum, standardized tests to measure attainment, rewards and punishment, and competition are retrograde. Interestingly, these positions are seriously at odds with public expectations about the schools. While professors of education contend that tests don't count or don't matter as much as conventional wisdom suggests, the public wants to make sure Johnny and Mary score well on basic tests so that they can get in to the college of their choice. According to the report, "Seventy-nine percent of these teachers of teachers say 'the public has outmoded and mistaken beliefs about what good teaching means.'" Although I do not have evidence to support my claim, I'd wager that at least 79 percent of the public believes professors of education have mistaken beliefs about teaching.

Moreover, in a system in which credentialing is determined by professors of education, not the general public, it is the professors who dictate the direction of primary and secondary education. Perhaps the most profound dichotomy between professors and the public can be found in attitudes about student deportment. Professors assume the active, engaged student will not be disruptive; the public assumes an orderly classroom is the prerequisite for engagement. Despite strongly expressed opinion, education professors overwhelmingly harbor doubts about their teaching methods, admitting that they are often detached from contemporary schools. In some respects this finding is analogous to physicians who have strong opinions about medical care but haven't been to a hospital in years.

When it comes to the allocation of resources, professors and public opinion are on virtually different planets. Professors argue that more money is needed for modern equipment, smaller classes, and support services. The public favors high standards and strict discipline that do not require additional funding. But when it comes to the education of their own children, teachers of teachers act consistently with the position of choice advocates and a significant portion of the public: they seek out a location where they can have confidence in the schools. It is ironic that those in the position of training teachers are so disconnected from public sentiments. Even as professors of education exercise enormous influence over the public schools, their attitudes betray an indifference to public opinion.

The powerful report ends with a poignant question: "How can we possibly serve the nation's children well if more than 100,000 graduates of education programs—nursed by their professors' vision—enter the nation's classrooms each year prepared for an ideal but unarmed for the reality?" How indeed?

The Goals of the NEA Are Political, Not Scholarly

The NEA is the nation's most powerful union. Its politicized goals reveal why it is among the most harmful organizations in the country, and why it contributes so little to promoting high educational standards. The NEA lobbied for the following goals in 1990:

1. More money for public education from federal, state, and local governments;
2. Opposition to parental choice or open enrollment plans;
3. Opposition to tuition tax credits or vouchers and federal legislation prohibiting any government assistance to private or parochial schools;
4. Prohibition of home schooling unless the parent is "licensed by the appropriate state education licensure agency" and the curriculum is "approved by the state department of education";
5. Federally funded early childhood intervention and education programs and compulsory kindergarten classes;
6. Guidance counseling beginning at the pre-kindergarten level and specifically including guidance in sexual orientation;
7. A prohibition on parental-consent requirements for sex education courses. Moreover, such courses should provide instruction in the "diversity of sexual orientation";
8. Proposed courses on environmental issues, nuclear war, and "global interdependence";
9. Use of nonsexist language in all schools "regardless of grammatical correctness";
10. National government-provided health care.

While some of these proposals have arguable benefits, most fall into the realm of empty bromides and even baneful ideas. Educational expenditures, for example, have gone up by about 200 percent in the last two decades (controlling for inflation) without the slightest effect on student achievement.

In fact, one could make the case for an adverse correlation, since performance levels have declined as school-aid contributions have increased. The NEA's opposition to parental-choice schemes and open enrollment are designed to reinforce the public monopoly of the schools and the primacy of school administrators in making educational decisions. It is obvious that the NEA leadership fears tuition tax credits or vouchers since they would enhance enrollment opportunities outside the public school system. Most important, the NEA opposition to home schooling indicates that the organization will not loosen its stranglehold on certification requirements in many states.

The NEA also overtly lobbies for a political agenda. A prohibition on parental consent for sex education courses suggests that the NEA knows what many parents do not and that moral decisions, including sexual orientation, should be within the purview of teachers, not parents. Proposed courses on the environment, nuclear war, and global interdependence represent the application of radical politics to curriculum design. In 1983, even the liberal editorial page editors at the *Washington Post* described the NEA nuclear-weapons curriculum, "Choices," as "political propaganda." But the NEA has not relented. Its call for nonsexist language in the schools "regardless of grammatical correctness" is a clear indication that political goals transcend educational goals.

Perhaps the NEA should give up the façade of educational concern. It is by any measure a political organization that parenthetically draws its members from educational institutions. Its aims are planted in a view of the world that could be described as open, except when it comes to sexual choice, sex education, environmental purity, unilateral disarmament, and sexist language. In the end this union is the exemplar of what our schools have become: centers for indoctrination. The shallow thinking and adherence to resolution of "the latest issue" can be transmogrified into the curriculum most evident in the schools. In a way, if the schools have failed our children, the NEA has failed its teachers. Each in turn has lost sight of its mission; each is in the grip of the Zeitgeist whose hold militates against serious reflection.

While proposals to fix our schools invariably take on the coloration of curriculum reform and accountability, one rarely mentioned but essential reform is undermining the dominance of the NEA on public education and recognizing that it is ostensibly a political organization. Sometimes labeling things accurately helps.

Promoting Academic Excellence

More Money Does Not Improve Education

It is virtually axiomatic in higher education that more money spent on the educational enterprise yields better results than has been the case heretofore. Exactly what "better results" may mean has never been clarified to my satisfaction, albeit the nexus between money and quality education is rarely subject to challenge. The word most deplored by academics and administrators is *retrenchment*, a word that inspires fear and loathing.

While it is naive to assume that current educational enterprises can continue without money, there is something quizzical about the assertion that money in one side of the academic education yields comparable results on the other side. After years of constructing budgets, I have found very little evidence to support the claim that money buys sound education. In fact, at the risk of facing an auto-da-fé organized by my colleagues, I would argue that retrenchment has its virtues. Very often a college faculty, forced to cut its budget, must consider what is truly indispensable in the curriculum. In my opinion, this is a much-needed exercise.

In the flush period for higher-education spending, new programs and courses were added without much debate. Where there was a strong faculty inclination, new programs easily found their way into the academic program. These additions were not merely a reflection of a latitudinarian view of educational appropriateness: They were accepted because there was very little consideration of the financial implications of new courses. As a consequence, a carefully crafted, philosophically rationalized curriculum caved in to an academic smorgasbord, what some analysts have called the "academic supermarket." There is a dubious link between scholarship and such fashionable courses as peace studies, feminist literature, social activism, consciousness raising, semiotics, and a host of other trendy ideas. But since the argument could be made that these courses fall into the realm of "curriculum enrichment," and since taxpayers and unwary parents are often bewildered by the financial consequences of these academic experiments, there was relatively little resistance to the rise in spending and the creation of new courses.

If one were to assume time for preparation of lectures, grading of papers, and office hours, the typical professor today works a twenty-hour week. The defense of this limited work schedule is that scholars are using their time to explore the frontiers of knowledge. Yet as most surveys indicate, a small percentage of faculty members engage in research and writing and an even smaller number publish. It therefore may be fair to suggest that budgetary reductions can encourage an interest in teaching, an interest that has atrophied in the face of so few demands on the faculty work schedule. Moreover, a resurgent interest in teaching may have some effect on students even though the relationship between teaching and learning is often ambiguous.

It is instructive that from 1983 to 1991, New York State increased educational spending by 102 percent in real terms (after accounting for inflation). During this same period, median SAT scores of New York State students declined by seven points. While the spending achievement relationship is wrapped in a fog of misapprehension, there isn't any reason to assume that educational cuts will adversely affect institutions of higher learning. By focusing the attention of those faculty members now accustomed to peripheral concerns and routine spending increases, such cuts may have the unintended effect of improving the very condition of learning and teaching about which an intelligent public is justifiably upset.

Good Schools Can Produce High Achievement
Even for the Most Disadvantaged

In a 1990 study, Rand Corporation officials argued that successful urban high schools have sharply defined academic and social goals for students and have an administration that is capable of solving problems, taking initiative, and accepting accountability. By contrast, marginal schools have diffuse programs, allow students and staff to define their own roles, maintain rigid division of labor, and impose regulations from a central bureaucracy. The primary conclusion is that good schools "can work for even the most disadvantaged." In the successful schools, where 80 percent of the students graduated and 85 percent of the seniors took college entrance tests and scored relatively well, the study found an emphasis on student achievement, a determination to mold attitudes, and a basic curriculum that all graduates follow. The study noted that effective schools "unhesitatingly place burdens on their low achieving students," while ineffective ones "agree not to demand too much in return for the students' agreement not to cause trouble."

Good schools tend to have a distinctive character and a primary commitment to students and parents. Marginal schools tend to be rigid and accountable to authorities at a central bureaucracy who dictate rules and audit performances. Obviously, the way to make marginal schools good is to encourage a clearly defined social mission and develop a social climate, curriculum, and teaching strategy consistent with it. Like most reforms in education, this is more easily said than done. Little in this report violated the dictates of common sense. However, that in no way is a criticism of a study that restates the obvious in an area where the obvious desperately needs restating.

The key to learning is the establishment of well-defined, undeviating goals that are realized through teaching strategies and administrative plans. Students will know at the outset what the expectations are and what rewards and penalties will be for satisfactory and poor performance, respectively. While standards of performance can be established at a district or even state level, each school and each teacher should be free to determine the method by which the performance standard will be achieved.

It isn't easy to place an academic burden on students with low expectations of themselves and with little confidence in their ability to learn rudimentary skills, much less sophisticated ideas. Yet this is precisely the necessary task before our teachers and administrators. It is precisely the willingness to sell rigorous standards that separates the superior school principal from the average one. What has happened in American education is that for the last three decades, academic rigor has retreated before the onslaught of psychological well-being. Instead of cognition, teachers have become obsessed with emotional health. The consequence of this priority is that American students think they are very competent, but actually, are not.

Character Is the Key to Learning

What kids need as requisites for educational success are unrelated to spending. Learning is fundamentally dependent on discipline. Those kids unable to keep the seat of their pants in the seat of a chair are at a distinct disadvantage. Learning is dependent on building a solid foundation, that is, learning to spell before one can compose an essay. And learning is dependent on rewards, the satisfaction of being able to accomplish what one could not do before the learning experience.

These requisites are character traits. Without them, without the ability to delay gratification, without patience, without respect for those who know more than you do, learning is unlikely. If capital investment is needed in education, it should be made in character formation, not computers. I am not a computer

Luddite, but computers are not as fundamental to learning as those character traits that cultivate the "active mind." Unfortunately, there isn't a formula for character development and money doesn't buy it. Character comes from the home, the church, and the school. When these institutions fail and public expectations are in disarray, education falters. That, unfortunately, is where we are at the moment.

Willpower and Determination, Not Affirmative Action Quotas, Produce Excellence

When Soojin Ryu, an eighteen-year-old student at Bronx High School of Science, won one of the ten prestigious Westinghouse Science Talent Search Awards (1990), she demonstrated what a determined individual can achieve through effort in the United States. Soojin Ryu had been on American shores only four-and-a-half years at the time, having arrived from her native South Korea speaking virtually no English. "I only knew 'good morning,'" she recalled. Ryu used her $7,500 scholarship to study biology at Harvard specializing in immunology. Ryu overcame a language barrier, a racial background different from the white majority, and cultural differences in a scant four years and while attending a public educational institution. She did this during the time when proponents of bilingual education were contending that learning is enhanced in one's native tongue. Yet this young woman was able to transform her deficiency into an obvious asset.

While critics of American education say New York's public schools cannot provide an adequate education for the city's youngsters, a young woman unfamiliar with this alleged handicap demonstrates the improbability of this contention by excelling with a public school education. While educational pundits call for multicultural education so that all minorities are included in the curriculum, a South Korean girl demonstrates that she can be included without jury-rigging the curriculum to meet current political demands. While the Board of Education introduces affirmative action hiring programs to attract black and Hispanic teachers so that "the self-esteem" of minority youngsters can be "improved," Ryu demonstrates that self-esteem is encouraged by personal achievement, not the color of teachers in front of the classroom. Examples of this kind show time and again that if only common sense were applied to our education system, much that ails this system can be remedied. In this nation, anyone who wants to learn can learn.

With the appropriate application of willpower, any obstacle can be overcome. While many of our public schools are marginal, youngsters can still learn in these institutions when there is a genuine appetite for learning. All of the affirmative action programs, multicultural-educational reforms, and bilingual programs will not have the slightest effect on student performance as long as many students are uninterested in learning. The key to the future of New York's and the nation's educational system is to find the keys that unlocked learning in a South Korean girl who did not speak English, came from a poor family, did not understand this culture, and is not Caucasian. Could it be that a stable family life transcends all other considerations in educational performance? Could it be that the motivation provided (perhaps imposed) by parents served to overcome any impediments to achievement? Could it be that our tinkering with education reforms offers the wrong message to those most in need of assistance? These questions are pregnant with possibilities.

For Soojin Ryu, however, the questions are irrelevant. The streetlights on her road to success are synchronized in green. She doesn't need a special program; she is special. Perhaps the insight that we can all be special if we work to achieve our goals is the message New York's and the country's schoolchildren should be hearing.

Chapter Five

"Higher" Education

The Dumbing Down of American Universities

Greater Access Does Not Equate with Greater Success
   While many observers of higher education in the '90s agreed that standards in American universities were going to hell in a handbasket, some optimists continued to view undergraduate education as a success. Francis Oakley, president of Williams College, argued in *Chronicle of Higher Education* in 1990 that American colleges were opening their doors to increasing numbers of students, and this growth was characterized by "an impressive degree of energy, imagination, creativity, and flexibility." Alice in Wonderland was alive and well and residing at Williams College.
   The president argued that colleges were providing greater access to women and other groups "traditionally disadvantaged" on campus. In addition, the intellectual ferment on campuses brought about by the strains on the traditional curriculum "show[ed] as much promise of revitalizing education as it [did] of being a destructive force." According to Oakley, "critics preoccupied with the reinstitution of the core curriculum took little account of the extraordinary pluralism, adaptability, and variety of American higher education." Recognizing the degree of hyperbole that had by then become a requisite in the rhetoric of educational leaders, these claims are hardly surprising. One must also grant President Oakley another concession by noting that at no point was the word *quality* used to char-

acterize undergraduate education in the article from which these quotes are extracted, albeit within the confines of academe that word had ceased to have any real meaning two decades earlier.

However, after granting these acknowledgments, it should be noted that the Oakley argument had almost no relationship to actual conditions in colleges or to the stated purpose of the academic pursuit. Clearly higher education is more available than it ever was. But Oakley should understand that bigger isn't always better. The democratization of higher education could be seen against a political landscape in which a college degree is employed as a necessary credential for social and economic advancement. In the process, exclusion based on any criterion, however legitimate, was tantamount to discrimination, a word stigmatized by the radical egalitarians who came to dominate higher education. But the net result of the "greater access" Oakley admires is the general depreciation of standards for admission to and departure from American colleges.

The intellectual ferment presumably revitalizing academic pursuits was and is in reality an assault on the deposited wisdom of Western civilization. Multiculturalism, despite claims to the contrary, is an attempt to demonstrate that Western ideas, such as those that undergird the Constitution and works written by "dead white males," are not demonstrably superior to those found in non-Western works and among contemporary women. This is not, as Oakley implies, some arcane but invigorating debate between scholars such as Snow and Leavis about the basic nature of the humanities. This is a cultural war, with colleges as the battlefield. To describe this conflict as "creative" is to mistake a sledgehammer for a slide rule.

Oakley also confuses demographic shifts with alterations in knowledge. It is in my view the height of condescension to contend that women, blacks, or Hispanics should be exposed to a course of study different from that offered to white males. While this is fashionable, it is also a banal and destructive opinion. The obligation curriculum architects have to students is to offer the best that is known and written regardless of class, race, ethnicity, and gender. Clearly the best, the most highly regarded, the most universal, speaks across generations and across skin color and nationalities. In fact the works that should represent the core curriculum pay little respect to the status quo, and they ask questions fundamental to our basic humanity and speak to the multitudes in the past and the future.

Despite Oakley's belief that the core curriculum is "time bound," it is decidedly unconstrained by time. That is its essential value; it is for the ages, for all times and all peoples. What Oakley misunderstood is that the pluralists are engulfed in the present. For them, year one of human history is the Gulf of Tonkin Resolution. It is astonishing that a medievalist of Oakley's reputation doesn't apprehend that the trial of Galileo, the death of Socrates, and the dilemma of Antigone cut across time. Can the same be said of Franz Fanon, Malcolm X, and Shulimaith Firestone?

What Oakley describes as the era of imagination, energy, and flexibility has turned out to be the dark ages of higher education. Alas, the academy's energy has been directed at the trivial and purposeless; imagination for semiotics and deconstruction has rocked rationality to its foundation; diverse views are allowed only as long as that diversity is restricted to feminists, black activists, Native Americans, and homosexual boosters. The pedagogic challenge of the future is not to be found in the insertion of pedagogic disputes into the heart of teaching, as Oakley asserts. It is to be found in a resistance to puerile reform, in opposition to radical egalitarianism, and in standing true before the cultural pillars of Western civilization.

Is it any wonder that Alice is infatuated by the antics in Wonderland? After all, she has had the experience of presiding over educational matters at Williams College.

Postmodernists' Loss of Standards

Truly, we are now living in the dark ages of education, ruled by purveyors of pluralism who avoid making distinctions between excellence and mediocrity. For them, everything is as good as everything else. There is no genius or ignorance, there is only what exists. In the process, these educators are creating a curriculum that ignores the basic and timeless questions that examine issues fundamental to all humanity. This traditional core curriculum has been replaced by one that eliminates all distinctions between high and low culture, between that which ennobles the mind and soul and that which merely entertains. For postmodernists, all texts have value or don't have value as the case may be, but none is better than any other. Bugs Bunny is as valuable as Socrates, the death of Superman as notable as the birth of Christ.

Some would say that such illustrations are gross exaggerations of what is happening in the academy. But assuredly those in the academy—whether traditionalists or postmodernists—would easily recognize such examples. To some degree, the canon wars fought over the value of the Great Books could be examined from this perspective:

- The traditionalist contends that those books that address the fundamental questions of existence, that explore the essence of our common humanity, are more valuable to study than other, less significant books that merely entertain.
- The postmodernist would say that the book is less important than its text, which should be deciphered for its symbols and hidden meaning (read: race, class, and gender). In the mind of the postmodernist, anything goes. Distinctions in taste and quality are meaningless. Just as the Marxist resists the idea of class distinctions, the postmodernist resists the idea of cultural distinctions. Everything is as good as everything else.

Even when traditional texts are used in the college curriculum, they are frequently taught from a politicized perspective. The Modern Language Association's (MLA) 1991 survey found that the English professors surveyed on 350 campuses continued to include Dickens, Hawthorne, Milton, Spenser, and other canonical authors on their reading lists. Yet while the classic texts were still emphasized, new questions were being asked and a host of experimental pedagogical techniques were employed, which supports the critics' view that educational standards have been falling. For example, while 75 percent of respondents used traditional texts, 61 percent used feminist approaches, 28 percent used Marxist approaches, and 21 percent used poststructuralist approaches, which hold that language has no meaning. When asked about their teaching goals, 62 percent said that it was important that students understand the influence of race, class, and gender in literature, compared to 51 percent who felt it important to teach about the enduring ideas of Western civilization.

It should be evident that the use of a classic text does not necessarily infer a commitment to the transmission of the deposited wisdom of Western civilization. Nor does the reading of these texts ensure an honest examination of the author's words. Grafted onto these experimental pedagogical approaches is often a political or social agenda that stretches or obscures the author's meaning. For example, Conrad's *Heart of Darkness* is sometimes read more as a justification for imperialism than as an examination of the evil lurking in the hearts of men. And I've seen *Hamlet* reduced to a feminist tract in which Hamlet suffers from an Oedipal complex.

While new approaches may certainly illuminate a text, the new approaches of the moment invariably reduce literature to formulaic political analysis shorn of story line and literary grace. It is not that critics such as I prejudicially discount new approaches to learning, but rather that the new approaches rely heavily on unidimensional analysis which rarely does justice to the texture of great literature. There is little comfort taken in the assignment of canonical texts when the texts themselves have been manipulated to conform to a current political agenda. In fact, asking a question such as how did the author view women, racial minorities, homosexuals, or non-Europeans often detracts from the meaning in the texts. While issues of class, race, and gender have their place in some texts, such as *Madame Bovary*, they are not pertinent to all texts.

Former MLA president Phyllis Franklin may contend that her survey proves that the canon is alive and well at American universities, but I would argue that the MLA survey shows that the canon is in a parlous condition infected by the crosscurrents from political science and sociology. What better evidence of radical influence on campus could there be than the fact that more professors in the survey consider race, class, and gender important than those professors who teach about the principles which undergird Western civilization?

Should the radicals have their way—which appears to be a fait accompli—literature will be taught to segment, separate, and politicize rather than illuminate. Ideas will be subject to the litmus test of what is currently fashionable. And university humanities programs will sink into the vast curriculum abyss under the weight of ever more demanding political requirements imposed from the inside by professors with their own narrowly constituted agenda.

While the Cost of College Education Continues to Spiral Upward, the Curriculum Is Becoming a Wasteland As Students Design Their Own Programs of Study

Today's college curriculum typically no longer requires the core courses of a structured curriculum that once provided a common cultural foundation for graduates. Instead, administrators and faculty members have accepted students' demands to take only those classes they "need." Accepting the false premise that students have the necessary perspective to identify their academic needs, administrators have caved in and allowed students to choose courses that take their fancy.

Indeed, at the University of California, students actually vote on the subjects they want the college to *offer*. In this ten-year-old program, a student committee surveys 1,500 undergraduates asking them to identify subjects for university-sponsored courses, including those in the core curriculum. The top ten listings are put on a ballot, and the four with the most votes are submitted to university officials for approval. The university lacks the resources to offer all suggested classes, and the ordained professors are paid $34,000 to teach the two quarters each quarter. Barbara Bertin, the director of undergraduate studies, believes that this program has a significant benefit to the university and contributes to its diversity.

The egalitarian view that students are as qualified as faculty members to make judgments about their course of studies gained a foothold on campuses in the '60s, and the effect has been to add course offerings such as the Kabuki theater. If the trend of letting students pick the courses offered continues, television appreciation may soon drive calculus from the curriculum. This egalitarian view that students can effectively select their own course offerings is wrong because colleges by their very nature are not democratic institutions. Teachers know—or should know—more than students. Teachers should determine grades. And a curriculum should reflect the thoughtful influence of faculty judgment. By abdicating their responsibility, faculty members are jeopardizing the public support colleges have generally received. Parents may wonder why they are sending their kids to college at all if the students are in charge of their own programs. It is only a short step from student selection of courses to the student determination of grades. This application of the egalitarian spirit has obscured the obvious status and knowledge difference between faculty members and students.

The lack of a structured core curriculum and students acting as their own academic advisers has led to a profound change in college education. What students are given to learn in the American university and the way that knowledge is packaged is very different from what it was during their parent's day. A study by the National Association of Scholars (NAS), *The Dissolution of General Education: 1914-1993*, postulated that a "radical transformation" had taken place in higher education in which basic survey courses had been purged from the curriculum. To test this hypothesis, NAS researchers examined the requirement for a bachelor of arts degree at fifty of the top-ranked institutions in the nation. What the study demonstrated is what many academics have long suspected: The nation's leading institutions have abandoned the core academic requirements once considered the essence of a sound curriculum and the basis for a democratic society. Overall, the study found that structured course requirements were the norm in 1914, 1939, and 1964, but by 1993 these requirements had declined precipitously. Moreover, graduation requirements incorporating general education courses dropped significantly. There are now fewer mandatory courses, fewer clusters, fewer courses with prerequisites and long completion times than heretofore. In addition, the study indicates that today's students at leading colleges are not held to the exacting standards that once prevailed in the academy. For example, more than 50 percent of the schools in the study demanded a thesis or comprehensive examination as a requirement for a baccalaureate degree between 1939 and 1964. By 1993, only 12 percent of the institutions in the study maintained this requirement.

With their roots firmly planted in the soil of the '60s, academics willingly, and in some cases reluctantly, accepted the proposition advocated by radical students that judgments could not be made about what should and should not be studied. I can vividly recall a graffito on an NYU facade circa 1968, which said, "Make them [professors] teach you only what you want to learn." Alas, this cri de coeur from the barricades became official policy less than a decade later.

Commitment to structured general education requirements and rigorous standards for the completion of a degree have been vitiated, as the NAS study demonstrates. For some, participatory democracy has had a natural and understandable effect on the curriculum. As Sidney Hook reported (eds. Hook, Kurtz, and Todorovich, *The Philosophy of the Curriculum*, p. 28) a student at a Washington Square College meeting (in the '60s) said, "the intrinsic value or interest of a subject isn't enough to justify prescribing it. Every subject has intrinsic value but not to everybody, and judging by some of our teachers, not even to those who make their living teaching it. If education is to be effective and relevant, it must be related to the personal needs of the students. Without us, you have no justification for your being teachers."

Here, in unadorned form, was the challenge of that decade and beyond, a challenge from which most academics have retreated. Some scholars (Nelson Polsby falls into this camp) contend that students should have the choice of a college curriculum—not merely the college one wishes to attend—but open-ended opportunities to select any course within the university's catalog of offerings.

It seems to me that this point of view underscores two conditions. One is that an education having any value should be related to individual needs, and the second is that students know what they want to study and the consequences of their decisions. After thirty years in the academy, it seems to me almost axiomatic that these propositions are mutually incompatible. What students want is often not what they need, need being defined as that common frame of reference that sustains a liberal society such as ours. To balkanize the curriculum by allowing students, as unfettered actors on the university stage, to select any course they wish is to admit that professors, with more experience and presumably more knowledge about what to study, should abdicate their responsibility and transfer it to untutored freshmen and sophomores. Yet, mirabile dictu, this is precisely what has been occurring for several decades.

As the NAS study notes, broad exposure to areas of knowledge and the attainment of skills have been declining rather dramatically since 1964. To cite one example: "percentage of institutions with composition requirements administered by English departments slipped from . . . 86 percent in 1964 . . . to 36 percent in 1993." The present university curriculum has gone very far down the road of student participatory democracy, leaving in its wake a hodgepodge of general education programs and ambiguity about priorities in undergraduate education. As some detractors of the academy have pointed out, the current university curriculum can be analogized to a Chinese menu—a student can choose two from column A and three from column B, without any particular pattern or coherence emerging.

Granted that students will ultimately make career decisions and select majors on their own, and granted as well that we have experienced a knowledge explosion, it is nonetheless incumbent on professors to identify what is to be studied. It is not arbitrary and inappropriate for the faculty to say that in its considered judgment there are indispensable courses all students should experience. Surely, curriculum decisions are not entirely one-sided. They unfold from the debate about curriculum that is never-ending. But a faculty, as I see it, should not abandon its authority to be at the very center of these decisions.

A former dean and present vice-president for information technology at Middlebury College, Eric Davis, argues that it is desirable to have fewer required core courses. "To expect all students to take the same course, read the same books, hear the same lecture, is a format of study that's too rigid and too restrictive for the modern world," he says. What Professor Davis does not say is that the humanities are predicated on an understanding of our common *humanitas*. The humanities are, in fact, based not on the superficial differences that separate us, such as race and ethnicity, but the common bonds of empathy, sorrow, loyalty, love, bravery, and cowardice that unite us.

A culture divorced from its common bonds does not have the amalgam to cohere. When students are unaware of common cultural cues, when the voices of deep human understanding, such as Shakespeare, are ignored, when the achievements of Western civilization are derided and subsequently subordinated to the study of other civilizations, then the die for cultural dissolution is cast. I have given lectures with passing reference to phrases rooted in the culture— "Panglossian," "Achilles' heel," "Alice's rabbit hole," "The Ides of March," "Hobson's choice." Yet, to my astonishment, the college students I encounter often do not know the meanings. Admittedly, this does not exhaust the range and depth of liberal education, but it is symptomatic, in my judgment, of a loss in cultural coherence.

Lacking perspective, students are often unaware of the disparity between ideals and reality. Without some grounding in the essential works of our civilization, the Great Books, if you will, students confuse the possible with the probable. Moreover, even the radical sensibility cannot be nourished unless there is some understanding about what one is rebelling against. Education is not existential. Whether we like it or not, we are tied organically to the past. To neglect that means that in every course the wheel must be reinvented. Either we recognize the role of higher education as a transmission belt of the past to the present, or we are caught in a seamless web of enigmas and relativism. John Dewey notwithstanding, I am persuaded that Aristotle was right: Education should pass on the previous contributions of human thought.

Unfortunately, universities often fail to appreciate this aspect of their mission, albeit most give lip service to the idea of cultural transmission. A curious condition of inventiveness without background has insinuated itself into much of what passes for higher education. Perhaps the following illustration makes this point, although I do not pretend to believe that generalizations can be derived from a sample of one, and I realize that even courses grounded in tradition can be taught poorly and have little value. A student interested in playwriting came to see me about his course of study. Since he expressed an interest in contemporary drama, I asked if he had read Brecht, Pinter, and Growtowski. "Oh man," he exclaimed, "I don't even know those cats."

"Well," I replied, "don't you think you should at least read other playwrights?"

"Oh no," he proclaimed, "that would only screw up my head. I've got to keep myself open for new experiences." Of one thing I am sure: his head is very open. While this student may represent an extreme example, he is not atypical of those who contend that freedom translates into a lack of regimen and few constraints. Apparently many soi-disant artists in the academy have not read André Gide, who wrote, "Art is born of discipline and dies of freedom."

In *The Paradoxes of Freedom*, Sidney Hook argues that a freedom cult can develop an orthodoxy so rigid that it inhibits the very action it was designed to promote. How, it might be asked, can students write novels when they have not read novels? How can students measure results in an experiment if they haven't studied basic math? How can students criticize Western civilization when they haven't been exposed to the best of Western thought? Indeed, how can professors claim to have educated their students when course selection is largely arbitrary and professors have lost confidence in their ability to define the bachelor's degree?

Critics like Nelson Polsby are right to contend that individuals learn at different paces and with different aptitudes. But I disagree that autonomy of student choice flows from these assumptions. There is material that all students should know, even if they learn it at their own pace and under conditions consistent with their readiness to learn. Not everyone should read Shakespeare as a first-year college student, but every college graduate should have read some Shakespeare.

What does a college education mean without exposure to Shakespeare, Plato, Aristotle, Dante, Homer, Milton, and Tolstoy, to cite only a few examples? For graduates who have not been exposed to great works, there is only a discredited degree, one that suggests that students have merely passed through an institution of higher learning without dramatic effect. Napoleon once said, "A form of government that is not the result of a long sequence of shared experiences, efforts, and endeavors can never take root." So it is with the relationship between society and university education. Without a shared experience, citizens are open to any claim and stand naked in the public square unable to defend what they believe or deny what they do not.

Dr. Johnson pointed out that "teaching a horse how to count doesn't make him a mathematician." George Bernard Shaw once said, "Taking an ass around the world doesn't make him a horse." The study of the humanities does not necessarily lead to humanitarianism. And reading philosophy does not necessarily mean that one will lead a successful life. But learning how to count is the basis for math; experience can be a great teacher; the study of the humanities can awaken insight about oneself and others; and philosophy can pose the questions from which a good life is derived.

If a university loses sight of its core purpose, if faculty members retreat before the "nonnegotiable" demand for student freedom, then the university as we have known it and on which our society depends will be an institution marginalized by its unwillingness to uphold the best that is known and written. As I see it, the NAS study still represents a wake-up call for the academy. There is yet time to save our universities, but only if academics realize how poorly the student body is being served with the present pick-your-own-courses curriculum.

Cultural Faddishness Contributes to the Erosion of the University Curriculum

There was a time when universities remained insulated from cultural faddishness, but those days are long gone. The obsessive interest in human sexuality has moved from the tabloids to the classroom, as the University of Minnesota, NYU, the University of California, the University of Chicago, and a host of other well-known institutions explore every dimension of sexual identity. These schools have instituted gay, lesbian, bisexual, and transgender programs, and students receive credit for explicit classes that include hands-on exercises such as sculpting genitals from Play-Doh. The State University of New York (SUNY) at New Paltz sponsored a conference where sadomasochists demonstrated their "techniques" for interested students and sex toys were on display for the uninitiated.

Although one might argue that any subject might be considered for the curriculum if it meets rigorous academic standards and has an empirical body of evidence to substantiate its claims, most of these courses on sex have more to do with expression and feelings than research and scholarship. Dr. John Bancroft, who heads the Kinsey Institute at Indiana University, contends that "there is still a lack of good, basic research into the fundamentals of human sexualities." Since there isn't a sufficient body of consistent scientific findings to build a discipline, it is appropriate to ask why there is this current fascination with sexuality on campus.

The answer to that question, like the answer to so many other questions in contemporary society, is political. Invariably the instructors in these courses are trying to undo bourgeois morality. Susan Tate, an instructor at the University of Virginia, put it bluntly: "If we can discuss the heart, stomach, and elbow without embarrassment, we should be able to talk about the penis, clitoris, and vagina without laughing." The only problem with this effort at proselytizing is that sex is not elbows and even if it were, what do these classroom discussions have to do with getting an education? I often wonder whether parents who have sacrificed a great deal to send Johnny and Jane to college are pleased to learn that instead of reading Aristotle, Jane is learning how to use a dildo.

Moreover, much of the programmatic basis for sex courses is the growing tolerance for and political muscle of homosexuals. Whether this movement serves the interests of the nation remains undetermined, but at universities, homosexuality has become an extension of the civil rights movement. Hence courses on sex assume that sexual orientation is a preference not unlike the selection of bow ties. Should one contest the claim by arguing that homosexuality is a sexual aberration, insults and worse are forthcoming.

In this faux discipline, all the questions have predictable answers that fit neatly into clearly defined political parameters. Same-sex relations are natural, sex should be discussed openly and objectively, and there should be no shame in expressing oneself on this matter. Since expression is the sine qua non of these sex courses, adolescents curious about sexuality gravitate to the classroom. What these classes often encourage is personal examination, as if self-absorption weren't already a national contagion.

In a higher education environment in which students often do not know when Columbus came to the New World or how to figure out the area of a rectangle, it is astonishing that resources are being spent for courses on sexuality that have neither rigor nor an empirical body of evidence. Professor George Chauncy of the University of Chicago notes that from 1987 to 1992 there was a tenfold increase in the number of attendees at a conference on gay and lesbian studies. I would not question the veracity of this claim or his belief that this subject has newfound adherents. But what Dr. Chauncy has not noted is that the increased numbers at this conference may reflect the propaganda in sex courses, the legitimacy the academy has accorded the subject, the belief that homosexual rights are consistent with a civil rights agenda, and students' inclination to express themselves rather than engage in the hard, painstaking effort of genuine scholarship.

When the stew is served, we shouldn't be surprised at a tenfold increase of young diners.

Political Correctness (PC) and the Blossoming of Ethnic Study Programs Do Not Promote Higher Educational Standards

That free exchange of ideas and free speech can be in jeopardy on American campuses is unbelievable, yet that is a legacy political correctness will leave if not challenged. While there are thousands of diverse colleges in the states, and few professors have been fired for unpopular views, it cannot be ignored that open debate among professors and between instructors and students has been chastened by the orthodoxy that is so widely prevalent on most campuses today. One is not allowed to challenge homosexual, radical, or Third World agendas. The excellent PBS documentary *Campus Culture Wars: Five Stories about PC* captured scenes illustrating the scope of the problem.

The first deals with the campus minister at Harvard who, in the wake of a student publication, declared himself homosexual, thereby triggering a bitter dispute between gay activists and devout Christians. The second deals with a popular instructor at the University of Pennsylvania, who in a class session—as a pedagogical device—referred to black students as "ex-slaves." For this infraction of PC etiquette the professor was obliged to attend a sensitivity workshop on race relations and was later suspended. Perhaps that is why one member of the university faculty dubbed the University of Pennsylvania "the University of Peking." The third segment deals with campus administrators at Stanford University who reportedly ignored tactics of physical intimidation employed by the PC police in order to seize control of the Chicano student organization. The fourth is based on a controversy at Penn State University over a reproduction of Goya's *Naked Maja*. The painting was removed from a classroom because it created "a climate of sexual harassment." Needless to say, the instructor leveling the complaint is not an art historian. Last is arguably the most poignant section. It tells of a business student who was removed from a University of Washington Women's Studies course for asking questions inconsistent with the approved feminist doctrine.

Defenders claim that PC is little more than being sensitive to racial, gender, and ethnic slights, being opposed to rape, and being vigilant toward possible ecological disaster. Overlooked by the PC defenders, however, is the effectiveness of chilling measures that intimidate and silence all but a hardy few. If scholarship is to have any meaning at all, it should encompass the notion that ideas may be pursued wherever they lead, unfettered by suspicion or distrust. Julius Lester, a professor at the University of Massachusetts, was ostracized after deviating from the party line a single time. This caused him anguish and despair, and he found that "It took every ounce that was in me to write again." PC works by using every means short of clear-cut dismissal or censorship to intimidate the critics of the educational establishment. Defenders of PC maintain that professors' jobs aren't in jeopardy because of a political litmus test. But these assertions miss a fundamental point: There are conditions worse than job loss. They are the conditions that inhibit the free and open exchange of ideas and the pursuit of truth in an atmosphere where evidence is evaluated fairly and political beliefs are irrelevant to scholarly discourse.

Another insidious effect of PC is that it trumps truth. The autobiography *I, Rigoberta Menchu* published in the '80s, told the tale of a poor Guatemalan woman whose family was brutalized by right-wing soldiers and oppressed by reactionary landowners. The book became a symbol among professors and students and led to a Nobel Peace Prize for its author in 1992. However, David Stoll, a Middlebury College professor, investigated key allegations in the book and showed that the Menchu story was a hoax. Professor Stoll revealed inaccuracies in her account in painstaking detail and refuted many of the book's key details. For example, Menchu claimed that her brothers died of malnutrition, which proved to be untrue. She also argued that there was a struggle for the land between her family and light-skinned Guatemalans of European descent. It turned out that the struggle was between her father and his in-laws.

Yet politically correct scholars were not happy with Professor Stoll's finding, and he became very unpopular in academic circles. Seeming unable to distinguish between the requirements of autobiography versus fiction, many of Menchu's defenders adopted the position that truth was less important than the need to teach students about the brutality of the Guatemalan military and how the United States financed it. Faculty members wrote to the *Chronicle of Higher Education* claiming that Stoll had "exaggerated the importance of the discrepancies he claim[ed] to have found," even though the *New York Times* had already verified his contentions.

Joanne Rappaport, president of the Society of Latin American Anthropology, called Stoll's work "an attempt to discredit one of the only spokespersons of Guatemala's indigenous movement." Since the humanities are predicated on the pursuit of truth, there is something fundamentally wrong with scholars who say that facts don't matter. If facts don't matter, fabrications that meet the test of political correctness may be all that remains. Would it still be acceptable to teach the *Autobiography of Benjamin Franklin* if we were to learn it was written by his mother? Would the *Diary of Anne Frank* be as moving and authentic if it were written by an American girl who imagined experiences with Nazi storm troopers?

Devotion to ideology has taken us down a slippery slope in which lies are defended as "larger truths" and facts are denied as unimportant. The revelations about Rigoberta Menchu tell us something about her, but they tell us even more about the sad state of the academic enterprise.

As Student Radicals Agitate for Ethnic Diversity, Administrators Cave In

Students at Columbia are well known for their protests, and no matter how absurd the goals of the protestors, administrators often respond seriously to the agitation, believing deeply in the principle of "no trouble on my watch." During early 1996, thoughts of protest turned to the student concern that too much weight was given to Western thought in the well-established Contemporary Civilization-Humanities curriculum. To illustrate the rioters' concern about this weighting, names of their homegrown heroes—Caesar Chavez, Fidel Castro, and Malcolm X—were placed over those of Homer, Dante, Plato, and Cicero on the facade of Columbia's Butler Library.

Students demanded an ethnic studies department in which a half-dozen new professors of Asian and Latino programs would be hired. Students chanted, "Students, united, will not be defeated." And as is often the case with student rebellions, the administration did concede to one tenured professor and one assistant professor for each program, even though a new department is not in the offing.

Student protestors insisted that their concern is for greater emphasis on the experience of immigrants than was the case heretofore. "You can't grab someone from East Asian Studies and say 'Here, go teach Asian-American studies,'" said one student. Of course, unbeknownst to this student, Columbia has a distinguished East Asian studies program that is world renowned. Moreover, Columbia founded an Institute for Research in African-American Studies in 1993 that has several professors. And the core curriculum, in addition to the Contemporary Civilization-Humanities offering, requires students to take two courses on non-Western civilization.

Recognizing the signs of a radical sensibility among the protestors, Professor J. W. Swit, a European historian, noted that what students really were seeking was "a department of discriminatory practices. And that," he added, "is not a useful way of organizing a department." Indeed it is not, albeit the practice of organizing departments in precisely that way is all too common in contemporary American colleges.

Students view protest as a rite of spring, and it is hard to accept claims of oppression from students who are continually indulged and have every privilege the well-developed collective of college administrators can conjure. When the temperature rises and young men and women's fancy turns to thoughts of what cause can be adopted for a protest, it is increasingly difficult to take these demonstrations seriously. The only people who do engage in hand-wringing over this annual ritual are the university administrators who feel obliged to respond as they do.

Administrators View Black Students' Confiscation of Newspaper As an "Opportunity for Education," Not a Violation of Free Speech

At the University of Pennsylvania in 1993 a group of black students confiscated an edition of a student newspaper because they were dissatisfied with an editorial written by a conservative white columnist. Rather than discipline the students, administrators decided that this situation presented a case where "mistakes by students must be seen as opportunities for education than as occasions for punishment." Administrators argued that the students had no way of knowing that their behavior went counter to university policy because "confiscation of publications on campus policy" was not explicitly condemned in the school's *Policies and Procedures* manual. The administration therefore decided to "look forward" and prevent further conflicts and concentrate on "healing."

But if a lack of knowledge about university policy on theft is an appropriate rationale for dropping charges, why can't all students claim ignorance of university policies? Does one really need a policy statement to know that theft is wrong?

Suppose, for the sake of argument, that a group of white students had confiscated a black student publication. Would the administration be so lenient in the treatment of guilty students if they were white? As history professor Alan Kors argued, if the conditions were reversed "the administration would be leading candlelight teach-ins on freedom of the press."

"What hypocrisy!" Kors said.

Harold Arnold, an associate professor of social work in the university, found that the Black Student League (BSL) orchestrated the confiscation, which involved as many as sixty students, but only nine were charged. In his report, Arnold said that the leadership of the BSL "believed that taking the student newspaper was a legitimate and appropriate form of protest through which they could secure the attention and response to the concerns they had expressed repeatedly during the course of the year."

Here in undiluted form is a rationalization for breaking the law and violating First Amendment principles. Presumably, if you are aggrieved you can simply ignore the rights of others. As one might guess, the Arnold report suggests that the university "take seriously the educational challenge" by establishing seminars, courses, and symposia in which students can explore the interrelationships among freedom of speech, freedom of the press, the right to protest, and 'the needs and responsibilities of a diverse and inclusive society.'" What this mumbo-jumbo means, of course, is that you can't say something is wrong at the University of Pennsylvania if it is committed by a designated minority group. In language equating diversity with free speech, University of Pennsylvania officials demonstrated their confusion of issues and their cowardice in the face of obvious malfeasance by black students.

Racism Cloaked As Racial Solidarity Breeds Hatred

When Leonard Jeffries, a professor at the City University, uttered a hateful anti-Semitic diatribe, it was appropriately criticized by a variety of New Yorkers. There simply is no place for Jeffries's kind of hatred. Moreover, there isn't any reason for taxpayers to support Jeffries in a public institution. Although some supporters contend that academic freedom shields Jeffries from any criticism, most of these defenders have a misguided view of academic privilege. Academic freedom decidedly does not afford scholars the freedom to say anything at any time. It provides them only with the opportunity to express views in areas where they have expertise. When Jeffries contends that Jews were engaged in the slave trade or involved in a Hollywood conspiracy against blacks, he forfeits—by dint of these violations of truth—the privilege associated with academic freedom.

Yet as vile as Jeffries's comments may be, they seemed no longer aberrational when 500 people filled the Bethany Baptist Church in Brooklyn chanting encouragement for their "heralded hero." Reports of this rally should be evaluated against the backdrop of a State University of New York African-American Institute "study" claiming that "many" New York City Jews and former mayor Edward Koch were racist. Incidentally, the African-American Institute cosponsored the event in which Jeffries made his anti-Semitic remarks. It should be noted, furthermore, that not one of the black representatives in the legislature formally repudiated Jeffries's comment. And one, Albert Vann, said that an investigation into the veracity of Jeffries's claims should be conducted.

This is not the first time Jeffries has made racist and anti-Semitic statements. A City College newspaper account in 1989 revealed his hatred of whites and Jews. But what distinguishes this incident from those in the past is the degree of tacit and overt support Jeffries has received within the black community. It is no longer possible to rationalize his remarks as the rantings of a single bigot. Jeffries has been described by his admirers as blunt and fearless, "a brother willing to take on whitey and the Jewish establishment."

Undoubtedly there is much posturing in this incident, as there was in previous anti-Semitic comments by Reverend Jesse Jackson and Louis Farrakhan. Yet it should be obvious to Jews that even if Jeffries's remarks represent a small minority of black opinion, there are enough rabble-rousers in this community to sever the civil rights alliance that brought Jews and blacks together for several decades. The names Chaney, Schwerner, and Goodman are emblazoned in the history of civil rights as white and black joined in a phalanx for fairness. These names also symbolize the union of blacks and Jews fighting for human decency. That alliance may well be over.

Jews cannot countenance anti-Semitism of any kind, much less anti-Semitism that is not even condemned by black leaders. There may indeed be much that will have to be accomplished before blacks reach "the promised land," but this odyssey is unlikely to occur with Jews and blacks marching side by side. On the Jewish side is a fear that scapegoating is subscribed to by many more blacks than the Jeffries incident suggests. And on the black side is a growing belief that any comment by a "brother," however outrageous, must be accepted because it is a show of racial solidarity. Emerging in some black communities is a form of melanin determinism. That which would most certainly be condemned if committed by a white is excused if committed by a black.

The civic bond on which human relations depends is in danger of unraveling. Jeffries has become a symbol of racial antipathy, in part because white and black leaders averted their gaze from the hatred percolating below the surface in many black communities. As racism in the past was employed to deny blacks fundamental human rights, racism in the black community is employed as rationalization for disappointments and fears. The dawn of a new era in race relations arrived in the '90s, and "We Shall Overcome" gave way to rap lyrics that promote hate, violence, and racial separation.

College Tuition Plans Are Often Not Fair to Students

By 1998, America's private colleges were reportedly increasing their tuition at the lowest rate in decades. Colleges, it seems, arrived at the unpleasant conclusion that only by squeezing costs and controlling tuition would they remain affordable. Many tuition hikes still outpaced the inflation rate. In that year, the consumer price index was 1.6 percent; the average tuition increase was 3.0 percent. Nonetheless, this increase compared favorably with the tuition increases of recent years, which were three and four times the rate of inflation.

A report issued several months previously by the National Commission on the Cost of Higher Education may have influenced university tuition increases; the report warned that unless tuition was brought under control, government intervention might be necessary. Thus, market forces were at work in this decision. Some college administrators readily admit that the single most important factor in setting tuition is an estimation of what the wealthiest families might be willing to pay.

In reality, tuition increases mean less than might be assumed, as relatively few students pay the "sticker price." Several colleges have simply slashed tuition—and cut the financial aid budget commensurately. The Washington-based National Association of College and University Business Officers, which since 1990 has examined the price of higher education, reported that private colleges are "discounting" a record proportion of tuition income. For every dollar colleges have tacked on to tuition since 1990, they have kept only forty-six cents. Overall, colleges are giving back 31 percent of the sticker price as student aid. The survey showed that three-quarters of freshmen students receive some scholarship assistance.

A question emerges from these data: When so few students are paying full tuition, why aren't more, if not most, colleges cutting tuition? According to Lucie Lapovsky, vice president for finance at Goucher College, a high-tuition model "tends to work best." It can use merit scholarships to entice good students and discounts to lure students who can pay most of the tuition freight. What appears to be in play is a Robin Hood plan in which the rich are obliged to give to the poor. In some instances, it might also be viewed as a redistribution plan that takes from those willing to pay and gives to those unwilling to pay.

In either case, college tuition defies logic. Those who realize that discounting is widespread—and ask for it—often get financial aid. While need is the singular criterion for assistance, it is often difficult to measure and increasingly an unfair method for judgment.

Suppose, for example, two families have the same incomes. Family one sacrifices to send its son to college by buying bonds monthly, husbanding resources, avoiding unnecessary expenditures, and foregoing summer vacations. Family two refuses to make financial sacrifices for its son. It does not save; it engages in frivolous expenditures, and it satisfies every craving for new purchases. Even though their incomes are the same, family one will be penalized for pinching pennies and acting in a responsible manner. A financial aid officer will invariably contend that savings are a reflection of the ability to pay. As a consequence, need is sometimes self-imposed and tuition assistance is granted to the profligate and irresponsible.

Needless to say, there isn't a completely fair system even when colleges have the lowest possible tuition rate without discounting. Presumably, students with genuine financial need might be adversely affected by this arrangement. However, the present tuition plans often reward the wrong students, penalize those who are willing to pay the sticker price, artificially inflate tuition, and discount arbitrarily. Is this any way to run a college? I think not.

Diversity Standards for Student Aid Contribute to Unfairness

Just as families who save are penalized by colleges that deem them capable of paying maximum tuition rates, so students who are not members of designated minority groups find themselves faced with huge bills. The quality of student performance often does not enter into the equation of who takes home the largest piece of the financial pie.

While a needs test might be a reasonable standard on which to proceed if it were applied with reference to other criteria, this is not the case. Instead, certain minorities find themselves in a bidding war that has race as the primary standard for assistance. Clearly the pursuit of a racial diversity standard at American colleges has fostered a bidding war for the relatively small pool of black students who have achieved academic excellence. And there is growing evidence that some of these students from affluent families are receiving scholarships beyond what federal guidelines would suggest, depriving needy white students of help. As one admissions officer told me: "Black students scoring above 1200 on the SATs are the academic equivalents of Shaquille O'Neal."

While many colleges use a needs-based standard for student aid, when it comes to minorities this principle is often ignored. Fred Hargedon, dean of admissions at Princeton University, said the use of financial aid to attract black students is tantamount to buying them. In an environment where the demand is great and the supply limited, black students, even very wealthy black students, are in the driver's seat. With diversity now largely a racial head count, colleges and universities are eager to demonstrate their adherence to the prevailing view of political correctness.

While top black students are getting more financial aid than was the case heretofore, the proportion of blacks who attend colleges remains well below that of the white population. That doesn't seem to concern those who are in demand at the moment. Abraham Walker, a black high school student from Richmond, Virginia, has a combined 1000 score on the SAT—marginally better than average. Nonetheless, elite institutions are tripping over one another in an effort to recruit him. Mr. Walker notes, "I think I might have a better chance because I'm black. That doesn't bother me. It doesn't bother people that Princeton is terminally Caucasian." Apparently Mr. Walker hasn't yet spoken to the Princeton admissions director. Mia Mends, a Houston high school student, notes, "I'll admit it myself: if I was a white student I probably wouldn't be out of the ordinary."

Where does that claim put white students who do excel and are out of the running for financial aid? The answer is obvious: Reverse discrimination is a key factor in university financial aid decisions. A top black student unquestionably has a better chance of receiving assistance than a top white student, even if the black student isn't as talented as his white counterpart and even if his parents have a higher income than that of white parents.

Surely something is wrong when race is the central criterion for aid. But as long as diversity is defined by race and as long as elite institutions want black students, many of those who don't need aid will get it, and people like me will sit on the sidelines paying full tuition and seething.

Demands for Multilingualism Add Fuel to the Fire of Multiculturalism

While America has historically been a nation united by a common language, bilingual educators are arguing that only the use of multiple language can assure fairness to nonnative speakers. An education commissioner in New York proposed that the state Regents exams, which have long been used to evaluate students' college preparation, be translated into four foreign languages.

Under Commissioner Richard Mills's plan to raise academic standards, passing grades on Regents tests in English, math, social studies, and science will be required of all high school graduates. Mills contends that offering the tests in the state's most common immigrant languages of Spanish, Creole, Russian, and Chinese would ensure that students with limited English facility had a chance to display their knowledge in other areas of study.

Groping for a compromise between bilingual educators and assimilationists, Mills would allow students to take exams in their native language and, at the same time, require them to pass the English Regents exam. As he notes, "It is going to be very, very hard for them to succeed in this country without English." Alas, that point is virtually self-evident. Then why are students permitted to take other exams in their native tongue? Mills maintains that students with limited English skills might score poorly in science, math, and social studies even when they possess the requisite knowledge to score well.

If this answer appears Orwellian, it probably is. If foreign students can pass an exam in English, it stands to reason that they are sufficiently familiar with the language to take all their exams in English. Admittedly the Mills approach is a compromise rendered after debate and negotiation. Nonetheless it remains a flawed compromise. Will employers offer training in Russian? Will colleges give science courses in Creole? Will state bonding propositions be translated into Chinese? I will never forget an elderly Spanish woman who, when told her son was not required to learn English in an American school, said, "I didn't bring my son to the United States to be a busboy. Without English that is what he will become."

Ramon Cortines, former New York City schools chancellor who became acting assistant secretary at the U.S. Department of Education, offered another view. "There are people who feel the predominant language of the land is English and that is what children should be tested in. I feel children should be assessed for what they know." The problem with this assertion is that the only way society will know what these students know is if the predominant language were Creole or Russian. While it was once axiomatic that immigrants would adapt themselves to the standards of their host nation, it is now apparent that the nation will adapt itself to the immigrant population.

David Merkowitz, a spokesman for the American Council on Education, notes that the proposal would allow more students with limited English language skills to enter four-year colleges. He added that the City University has a long tradition of accommodating students from varying ethnic and class backgrounds. "It's a recognition that we have an enormously diverse society," he said.

Indeed, this society is diverse, and the City and State Universities provide enormous opportunities for the children of immigrants. In the past, however, immigrants entering the City University had to demonstrate familiarity with the English language. The university of yesteryear was as diverse as that of today, but it did not cave in to the avatars of multiculturalism. In fact, universities assisted in the assimilation process by making the many one. By contrast, universities of the moment are often in the business of making the one many. Merkowitz notes, "There is a recognition that it doesn't pay for this society to create obstacles." Presumably, higher education should not place impediments in the path of foreign-speaking students unfamiliar with the English language. So what if foreign students unfamiliar with English wish to gain admission into American universities? Aside from the extent to which university standards have been and continue to be compromised by various multicultural themes, Mills's proposal has the added effect of balkanizing the society, of erecting barriers that separate and divide.

While one might applaud the intent to raise standards—a somewhat dubious point when any score above the fifty-fifth percentile passes the English Regents exam—it is not clear that the Mills proposal will do any more than keep foreign-speaking students in a state of perpetual disadvantage. Moreover, if one rationalizes exams in four languages, why not ballots, licenses, road signs, advertisements? Although this is certainly not Commissioner Mills's intent, his proposal is moving the nation one step closer to Canadian bilingualism, Swiss trilingualism, and a polyglot of language ghettoes. Ironically, it was reported that only 13 of 104 "graduates" at Hostos Community College in New York City could pass an English proficiency exam. Moreover, an English language exemption for graduation, I learned, has been in effect at the Borough of Manhattan Community College and LaGuardia Community College.

The exceptionalism of a nation that brought people of many backgrounds together and united them under a banner of one language and one flag is in jeopardy of sacrificing it all on the altar of multicultural ideology. Mills's proposal was only one example of educational compromise that took us one step closer to America's tower of Babel and national disintegration. When administrators cave in to what are often naive student demands for ethnic diversity, they are not contributing to campus unity. Indeed, when a university emphasizes what divides students rather than stressing what unites them, it is asking for trouble. The conditions that unite students and are universal have been subordinated to that which separates and keeps them apart. Pandering politicians claim they are working to counter the effects of discrimination and bigotry. In actual fact, their programs often promote the very conditions they were organized to prevent. The separation by ethnicity and the curriculum concession to cultural hegemony acknowledge the supposition on which discrimination is based.

When City University of New York proposed to convert the John Calandra Italian-American Institute from a recruiting, counseling, and teaching program into a research center specializing in Italian and Italian-American issues, citizens of the Italian community protested vigorously. The critics contended that the proposal was simply a means to dismantle the organization and punish its longtime director for participating in an antidiscrimination complaint filed by Italian-American faculty members against the university. University officials denied any discrimination against Italian-Americans. The Calandra Institute, named after the former state senator, had been established by the state legislature fourteen years earlier after complaints of discrimination and neglect of the Italian-American community. What the state legislature, critics of the university plan, and university officials overlooked was that any unit of the university organized to promote the interest of one ethnic group or race will invariably generate anger and frustration.

Once the proposition of ethnic studies is recognized and given legitimacy by the university, there is no way to deny claimants for similar status. If one accepts Italian-American studies, Black studies, Hispanic studies, or Jewish studies, what rationale can be employed for denying the claims of Muslims, homosexuals, left-handed people, or any group organized by fate, culture, or history as distinctive?

And if one does not deny these claimants, the university becomes balkanized—organized solely around the superficial conditions of what separates us.

Ultimately multiculturalism is a war of cultures. Since there are no ground rules for such competition, political influence is all that counts. Power, not scholarship, prevails, and politics, not the canons of scholarship, is the handmaiden of curriculum reform.

It is not surprising that the Calandra Institute generated turmoil. Any other response would have been the real surprise. As long as universities deny the universal and emphasize the divisive, they vitiate an essential purpose for their existence. Universities don't exist to combat discrimination. In fact, no matter what steps are taken, that goal is unachievable. Universities exist to promote learning, the search for truth, to consider what is universal and transmit an understanding of the past. Any other mission imposed by political solons is likely to dilute the purpose of the university at best or generate anger and turmoil at worst.

Student radicals at Hunter College in New York developed a longer laundry list of demands. Paramount on their list was a condemnation of the state legislature for proposed budgets cuts and a demand for a "tuition freeze and rollback." In addition, the students demanded a "legitimate evacuation plan for disabled students." They wanted to see the budget for the past ten years. They wanted the immediate removal of Professor Michael Levin of City College, who said he believes that whites are more intelligent than blacks. They wanted free tutoring services. They wanted the college to procure buses so students could travel to Albany for "political mobilization." They wanted "a multicultural core curriculum reflective of the ethnic composition of the Hunter College student body."

Though it may be tempting to dismiss these requests with the usual, "Oh, what can you expect from students?" the expectations should indeed be higher. Students should recognize that if they want to freeze or even roll back tuition that is already subsidized, their demands should be evaluated against a backdrop of diminished revenue from tuition.

What judgments can students possibly make from an examination of the budget? I can predict they won't approve of the present allocational pattern. Should Professor Levin be fired because students don't like his views? If Levin goes, every professor with unpopular views becomes a candidate for dismissal. Should administrators be dismissed because students are dissatisfied with their stands on various issues? Should condom dispensers be available at the college even if this open display offends some students? And anyway, aren't condoms readily available in the drugstore down the street?

The students' demands bring up more questions than they answer. If students wish to demonstrate, they can do so without the support of the administration. Similarly, if students want a convention on public education, they can organize one without the assistance of the college administration. The organization of a multicultural curriculum reflective of the college's ethnic composition is tantamount to institutionalizing a war of each against all. A curriculum should seek to address universal questions which cut across ethnicity and race. To accentuate ethnicity to the exclusion of other factors is ultimately to deny students an understanding of the world in which they reside.

What these demands reveal is an insulation from the world as it is. The students are saying what they believe the administration wants to hear from them. Their views are formulaic—a dash of ethnic loyalty, some environmental concerns, the de rigueur fiscal investigation, an acknowledgment of sexual openness, a nod to political activism and voila, the radical soup is ready to be served. If administrators had some backbone, they would take these proposals and use them as an exercise in logical exegesis, pointing out with cruel irony the illogic in each contention. That probably won't alter the new rite of passage for these students, but it may introduce a degree of levity in what should be taken as the ludicrous exercise it most assuredly is.

Even the Awarding of Honorary Degrees Is Influenced by Affirmative Action

At a university graduation ceremony I attended, the president introduced the honorary-degree recipients by saying, "These people represent what we consider valuable and worthy." In ways he never intended, his statement is undeniable.

There was a time, not so long ago, when an honorary degree was conferred because of a genuine achievement, such as the discovery of the polio vaccine or the translation of an ancient and hitherto undecipherable text. But honorary degrees, like everything else in the university system, are determined today by the Zeitgeist, the cauldron of political correctness. At almost every ceremony I witnessed or read about in the '90s there were a disproportionate number of minority members and women receiving honorary degrees. I haven't any quarrel with women or minorities receiving such honors, but I do dispute those whose contributions are slight receiving high accolades from a university. There can be little doubt that the reason this practice continues is because university administrators want to mollify potentially angry students and faculty members. It is what I describe as preemptive surrender. You can prove you are sensitive by cooperating in advance with the university thought police.

The affirmative action policies that have insinuated themselves into every other dimension of university policy now affect the selection of honorary-degree recipients. When members of the selection committee meet, they have a profile in mind that includes a woman, a black, a Hispanic, and, perhaps, a homosexual. It is only after this game plan is established that they seek out "appropriate" candidates. This is a lot like the old-line New York City Democratic Party slates, which invariably had an Italian, an Irishman, and a Jew for the top three electoral positions. The only matter that had to be brokered was who would get which position.

It is only a matter of time before the value of honorary degrees is depreciated. Sensible students will most certainly understand what is going on, and even the recipients themselves might see through the charade, in which genuine contribution is not distinguished from inauthentic contribution. Daniel Boorstin, author of *Image in America,* predicted that the inauthentic might replace the genuine in practice and meaning, as a filtered cigarette has replaced the unfiltered variety. That, it seems to me, may have occurred already in the matter of honorary degrees.

If universities persist in this charade, they should remove the honorific adjective and simply describe the honors as alternative degrees, degrees achieved for nothing of any significance. Those who receive the degrees solely because of race, sex, or ethnicity should receive "life" degrees. They are therefore recognized for having lived, but no special honor should be attached to that accomplishment. This innovation, by the way, would deal squarely with the unfairness charge. After all, if X gets a degree, why shouldn't Y. In my arrangement, everyone would be equally eligible to receive a meaningless document. It is also apparent that since women and those of color—to use an expression favored on campus today—are more likely to receive such honors, there should be a specifically constituted award for white men, simply called the Consolation Prize.

The absurdities to which universities will go in an effort to accommodate the dictates of politics know virtually no bounds. Caught in the vortex of a tornado, even the sensible practice of recognizing real achievement has been contaminated by the avatars of political judgment. As a consequence, the quaint practice of honorary degrees will soon be subjected to late-night talk-show ridicule. Deservedly so.

Racial Politics Lead to an Absurd Quota System in Admission Policies in California

Public policy can drive a wedge between the races. Such was the proposed California "educational equity act" of 1992, which advised that state colleges must admit ethnic minorities in the same proportions as their numbers in the state's high school graduating classes. It further proposed proportional graduation rates "for individuals from historically or currently underrepresented or economically disadvantaged groups."

In addition, the bill required colleges to submit "specific step-by-step plans" for achieving these numerical goals. The bill also instructed governing boards to "hold faculty and administrators accountable for the success of the institution in achieving equity." Efforts fostering "diversity" were to be "granted significant consideration" in general performance evaluation.

Incredible as this proposal was on its face, it should be evaluated against a backdrop in which the disparity in math SAT scores between blacks and whites was 140 points on average and the disparity between blacks and Asians 169 points. What this means in effect is that a large number of Asians and whites in the bottom quartile of their racial groupings have scores that are higher than blacks in the top quartile of their grouping. In this schematic, equity has a very peculiar meaning indeed. It is hardly surprising, based on the aptitude demonstrated on SAT scores, that there is a corresponding disparity in graduation rates. Brown's bill alluded to these performance differentials by noting a "hostile and intolerant academic environment." Yet whatever rationalization Brown employs cannot possibly offset the reality of SAT scores and graduation rates.

Brown's bill is symbolic of a political and academic trend to establish by fiat what cannot be accomplished in the normal course of events. Equal opportunity has yet again been confused with equal results. However, the Brown proposal is very far from an equitable arrangement; if anything it is a fixed arrangement in which achievement is subordinate to racial ascription.

Where the differences in measured academic ability among the races continue to be pronounced, latent racial animus will most assuredly be reinforced as the system continually uses "unfairness" to explain why blacks don't perform as well as whites and Asians. This is an argument that most students know to be inaccurate despite all the vocal remonstrations to the contrary.

Admitting ethnic groups on the basis of their proportion in the larger population is a violation of the Civil Rights Act of 1964. Proposing proportional graduation rates is a violation of logic, since no matter how one orchestrates such matters a final determination on the basis of race can be made only through administrative engineering. And if either of these goals was to be established, the foundation stone of performance on which colleges are predicated would be vitiated by this effort to accommodate fashionable views.

Such proposed legislation is an exemplar of attitudes about affirmative action and racial equity. Down a slippery slope, civil rights advocates have taken us where standards and quality are mere pawns for the large and profound issue of racial adjudication. In a political climate where a Brown bill can be proposed and endorsed by the majority in his house, it is somewhat understandable that cynicism will be on the ascendancy and racial antagonism will be engendered.

One can only wonder what Mr. Brown would say if the shoe were on the other foot and he were Asian. Would he then argue that standards should be abandoned in an effort to assimilate racial minorities into the state system by head count?

Racial Head Counts, Not Academic Excellence, Characterize Affirmative Action Hiring Policies

The substitution of political standards for educational judgment can be seen in the growing practice of using a college's minority representation and diversity of the faculty and administration as criteria for accreditation. The Middle States Association of Schools (MSA) conducts an accreditation process every decade at member colleges. The Baruch College program review illustrates how colleges that are supposedly dedicated to the pursuit of truth have caved in to the political pressure for justice now determined by racial head counts.

The evaluation team issued a favorable report on Baruch College in December 1989 reiterating the deficiencies already identified by the faculty. In fact, Professor Bonaparte said he would recommend that Baruch be reaccredited with the second highest possible rating. However, by March 1990 a letter was sent to the Baruch administration indicating that reaccreditation had been deferred. Obviously something happened between December and March that altered the view of the evaluation team.

While the evidence is not incontrovertible, it would appear that a conflict of interest bore directly on the decision. In mid-January chairman Bonaparte applied for the position of provost and vice president at Baruch College. By mid-February Bonaparte was one of the two remaining candidates for the position, and the only black candidate. But he did not get the job. Bonaparte claims he "cleared his application with the Middle States authorities," but it nonetheless had the appearance, if not reality, of a conflict of interest.

Emerging from this are some disturbing developments. One is that college administrations had become so inured to the climate of affirmative action that they subordinated the truly critical issues of teaching and research for head counts along racial and ethnic lines. It would seem that the central college concern should be an assemblage of the most talented faculty whatever their racial and ethnic mix. To be obliged to mention this obvious commonsense concern itself demonstrates the slide of reasoned argument on campus.

A second disturbing development is the seeming use of one's exalted position on an accrediting board as a lever to extract advantage or to penalize those who would not confer advantage. If Bonaparte sought and received clearance for his job application, then the MSA authorities engaged in a serious dereliction of responsibility. By allowing him to be a candidate for a position at the same institution he was evaluating, the appearance of either extortion or punishment was engendered, thereby compromising either the job search or the evaluation.

It should be apparent from this incident that an evolution of vitiated standards has been under way. At first it was merely misguided professors using the privilege of academic freedom, who proselytized for a radical agenda in their classrooms. Then whole disciplines were either created or altered to accommodate the emerging sensibility of professors. Now one can observe that the standard for evaluation of colleges as well as the methodology employed in this accreditation process is in the service of a radical agenda.

What does it mean that colleges must promote ethnic diversity in their faculties? In 1989 there were six blacks in the nation who received Ph.D.'s in mathematics, five of these in math education. What can one say about the lack of ethnic diversity in math departments; indeed, what should one say?

If evaluators were truly interested in enhancing the education of youngsters, the criteria for faculty appointments would be color-blind. Of what possible value is there in hiring an incompetent black professor to satisfy an arbitrary standard for affirmative action?

The Shifting Climate on the American Campuses

Permissiveness prevailed on American campuses throughout the '90s, and the principle of in loco parentis became an anachronism. A nontraditional orthodoxy still permeates many campuses, where tolerance exists only for what is politically correct.

Very little occurs in higher education that shocks. Segregation by race, which I regarded as a well-dismissed practice in the rest of society, has, to my horror, been reintroduced in the academy. Meritocratic standards have retreated before quotas, or what are euphemistically called goals. A radical orthodoxy, which includes concessions to race, ethnicity, class, gender, and sexual orientation, has insinuated itself into the curriculum as rational discourse has diminished.

Some vignettes from '90s campuses illustrate how once-taboo subjects have been taken out of the closet and students with little experience are asked to reflect on the perverse and obscene. At the same time, traditional values and decency have come under attack. Open living arrangements, tolerance for homosexual activity, and the general denunciation of religious convictions have been the vogue on campus for years. Students often wish to separate themselves by race, ethnicity, or "sexual preference."

Harvard Divinity School, once a bastion of conservative religious thought and the center for the training of establishment Protestant ministers, sponsored an art exhibit of colorful objects and tiny sculptures—one a bust of C. Everett Koop, the former surgeon general—constructed with condoms. This display, according to Andrew Rasanen, a divinity school spokesman, was intended to teach students "how to counsel people about sexuality." This educational tool included condoms covered with beads, fur, yarn, leather, charms, and feathers. In addition, there were dolls dressed in condoms, images of condoms as if fossilized, and condoms filled with honey, alphabet soup, a baby's sneaker, tiny globes, and sunflower seeds.

At the State University of New York at New Paltz, as noted earlier, a women's studies conference featured sessions on sadomasochism and sex toys, including explicit dramatization of techniques. At one workshop, a stripper and S/M aficionado mounted a male colleague and began whipping him. Roger Bowen, the political scientist who gave the opening address, characterized John Milton, John Stuart Mill, and Supreme Court Justice William Brennan as defending free speech "no matter how odious." He suggested that the conference was important because "we are the last chance to help students develop a sense of civic responsibility." So far down the rabbit hole of depreciated expression have we gone that perversity and tastelessness are defined as First Amendment rights.

At Yale University, Orthodox Jewish students protested that living in coeducational dormitories where alcohol flowed freely and weekend orgies started on Thursday night was akin to residing in Sodom and Gomorrah. Explaining that these dormitory living conditions conflicted with their religion's rules of modesty and sexual abstinence until marriage, the students asked to be excused from the university requirement that all freshmen and sophomores live on campus. Yale's administration, which bends over backward to accommodate feminists, homosexuals, and a variety of other activists, resisted the request. Administrators in effect told the students they had to conform to secular standards or be unwelcome at the university. While tolerance exists for what is politically correct, intolerance prevails for traditional religious adherence.

At Princeton University, *The Daily Princetonian* reported a lecture given by Suzi Landolphi before a capacity crowd, titled "Hot, Sexy, and Safer." During the frank sexual discussion, women were encouraged to hold the microphone "tight" and men were instructed, "the clitoris, it's about time it got the respect it deserves. Most of you guys haven't found it yet." Writing in *On the Campus*, Maia Batlin described how students routinely shoplifted from a convenience store near campus. The store's manager estimated that there were at least twenty-five shoplifting incidents in the store daily, and "Every person arrested this fall has been an undergraduate." Some students claimed that the store's high prices made "you feel like ripping it back." Others shoplifted to vent their frustration at the high cost of a Princeton education. One student argued that minor theft is not inherently wrong and justified shoplifting as a statement against capitalism.

Who is telling students that sex is a private matter? Who tells them that "letting it all hang out" is not appropriate student conduct even if it masquerades as honesty? And who says that theft is wrong, period, notwithstanding budding Marxists' rationalizations for their miscreant behavior? Clearly, the campus of the '90s was not the same as the campus of the '50s.

Perils of Conformity

The atmosphere on college campuses is now charged by priests of political fashion who decide what can and cannot be said. Free speech has been compromised by professional tastemakers who use their influence on campus to chasten dissenters. Opposing views are suppressed, most often by a subtle form of censure. Charges of both sexual harassment and politically correct speech have created a political climate that has corrupted the disinterested examination of knowledge. The effect on both students and professors has been chilling.

Some students have resorted to violence. At Weber State University near Salt Lake City, a student grievance hearing erupted into a shoot-out that killed one and wounded several during a hearing involving Mark Duong, a twenty-eight-year-old computer science major who had been accused by a female student of physical and verbal harassment. At the University of Houston, a graduate student, Soviet émigré Fabian Vaksman, frightened some faculty members by writing a 316-page poem in which an angry student kills five history professors. Vaksman contended that a Marxist cabal at the university objected to his anti-Communist opinions in "R Racist," which he dedicated to William Shockley, the Nobel prize-winning physicist who espoused the theory that blacks are genetically inferior to whites. Such violence cannot be justified, and these extreme reactions were at least partially responses to institutional bias.

A charge of harassment has political meaning on campus related to the influence of feminists. Clearly real harassment should be punished, but in the university hothouse it is often hard to distinguish the real grievance from the questionable. Similarly, speech has been limited by what professors consider acceptable. If a student were to challenge a professor who endorsed Shockley's views—as unlikely as this scenario is—the professor might be sentenced to a sensitivity program. Instead of relying on evidence as the final arbiter in the adjudication of differences of opinion, political influence at universities is rapidly replacing the canon of scholarship.

It is precisely this political influence that has corrupted the disinterested examination of knowledge. Epistemology has been socialized. For students the effect is chilling. One must be careful not to offend specially designated groups; the sensitivity troops are always on guard. In the febrile atmosphere at most colleges and universities, the airing of many views, extreme or otherwise, is unacceptable. There was once a time, not so long ago, when unpopular expression was encouraged in order to sublimate extremism into moderation. That time has passed. In a different era, professors would raise issues that were intentionally contentious. The challenge was the essence of learning. A student was asked to defend his views with an appeal to evidence. Even if an argument was substantially correct, it was unacceptable to apply ipse dixit argumentation. Pedagogy was dependent on logical discourse and empirical substantiation. At the risk of hyperbole, pedagogy now uses the sledgehammer of "correctness"; truth is known, not revealed; ideas are a priori true or false and are rarely tested.

That nonconformist students might behave in a bizarre manner is not entirely surprising. Their views aren't tested; they are simply dismissed. Like the inmates in the gulag Solzhenitsyn described, the enforced homogeneity demanded by totalitarianism leads to acts that, under normal circumstances, would be considered bizarre. I am not trying to justify the behavior of Duong and Vaksman, nor am I equating their actions to those in the gulag. I am, however, persuaded that in an environment where power is employed to enforce conformity, strange and even violent acts might well be expected.

Imposed conformity in the name of politically correct speech leads to intimidation, which in turn produces ignorance. When Professor Richard T. Hofferbert gave a lecture at the State University of New York (Binghamton) in 1991 entitled "Letters from Berlin 1990: Fall of the Wall," his audience consisted primarily of black students who were responding to an erroneous and mean-spirited rumor that members of the Ku Klux Klan (KKK) would be present and to an equally vicious and false rumor that the National Association of Scholars (NAS), which sponsored the lecture, promoted racist views. The effect on the audience was predictable.

Before the talk began, students organized outside the lecture hall to listen to Gonzalos Santos, an adjunct lecturer, and Edward Pichardo, president of the Black Student Union, excoriate the university for inviting the KKK to campus and for allowing the NAS to sponsor a lecture. Pichardo said, "We must let the organization (NAS) know that we are not going to stand for their discrimination against minorities. We must question what the NAS is about." Santos added, "We will not allow them to paint us as the barbarians." Yet neither Pichardo nor Santos offered a scintilla of evidence to support the argument that NAS discriminates against minorities or that NAS has "painted" minorities as barbarians.

Once inside the auditorium, several students verbally abused and physically intimidated participants. Some students brandished sticks. One student paced behind Professor Hofferbert. And another student (the word is used advisedly) threw a framed picture of Hofferbert's granddaughter across the hall, narrowly missing several professors. Although the black student leaders and the radical caucus deny any attempt at disruption, there was more than a whiff of intimidation in the air. On the way back to his dormitory, a student named Adam Bromberg was punched in the face and kicked while on the ground because he was seen chatting with an NAS professor at the Hofferbert lecture. Fortunately, he was able to walk away from this incident without injury. When an adviser came to Adam's assistance, he asked the attacker his name. The response was "John Smith."

Clearly, these actions beg for condemnation. Yet neither the president of the university nor the faculty condemned the student actions in unequivocal terms. In fact, President Lois De Fleur insisted in oral and written commentary that the reports of the incident were "overblown," albeit when the publicity attendant to this matter could not be contained, De Fleur had only exculpatory comments. A statement released from the president's office noted, "Thoughtful persons are wrestling with pressures on campuses to broaden traditional curriculum and perspectives while preserving an open and respectful exchange of ideas." Peter Wagner, vice president for academic affairs, said the president "want[ed] to take the high road."

It is instructive that De Fleur seemed to be far more interested in containing the publicity than in dealing directly with the incident. My suspicion is that the risks associated with potential campus demonstrations organized by radical groups far exceed, in a college administrator's mind, the risks associated with challenging the very essence of academic freedom. In far too many instances, college presidents contend that there will be "no trouble on my watch." How else can one explain President De Fleur's contention that disruption and intimidation could be explained by "festering social ills in the nation"?

That university administrators have an obligation to encourage a rational exchange of views, no matter how unpopular some of them may be, seems to have been forgotten in an era where radical reform orthodoxies on campus are in the ascendancy. After visiting SUNY—Binghamton recently, I can testify that humorless radicals are insinuating their agenda into university affairs. It may be an exaggeration to describe them as contemporary Brownshirts; they are more or less the tie-dye shirts suffering from sloppy thinking, and mere pawns in the hands of self-serving political manipulators. Their questions at my lecture bespeak untrained minds filled with evocative and fashionable clichés about race, gender, class, and the "evils" of Western civilization. It is difficult for these students to appreciate the canon they generally have not read, and it is equally difficult for them to be disinterested observers of the social scene when they are indoctrinated by campus rabble-rousers.

I have long argued that ignorance should never be underestimated as an explanation for strongly held ideology. It would appear that ignorant rumors incited the disruption at the Hofferbert lecture. And the manner in which that ignorant rumor was manipulated led directly to the unconscionable behavior of several *bien pensant* students. What is most curious is that taxpayers, who subsidize the state system, did not call for a public hearing about the incident. Why was the chancellor of the SUNY system, Dr. Bruce Johnstone, conspicuously silent? Why weren't the students who hurled a framed picture and engaged in jeers and taunts not expelled immediately? Why didn't the entire faculty unite behind Hofferbert and his colleagues in the NAS chapter?

Affirmative Action Can Be Unfair to Its Recipients

Using the standard of the moment, Frances Lawrence, the president of Rutgers University, did more for black students than any university president in recent memory. He increased black enrollment significantly through affirmative action policy. He opened an Afro-American campus center. He raised substantial scholarship money to increase student diversity (read: black students). He hired several high-level black administrators.

Despite these achievements, however, President Lawrence said the unpardonable. At a faculty meeting to discuss tenure review policy, he asked, "Do we set standards in the future so that we don't admit anybody with the national test [the Scholastic Aptitude Test]? Or do we deal with a disadvantaged population that doesn't have the hereditary background to have a higher average?" Once those remarks were made public, a firestorm began. Demonstrators prevented the completion of a basketball game. Several classes were suspended. Lounges and cafeterias were forcibly closed. Rutgers was under siege.

It is instructive that in accepting the premise behind affirmative action, President Lawrence was hoisted by his own petard. Sensible people realize that there is a bell curve in the black community as there is in the white community. Some students are very smart, most are very average, and some aren't smart at all. But the assumption with affirmative action is that race is the sole criterion for this judgment.

As a consequence, the proponents of affirmative action, of whom President Lawrence is one, assume inferior performance from black students or at best that black students are incapable of performing as well as whites. Not only is this not true for a sizable portion of the black population, this assumption causes doubts in even the most talented, who often believe they would not have succeeded without an affirmative action program.

It so happens that I believe in affirmative action, but not in programs that rely on race as the only consideration for special assistance. If affirmative action were based on parental income, for example, it most likely would be perceived as fair policy and it would certainly not generate the hostility associated with a racial standard. The man-on-the-street is increasingly hard-pressed to support a policy that rewards some rich students over some poor students simply because the rich students happen to have the "designated" skin color.

The irony of the Lawrence position is that in advocating affirmative action based on race, he accepted precisely what the student demonstrators were espousing. Of course, the difference is that the president uttered the ineffable: he said that affirmative action is needed among blacks because of inherited disadvantages. If that position is not true—and I would contend that it is indeed not true—then affirmative action in its present form is unnecessary.

It might make sense to revisit the issue. Perhaps the student population exercised about the president's remarks might ask what affirmative action has wrought and what policy would be in the best interest of black students.

This country has demonstrated an extraordinary capacity for compassion. That compassion is usually constrained by fairness. At the moment, however, affirmative action is neither fair to its recipients nor fair to the general public. The civil rights acts of the '60s suggested that people should not be evaluated by the color of their skin. Martin Luther King Jr., in his much-quoted statement, argued that people should be judged "by the content of their character, not the color of their skin." In my judgment, it is time we returned to that color-blind standard. It might even have the collateral effect of taking President Lawrence off the hook.

Hypocrisy of College Administrators Undermines Traditional Culture

While this generation of college students may not be so different from its predecessors, who also engaged in hard drinking as an act of adolescent rebellion, what distinguished past from present is that the authority figures of yesteryear frowned on the practice. All dorms were once theoretically "chemical-free." Today, many students are asked on college applications whether they would prefer to live in a "chemical-free dorm." Never mind what the laws of this land say; college today is a sanctuary for underage youth who want to get high and plastered. And presumably, only the nerds sign up for chemical-free dorms.

At one large urban university, marijuana smoking is tolerated in nonsubstance-free dorms as long as it is conducted in the privacy of one's room. At another, a floor counselor has to catch a student in the act of smoking marijuana three times before expulsion proceedings can be considered. In fact, even though every college has stated parietals against drug use, nonsubstance-free dorms are notorious for pill popping and marijuana use. At one large university, drinking and drug use start on Thursday night and go on until Monday morning. Invariably someone gets sick and an ambulance is called. A dorm counselor told me that this is a regular weekly occurrence.

While university officials will invariably decry drug use, university hypocrisy is palpable, especially to students. Those adolescents who opt for non-chemical-free dorms know full well that drug use will be tolerated. And university officials who give lip service to a zero tolerance policy defy their own regulations by averting their gaze to what happens in some dorms. As the *Chronicle of Higher Education* pointed out, several students lost their lives to alcohol consumption or drug overdoses during this permissive period.

What this report did not note was university complicity in these matters. When students who are not yet drinking-age consume alcohol, and when students buy and smoke marijuana, they are violating the law. And by extension, universities are in violation of the law as well.

What college administrators do is wink as they refer to strict drug-use regulations. That wink is a manifestation of gross hypocrisy. It is a demonstration of how universities have become agents for the undermining of traditional culture. Every university catalog I have examined said that drug use is a reason for dismissal. Some even said that the university will apply the full weight of the law when drug rules are violated. Yet, curiously, these same universities have dorms that are openly not chemical-free.

A Contemporary Campus Where Time Has Stood Still

As college campuses accept the call to commit to diversity, higher education is unquestionably in a political hothouse. What was once an atmosphere of serenity with occasional winds of controversy has been converted into an environment of political bickering with rarely a serene moment.

It was with this in mind that I entered a time machine and went to the commencement at Grove City College in Grove City, Pennsylvania, in May 1993. At Grove City the clocks don't move; it feels as if it is still 1955. No, this wasn't Bill

Murray in *Groundhog Day*, it is a real world of manners and morals, of discipline and respect, of sweetness and innocence, characteristics seemingly lost in the rush to modernity and the politicization of the universities.

Grove City College is perhaps best known for its unwillingness to accept government money or government mandates. It is indeed the last bastion of independence in higher education. It is also an anachronism. Students follow parietals, young men call on women for a date, curfews exist, and students respect the well-manicured quad—no Frisbees allowed.

Students routinely say "Sir" and "Madam" and, with the exception of one obvious rebel, every student wore a suit or dress to the graduation ceremony. Men are asked to take off their hats in public places and, to my knowledge, no formal protest against this regulation has been registered. Students are required to read classic texts—in fact, the supermarket approach to the selection of courses is frowned upon. Learning of basic subjects is admired and emphasized.

The college is located in an idyllic corner of Pennsylvania far from the madding crowd. Doors are left unlocked in town. Grove City is a "dry" town. There is one movie theater that charges $2 to see *Aladdin*. The kids in this city are as refreshingly bright-eyed and bushy-tailed as if they walked off a set at Disney World.

I compare this scene with what I usually observe: The jean and T-shirt set I refer to as unmade beds, the profane-talking and hip-swinging poseurs who believe that sophistication comes from converting a four-letter-noun expletive into a seven-letter adjective; the defenders of a new orthodoxy based on race, class, and gender, and believers in a "democracy" dependent on breeding and privilege.

Grove City College is most certainly a new world for me. When a faculty member said he wished to comment on my remarks, I responded reflexively, expecting unvarnished scorn. Instead he said, "I agree with what you said—the speech was wonderful." I almost passed out. Could it really be that a faculty member somewhere in the Western Hemisphere agreed with me? As I was about to leave, a student came rushing up to me saying, "Dr. London, I would really appreciate the opportunity to introduce my parents to you." The parents looked and sounded like Ozzie and Harriet Nelson. I wanted to put them in a cryonic state so that I could take them back to New York and occasionally remind myself of the way the world used to be.

On the trip back to Pittsburgh, I found it difficult to believe that what I had experienced was real. Is there a place where sweetness exists? Are there other places like Grove City College, or is this a lone oasis in the higher-education desert? A college administrator driving me to the airport said, "This place is unique." He must have been reading my mind.

When I returned to the foul odors of Washington Square, the ubiquitous drug dealers on the street, and the shrill sound of student radicals, I wanted to go "back to the future," to recapture another time as Grove City College manages to do so well. Grove City is not merely a center for learning, it is a place for the development of character and the deepening of the soul.

The Dangers of Closed Doors on Campus

"Theme" housing programs on campus should be abandoned as inconsistent with the essential mission of the university. In the era of special-interest politics, it is hardly surprising that students want to separate themselves by race, ethnicity, or "sexual preference," to use the vernacular of the moment. But such separation is part of the problem, not the solution.

Homosexual students at Cornell University lobbied vigorously for their own dorm spaces, but the proposal was rejected by President Frank Rhodes. Rhodes explained his decision by saying that he had "the deepest reservation about the increasing tendency within the campus to define ourselves in terms of groups and factions." Alas, he is right, in my judgment, but one wonders whether this opinion is widely held among Mr. Rhodes's colleagues. Even at Cornell there are "program houses" for American Indian culture, black culture, international life, and environmentalists. If Rhodes is right, what is to be done about housing arrangements that systematically balkanize the campus? And if homosexuals are denied separate residences, why should the university countenance such an arrangement for blacks? Presumably, what is good for the goose is good for the gander.

According to the *Chronicle of Higher Education*, the University of California introduced Asian-Pacific and Hispanic "theme" floors in a new dormitory, and Wesleyan University approved a "queer positive" house much like the space requested by homosexuals at Cornell. Those who live in these separate quarters invariably justify the separation by noting that "they feel at home with their own kind" or "this is a space free of racial tension."

The question that remains, of course, is whether segregation—either voluntary or involuntary—is a racist echo from the past. It may well be that the voluntary segregation of the present inspires the very discomfort among white students that justifies further acts of separation and a gulf in interracial relations. I recall that when I enrolled in a university for the first time, many years ago, I was told that I had stepped over the threshold of a narrowly defined community and entered one without boundaries, called the academy. The very definition of the academy was ecumenical, universal, and open. How different most campuses have become!

Many white students with whom I've discussed this matter lament a campus torn by racial enclaves, yet only disturbingly few have the courage to speak out against the practice. It is the enclaves themselves that promote racial tension and, ironically, are the rationale for an environment "free of racial tension." So powerful is the peer pressure for racial separation that if a black student breaks ranks and resides with a fellow white student, he may be chastised as an Oreo or Uncle Tom.

If college administrators had the courage—surely in short supply in higher education—random selection would be employed as a housing policy for freshmen. I don't expect this result in the near future. But what the Frank Rhodes decision does indicate is that there is a growing realization that balkanization has gone much too far, transforming colleges from centers of openness for all kinds of people into parochial ghettos.

If one also realizes that the overriding purpose of a college education is to liberate youngsters from their narrowly perceived backgrounds and open them to the received wisdom of civilization, it becomes clear that housing separation, and its current curriculum variant, multiculturalism, often undermine the college mission. This act of liberation doesn't suggest a negation of the past but rather an embrace of the new. It isn't an attempt to trivialize racial or ethnic history but to contextualize it against the backdrop of the global experience. President Rhodes admitted as much when he finally vetoed the housing plan for homosexuals at Cornell. The next step is for a college president to assert the danger separation represents to the purpose and goals of the academy. I eagerly wait for this hero to emerge.

The Quagmire of Sexual Harassment

Just when some analysts had assumed that every pathology the mind can conjure had been inflicted on higher education, a new one presented itself for derision. While radical feminism holds an exalted position in the academy, its influence on every dimension of education is not, in my judgment, fully appreciated. The influence of these feminists was made manifest in the '90s by the City University Sexual Harassment brochure.

Now, before I am accused of insensitivity, it should be said that I oppose groping, intimidation, imposition of position, and any other form of genuine harassment. However, as I see it, the issue emerges from the present obscurity over what behavior constitutes harassment. According to this recently published brochure, the intended policy is designed to promote an environment of mutual respect among students, faculty, and staff. Clearly, this is unobjectionable. What is objectionable is what follows: "Sexual harassment is not defined by intentions, but by impact on the subject." Presumably, an innocent gesture by a professor could still be considered an example of harassment if so interpreted by a student.

It gets better. "Sexual harassment is not only about sex. It often involves the use, misuse, and abuse of power or perceived power (professor over student, supervisor over employee, etc.). Sexual harassment can also occur where no obvious power relationship exists (student to student, student to faculty)." Moreover, "all complaints will be held as confidential as legally permissible."

If sexual harassment is not only about sex, but the abuse of power, one must assume that student and faculty member are equally possessed of power or that role differentiation is nonexistent. While students since the '60s have been attempting to transform the academy into some form of representative democracy, if students are not there to learn from and be evaluated by instructors then the purpose of the academy is rendered moot.

If the subject believes that harassment has occurred, that, in the view of City University officials, is a sufficient condition for an investigation, even if the allegation is manifestly devoid of corroborating evidence. Since complaints are kept confidential only to the extent that is "legally permissible," reputations may be ruined—and in several documented examples, have been destroyed—by unsubstantiated charges.

Sexual harassment is illegal under federal, state, and city laws, but under what circumstance can the laws be applied when the accuser merely suggests how he or she felt in a particular situation, when sexual behavior or at least innuendo need not be factors in determining whether harassment has occurred, and when disproportionate power exists on one side of a relationship? While it is easy for a complainant to register his concern to a designated Sexual Harassment Education Committee, it is not so easy for the accused to defend himself. After all, accusations are based on "impact," not intention. Therefore, the accused is guilty if the accuser believes him to be guilty.

If this all has an Alice in Wonderland quality to it, that's because rationality has gone down the rabbit hole. The City University is not alone in its absurd stance. In fact, every university in thrall to political correctness has a standard very much like the one at the City University.

As a consequence, faculty members don't know how to address students, students don't know how to talk to fellow students, much less engage in courtship, and administrators are perplexed about appropriate behavior on campus. Everyone in the academy walks on eggshells. On one occasion I gave a colleague flowers on her fortieth birthday only to have her ask what intentions I had with this gesture.

Now I avoid any human gesture. I don't look, I don't ask, I don't communicate. I stay in my office with my door open in case someone should wonder what goes on behind closed doors. You can't be too careful with the Red Guard at American colleges.

The General Knowledge Once Associated with a Baccalaureate Degree Is in Dramatic Decline

With a societal expenditure of $210-plus billion on public and private higher education, one might expect graduates to know fundamental facts about the polity in which they reside. One might also expect that graduates would know how to write, compute, and reason at a fairly high level of sophistication. While these are reasonable expectations, they are not evident conditions.

Evidence suggests that basic knowledge about the nation's history is either not being required, not being taught, or not being imbibed by the current crop of college graduates. A few years ago, pollster Frank Luntz asked University of Pennsylvania students questions such as in which half of the nineteenth century was the Civil War fought and in which century did Columbus sail for the New World. Luntz found that only a relatively small percentage of students could answer these questions correctly. According to the National Opinion Research Center, only 53 percent of college-educated men under thirty and only 34 percent of their female counterparts read a daily newspaper.

A later study of college graduates indicated that general knowledge once associated with a baccalaureate degree was in further dramatic decline. According to the Roper Center for Public Opinion at the University of Connecticut, only 8 percent of those surveyed could identify the phrase "government of the people, by the people, for the people" as part of Lincoln's Gettysburg Address. Of the twenty questions asked, only 7 percent answered fifteen or more correctly. A third of those polled answered five or fewer questions correctly.

The poll found that 84 percent of the respondents did not know that Harry Truman was president at the start of the Korean War. Only 24 percent could identify Italy and Japan as Germany's main allies during World War II. Seventy-one percent could not identify Martin Luther as the founder of Protestantism. Only 21 percent knew that Plato wrote *The Republic*. Seventy percent could not identify Geoffrey Chaucer as the author of *The Canterbury Tales*.

Since these results come from a poll of graduating seniors, one might well ask what America's twenty-one-year-olds know, and the corollary question, what they learn during their college years. It is increasingly apparent that the college experience isn't what it once was. "Training in incapacity" is the result of a curriculum that is in decline and standards that are in disarray.

Many parents are beginning to wake up to the bait-and-switch operation that characterizes higher education at the moment. For $30,000 a year at elite institutions, students can imbibe the latest psychobabble, read indecipherable books about what is wrong with Western civilization, and engage in jejune expressions of youth as long as racial segregation is honored, homosexuality is never questioned, radical feminism is embraced, and tradition is shunned.

A recent report issued by the National Association of Scholars indicates that the use of required courses is declining. That in itself would not be worrisome if rigor were associated with the courses students do select. However, there is sufficient evidence to demonstrate that this is not the case. Many fewer colleges require a thesis as a graduation requirement than was the case in 1964. Fewer colleges have history, math, or writing requirements for graduation than was true thirty years ago.

In an effort to "democratize" higher education—to use the jargon of the '60s, "be responsive to student needs"—colleges began to modify the once-sacrosanct core curriculum. I can recall a graffito on a university facade in 1969 that said, "Make them [professors] teach you only what you want to learn." Alas, almost three decades later that proclamation has come to pass. In the hothouse environment of higher education, most professors and administrators would prefer to switch than fight. The curriculum is now a reflection of participatory democracy at work.

Unfortunately for the society at large, this doesn't work. More is spent for less effect than ever before. If college graduates cannot distinguish Plato from Pluto, then something is rotten within the halls of ivy. This indictment is not leveled against every institution and program, but there are far too many colleges and universities that have abandoned rigorous standards to challenge my generalization.

Trying to Teach Nonreaders in College Is Impossible

The college experience is for many students a replay of their earlier education, and a great deception is being fostered in the process. While students and parents believe they are receiving a college education, the students have been engaged in child's play. Taxpayers who believe that they have made a worthwhile investment in human capital are misled. And university-trained professors are obliged to foster the ruse in order to justify their efforts and salaries.

Too many students enter college not knowing how to read college-level texts. As a result, the public must subsidize basic reading programs for college students. A report in the Nassau County Community College, New York, student newspaper illustrated the problem. On Literacy Day, the article noted, students were encouraged to participate in three sessions: "Alienation in the Classroom," "The Imperfect Decoder: Penalties for Non-Standard Language Production," and "Negotiating the Text Before You Read."

If Literary Day were the focus of a *Saturday Night Live* program, viewers might regard it as too extreme for plausible satire. The reality, however, defies logic. No longer is it possible for a professor to say what is empirically valid; for example, that "half the students will drop out." After all, John and Mary may not like this statement.

The Imperfect Decoder is little more than a euphemism for semiliteracy. A demonstrated need to discuss this topic suggests, in unadorned fashion, that students at Nassau Community College cannot read college-level texts. In effect, colleges have gone from remediation centers to kindergartens, all the while using a language of obfuscation to deny student deficiencies.

The last session encouraged students to "get a mind-set" before reading the text. Students were told, "Read the title of the book before reading the contents." One gets a mind-set, it is argued, by reading the title of a book. I wonder what mind-set the semiliterate get when they read a title such as *The Iliad*.

The fact that such silliness is countenanced at Nassau County Community College and other similar institutions is cause for profound concern.

Chapter Six

Science

Despite lip service given to fairness, objectivity, and independence, science in the '90s was afflicted by political fashions. For example, AIDS now cannot be discussed as a public health problem requiring identification and controls and communicability. As a result of homosexual advocacy, any inquiry into those possessing the disease is regarded as a civil rights violation. And while feminists have brought the public's attention to the scourge of breast cancer, prostate cancer—which kills even more Americans—does not receive the same attention or funding.

Increasingly the line between politics and science is blurred. Assertions about the "Greenhouse Effect" are often related to a political agenda. Similarly, clean air targets are sometimes a function of political lobbying and the interests of advocacy groups. Scientists, in short, can be as biased as anyone.

Moreover, scientists, with their statistics and "studies," are able to pull the wool over our eyes so easily because Americans can be remarkably gullible. Consider that a recent Daniel Yankelovich survey found a threefold increase in belief in fortune-telling, an almost threefold increase in belief in reincarnation, a two-and-a-half-fold increase in belief in astrology, a four-and-a-half-fold increase in belief in faith healing, and a four-and-a-half-fold increase in belief in spiritualism, or communing with the dead, between 1976 and 1998. Could it be that the paranormal is becoming normal?

Forget Einstein. In modern America psychics are to be found on cable stations selling their special insights for $4.99 a minute. And according to cable station spokesmen this paranormal exercise is very much in demand. What callers get, of course, is pure unadulterated nonsense.

If the psychics had special power you wouldn't have to give your name or a credit card number. Presumably the psychic would know. Moreover, if the psychic really has predictive power she wouldn't be fleecing her audience for $4.99 a minute, she'd be at the track betting on 100-to-1 shots or picking lottery numbers.

Why then are so many people susceptible to the con and why are those numbers increasing? Needless to say, the reasons are complex. But two things are clear. In a media world that assumes only bad news is newsworthy, people want to hear good news. It is also the case that scientific literacy is in decline. People want easy answers even if they are misleading or false. Good news and easy answers are in demand and, if the trend line is accurate, are more in demand now than two decades ago. The delivery system is unimpeachable for true believers since it emanates from another world or the stars.

As I see it, the most compelling reason for this phenomenon is scientific illiteracy. People capable of scientific reason are generally not candidates for superstition. However, science is a subject less rigorously taught than in the past and less favored by a population that takes its findings for granted or, worse yet, is suspicious of its accomplishments.

On international science tests, American students score near the bottom or at the bottom compared to students from other nations. This is ironic. There isn't any nation that has profited more from scientific and technical advances than the United States. The American standard of living and the remarkable growth in gross national product are due in large part to technical innovation.

Yet remarkably there has been a substantial interest in séances, fortune-telling, and faith healing. Admittedly there are limits to science and limits to positivism, but these limits do not stop at the doorstep of paranormalcy. Faith healing will not cure an inflamed appendix, even if gifted hands massage the lower stomach area, and all the incantations in the world will not reduce the size of a tumor.

Computers and Americans

As P. T. Barnum noted, and cable callers prove late every night, "there's a sucker born every minute." But it's hard to believe there's been such an increase in the sucker population, especially when applied science is changing our lives as computerization attests.

Almost every educator and politician in the nation has called for a cyberspace autobahn to cure what ails American students. The refrain reached a crescendo when President Clinton argued that we owe it to future generations to build an educational infrastructure in which every classroom is hooked up to the Internet.

Many computer enthusiasts have simply lost perspective. Computers have limits. Although they can be a useful adjunct to conventional instruction, they cannot replace teachers, despite any hyperbole to the contrary. What I have observed in my thirty years in the academy is that teaching is essentially a matter of building relationships with students. In some cases e-mail and Web pages can assist, but they aren't substitutes for face-to-face contact, the human transmission belt of knowledge and experience. Morality, imagination, appreciation, discipline, will, and emotions are not programmable in any computer language.

Much has been made of Garry Kasparov's chess game loss to the IBM supercomputer, Deep Blue. Opposing Mr. Kasparov across the chessboard was a 2,800 pound RS/6000 SP computer rigged with more than 500 microprocessors capable of analyzing 200 million chess positions *every second*. In the final match Kasparov gave up after nineteen moves.

While John Ruskin argued "no machine will increase the possibilities of life," Kasparov's loss has been the catalyst for commentary about a brave new world in which machines will outwit humans and artificial intelligence will consider a variety of puzzling issues. When René Descartes described "the ghost in the machine," he was arguing metaphorically for a mind-body dichotomy. The ghost in the contemporary machine, in the computer's memory, is the anthropomorphic quality attributed to technology.

With Kasparov's defeat, a popular belief is emerging that technology possesses Zeus-like power to solve our woes, eliminate poverty, make us feel better about ourselves, and make chess players invincible. Ironically, this chess match produced inferences radically different from the usual scientific intention.

Historically, philosophers of science sought an expression of man's power in harnessing the forces of nature. What is evolving, however, is a belief that technology may elude or transcend human will pursuing a direction of its own beyond our understanding and control.

In *2001: A Space Odyssey,* Stanley Kubrick presents a wonderfully illustrative moment of technological impotence. H.A.L., the computer on board the spacecraft, malfunctions, taking on totalitarian qualities alien to the original computer program. The astronauts are helpless at first. Faced with the Hobson's choice of working with a dysfunctional computer on which their life support system depends or destroying it, they opt for the latter. The degree to which they are dependent on technology and helpless in the face of a computer "gone mad" is an appropriate metaphor for this time and not inconsistent with Kasparov's angry outburst after being vanquished by a computer that clearly outwitted him.

While it is true that technology is creating an illusion that anything is possible, the Kasparov defeat by a computer doesn't, in itself, prove this point. The computer faced a board of finite moves and a stored memory of previous strategy. In a universe defined within narrow parameters such as these, artificial intelligence can excel. However, assume a battlefield with many soldiers and virtually infinite moves; assume as well a variety of changing conditions such as variable weather. In this situation, the computer may be an adjunct to, but not a replacement for, human ingenuity.

To assume that technology can solve all problems in the way that a computer evaluates potential moves on a chessboard is misguided. We may increase our reliance on computers and attribute grand powers to them, but in the end they are only an extension of ourselves. Technology may be able to clone an animal, but it cannot tell us whether life created in this way is desirable. The computer has made it easier than heretofore to transmit information, yet it is increasingly more difficult to tease out the trivial from the important on the Internet. In its way technology has forced people to examine the human dimensions of decisions at the very moment people seem reluctant to accept the responsibility.

Believing that tools of technology are within human control is more than halfway to achieving control. Through his masterful chess moves in the past, Kasparov helped to build the software program that proved to be his undoing. The computer is a mirror of information systems recording what is observable; it can see and hear, but it cannot create or affect the causes of despair and joy. A computer's potential for growth is limited by the human potential to unlock the mysteries of our past.

The limitations of computers do not suggest that these instruments of technology aren't powerful forces in reshaping our environment. But it behooves those who arrived at rash conclusions after Kasparov's loss to consider the deficiencies in Deep Blue's software program had there never been grand masters of the past whose moves were recorded for posterity.

We control the destiny of computers by recording the chain of knowledge in computer memory. If the links in this chain are missing, the software program will be defective. That is the rub. Computers are not perfectible; they inherit human frailties. To assume that the IBM defeat of Kasparov marks a significant departure from the past is mistaken. Human will has dominion over technology. Kasparov's defeat may be surprising and illuminating, but it doesn't disprove this point.

Science and Life

In an era where rational explanations are demanded for all social phenomena, where even hubris and greed have been subject to scientific exegesis, science itself has been enlisted in the effort to explain everything.

Clearly biological makeup affects temperament. Yet in 1998 at the Association for Politics and the Life Sciences—an offshoot of the American Political Science Association—the claim was made that biology is *the* major influence on human behavior.

"Genetic evolution and cultural evolution are interwoven," said Edward O. Wilson, emeritus professor of entomology at Harvard. According to Wilson, the natural and social sciences are governed by a small set of natural laws. Presumably, then, the nature versus nurture contention is a false distinction.

Yet, while one should acknowledge the role of genetics in behavior, it would seem to be a form of scientific overreach to conclude that genes can explain all of human behavior. For example, young men with high levels of testosterone are more likely to be aggressive than females or older males. But it is also true that crack cocaine can artificially induce violent behavior and in some societies young males are encouraged to be more passive than in other societies.

It may stand to reason that aspects of behavior have evolved over time as a form of adaptation for the species, but that is neither easy to prove nor subject to validation.

Some theoreticians contend that democracy, based on rationality, is inconsistent with the evolution of the unconscious dimensions of the brain's functions. George Marcus, a professor of political science at Williams College, argues that the conscious decisions demanded of democratic government are inconsistent with the unconscious parts of the brain. However, if this claim is true or even partly true, should we suspend rational judgment or should we assume that rational decisions in democracy cannot be made?

Dennis McBride, a professor at George Mason University, maintains that congressmen with liberal voting records are more likely to have beards than are conservative colleagues. McBride concludes that liberal lawmakers may feel the need to grow beards in order to offset a "maternal" voting record, a signal reinforcing their "maleness."

This claim, however, falls into the *post hoc* fallacy condition. A beard may be a generational statement having nothing to do with politics. It may be a reaction to razor blades. It may be a function of sheer laziness. Despite what McBride claims about the "hairy House of Representatives," not one senator, not even Paul Wellstone (arguably the most liberal) is currently sporting a beard. So much for grand scientific theory.

The problem with scientific explanations is that very often they claim more than can be delivered. Unless a theory can be subject to laboratory reproduction, it remains a theory. To apply it to every aspect of culture is absurd.

A new age is dawning in which expectations from science and technology will be obliged to be more realistic than at any time in the computer age. Hubris will give way to humility, and the so-called better life will have to seek advance from nonscientific breakthroughs. The computer chip, we will see, does not provide all the answers.

Might this development lead to a religious awakening? At this point one can only speculate. We are at least two, perhaps three, generations from a day of reckoning. However, when science has extended longevity to 150, allowed people to communicate with everyone on the globe in real time, eliminated cavities and the common cold, built airplanes that can transport someone from New York to London in one hour, virtually eliminated poverty, raised crops four times more quickly in artificial environments than on farms, and eliminated most genetically transmitted diseases, what else is there to do?

I would respond to that question by noting that affluence has not inoculated people from spiritual despair. A time awaits us when the exploitation of human contentment may take nonsecular forms. After all, better cars, a bigger bank account, a larger house, a longer life, have not in themselves produced inner satisfaction.

If a scientific and technological slowdown is in the cards, it may usher in an era of reflection, a time of assessing where we have come from and where we may be going. Clearly the financial markets may be both optimistic and apprehensive about the impending technological change, but for those who have reached the near limit of consumption, spiritual awakening can offer a more fulfilling existence than they have previously known.

Are We Alone?

For me, however, reflection about our existence may never be the same again. When paleontologists claimed that evidence of a one-celled creature, amoeba-like, was found in the crevice of a meteorite that landed in Antarctica, the fantasy of those who believed in life on Mars may have come to fruition. Clearly this is not life on which grand boasts may rest. Moreover, the claims will be examined and reexamined by other scientists before concrete judgment is offered. Already Stephen Jay Gould has punctured holes in sanguine estimates of life elsewhere in the universe. But this discovery has stirred the imagination as few scientific breakthroughs have.

If the conclusions are verified, all kinds of possibilities are opened. A Martian microbe could be as significant as the Copernican and Galilean discoveries combined. Surely theorists of creationism and evolution are not yet challenged by the finding and indeed may never be challenged. But the notion that life may exist on other planets suggests that humans may not be alone in the universe, that life on this planet may not be unique.

How vast is the family of extraterrestrial life will not be determined anytime soon and certainly not by a bacterium from Mars. If a life-bearing meteor came to earth four billion years ago about the time the earth was churning in primordial soup, it might mean that we are the offspring of extraterrestrial seed planting. Of course, it might mean nothing of the sort. This exciting potential find links science with fiction; speculation about space may never be the same again.

NASA's news lengthens the odds against the uniqueness of life on earth. Along with recent revelations about the virtual infinitude of galaxies, far greater than previous knowledge estimated, the notion of unique life forms on this planet may be supplanted by a belief in variegated life in the universe beyond our ken. The secret of human genesis has long been a quest for mankind. With interplanetary probes, sophisticated new tools for interstellar investigation, and the search for radio transmission in space, the answer to this question may soon be within our grasp.

Stephen Spielberg's *E.T.* may be pregnant with scenarios for scientists. Little green creatures pointing fingers at the sky and communicating telepathically may not be in the offing, but a new world of discovery may await us as exciting, if not more exciting, than the Age of Discovery. Who knows what secrets may be unlocked in the micro-biota of other meteorites?

The cynics have a ready response: "Who cares; life on earth is what we should concentrate on." Or, the corollary argument that NASA released this report to enhance its budget for interplanetary projects. But in the end it doesn't matter what the cynics argue, for the power of life beyond this planet is so compelling, so romantic, that it cannot be diminished by naysayers.

Every person staring into the night will now be inclined to ask not whether Venus is brighter than the North Star or whether the Big Dipper can be located, but rather are there life forms in some distant star that, such as a Rosetta stone, will unlock secrets from our past, provide translations of biblical descriptions, and awaken us to our limits and to hitherto unimagined possibilities?

Chapter Seven

Morality

Is there such a thing as morality independent of personal choice? This seems like an odd question with an obvious answer. Unfortunately, throughout the '90s, the question was neither odd nor obvious.

During that decade I was asked to serve as a TV commentator for a group of adolescents discussing "teenage morality." Since I could not distinguish between adult morality and teenage morality, I was at a distinct disadvantage. Nonetheless, comments about choosing one's morality were uniformly embraced. One young lady said, "I pick and choose what I believe is right. My parents told me I am the best judge of what is moral." Alas, morality, like behavior and ethics, has come through the social funnel of radical individualism and situational choice, and not much is left of it.

When I asked whether some behaviors are wrong, most of the teenagers dissented. They could agree on murder, but not much else. Is it any wonder that we cannot put right the moral chaos that surrounds us?

The muscle of moral behavior has atrophied from disuse as many people—not only teenagers—pick and choose their preferred morality. This era of post-modernism and relativism makes morality like an item on a supermarket shelf. You can choose it, ignore it, or select another item. The choice, however, is yours.

We have slid down the greased pole of deviancy rationalization. Any act, however, odious, can be rationalized. A robbery can be justified because the thief is hungry, his satisfaction bringing more pleasure to him than pain to the grocer. Even murder can be rationalized—as Communists and Nazis did—if it is said to promote a "better society."

Most people—even those holding traditional beliefs—make some accommodation with contemporaneity. After all, it is often said, the world is changing. But change isn't always for the better, and confusion is sometimes the result of incremental change. Plato's allegory of the cave is useful for those who encounter contemporary life as shadows on a cave wall. Most people do not realize that they dwell inside an epistemological inferno, a veritable Walpurgis Night of hollow ideas and relativistic beliefs. To extend the metaphor, when dwellers leave the cave they do not see the bright light of day but a mist that inhibits clear vision.

The language of autonomy has eviscerated society's common moral framework. As a consequence, there are only rights and privileges but rarely, if ever, duty. An independent moral order has not been abolished; it has been forgotten. Good and evil exist, but the line between them has been blurred by a deficiency of memory. An exercise of self-restraint, an acknowledgment that there are limits, is what is needed.

But where does one begin, when individualism is utterly unrestrained? We must tell the young that distinguishing between right and wrong is not a matter of preference. And we must establish consensus about morality by stigmatizing bad behavior. Admittedly, in the era of rap music, bad behavior is even worse than it used to be. Limits have been stretched beyond the point of rational judgment. But this is not a time for despair. Rather, determination is needed: The determination to say that morality is not personal and autonomy must be defined by the parameters of moral authority. "Anything goes" is the call to nihilism; only certain things are permissible in a social order confident about its beliefs. Belief in individual rights must not be allowed to subvert the distinction between right and wrong.

Abraham Lincoln was once asked what he did when lost in the maze of policy decisions. He replied, "It is very much like being lost in a forest. When you lose your way, retrace your footsteps." That is what we should do as a nation: retrace our steps. It's not an enjoyable walk, as the following examples show.

Value-Neutral

At a late-'90s dinner party, a guest at my table expressed what had become the conventional opinion about President Clinton's alleged peccadilloes. "I don't care if he had a sexual dalliance or encouraged someone to perjure herself," the guest said. "The economy is doing well, and that's all I care about."

Polls reinforced this point of view. Americans have apparently reached a new level of cynicism. If the president is above the law, any rationalization can be employed to excuse his behavior. It is inconceivable that anyone in the '70s would have excused the break-in at the Democrats' Watergate headquarters by saying, "All I care about are President Nixon's overtures to China." Such an excuse is analogous to a wife's rationalizing her husband's adulterous behavior by noting that he supports his family.

Contemporary morality, as this example suggests, is as relative as truth itself has become. It is entirely in the eye of the beholder. Right and wrong have been put in a cauldron that destroys norms. Those who rode the Eden express through the '60s and '70s were amoralizers. They were nurtured on the belief that anything goes.

"The United States is a laughingstock in Europe," my dinner partner said. And perhaps she is right. There is evidence that French attitudes are different from those in the United States (albeit not as different as they once were). Not long ago, the widow of former president Francois Mitterand stood next to his mistress at his funeral. But it is precisely Europe's cynicism, its amorality, that brought Europeans to the brink of totalitarian despair. Hitler, Stalin, Mussolini, Lenin, and Franco did not germinate on American soil.

Should Americans resemble Europeans? Alas, do contemporary Americans resemble Europeans? Consider the evidence:

- Tupac Shakur, who made a career out of defiance and bad behavior, is an icon among rap aficionados, even though he died in a shoot-out on the streets of Las Vegas.
- Latrell Sprewell, who choked and then punched his Golden State Warriors' coach in a fit of anger, now stars for the New York Knicks—while his old coach has been fired and is out of the NBA.
- The Reverend Al Sharpton and his colleagues C. Vernon Mason and Alton Maddox, defendants in the Tawana Brawley defamation case, converted the courtroom into a burlesque theater. Yet Sharpton almost won the Democratic Party nomination for mayor of New York, despite his continual display of demagoguery.
- Developer Donald Trump converted arrogance, egotism, and bad behavior into book contracts and parts in Hollywood films and consideration for the presidency. In our Warholian world, where celebrity status is everything, getting attention is critical—no matter how it's obtained.

The message is clear, from Tinseltown to the Big Apple, slouching toward barbarism is in style. Of course, when bad behavior is rewarded, remorse is another word in sad disuse. Why should anyone be sorry when the rewards for violating bourgeois standards are so bountiful?

Surely President Clinton understood this condition very well. When evidence of his bad behavior surfaced—as it did on so many occasions from Whitewater to Filegate, from Gennifer Flowers to Charlie Trie—he could not recall what happened. The amnesia defense became a White House perennial. Amazingly, the public seemed not to care or, at least, was not aroused by the daily White House scandals. When last seen, the president was trying to reclaim his tattered reputation by emphasizing the economy.

Perhaps this cynicism isn't amazing. After all, bad behavior is in vogue. With allegations, rumors, and investigations circling Washington like a perpetual cloud cover, the public has become inured to scandal. It is as if people are saying, "So what else is new?"

Now there are hundreds of cultural Oscar Wildes—without his wit, of course—openly intent on overturning manners, morals, legitimacy, decency, and taste. They believe that banal cynicism is instructive, that rejecting manners is liberating, and that coarse language is expressive.

Morality is now evaluated against a backdrop of individual will. It is as if the Ten Commandments had been rewritten by the Rolling Stones. The question young people are likely to be asked is not whether a given act is wrong, but whether they think it's wrong. Americans are becoming existentialists, with each the author of his own moral code. In a sense not fully understood by the nation's journalists, Bill Clinton is a symbol for his generation. His lies are casual, though borne of necessity.

Americans appear to have been lying to themselves as well, throughout the decade. It is not "the economy, stupid," but the culture that counts. A nation that cannot control its emotions cannot long sustain its prosperity. If norms can be discarded like used newspapers, then the characteristics necessary for success will at some point be undermined. Yet instant gratification remains in vogue.

It is the theme of almost every prime-time soap opera. Bill Clinton and his generation were weaned on the likes of J. R. Ewing and *Dynasty*. Do whatever you can get away with—that is the moral of these television programs. Having imbibed this lesson, it has become a generational view. It is therefore not surprising that the public wouldn't condemn a president clearly if culpable of the allegations leveled against him. In fact, as long as the economy remained sound, unemployment low, and opportunity high, there was little the president could do that would invite public opprobrium.

What this means for the nation is insidious. If Americans are shockproof, if a president can win support as long as the gross domestic product rises, political compromises of major proportions are possible.

Europeanization, both its widespread cynicism and the totalitarian temptation, may have been exported to these shores, despite a belief in the durability of our political institutions. But this is not a matter for rejoicing. Drawing the line between degradation of culture and Clinton's behavior is largely in the realm of speculation. But for those who despair over the president's behavior and seek explanations for it, it behooves them to consider the effects of cultural decline as a likely answer.

How could most Americans rationalize lying and venery in the White House unless they had already lost their moral sense?

Lost Churches

Even our churches did not escape the immorality shadow cast by the White House and other American leaders during the '90s. Remarkably, a group of ministers joined with academics and health professionals to prepare a manual for members of the Presbyterian Church (U.S.A.) based on the astonishing assumption that the church cannot and should not countenance conventional norms of morality. The panel concluded, according to a *Newsweek* report, that marriage itself, "though sometimes liberating is too often vitiated by 'patriarchialism' and 'heterosexist' assumptions." The report goes on to note that homosexuals are feared "because erotic passion between persons of the same gender is a sharp break with socially conventional patterns of male dominance and female subordination."

If the committee has its way, sin itself will be redefined to reflect contemporary mores. Instead of confirming that thou shalt not give in to lust, the committee urges Presbyterians to masturbate "from early adolescence through lively old age" and to avoid passing moral judgment on sexual intercourse between "responsible" teenage lovers. These sweeping changes are encouraged, so the report notes, to accommodate those who feel "marginalized" by a society that doesn't share its ethical sensibility.

The act of bearing children isn't mentioned except as a matter of contraception or abortion. Neither can one find words like *love, honor,* and *obey.* They have been replaced by the ill-considered *justice-love.* For the marginalized, this may be a clarion call for recruitment, but for the vast majority, who do not fall into this category, the committee statement is an unequivocal debasement of religious thought.

Although this manual may have been designed to widen the circle of the church's faithful, which has already understandably declined by half a million members over the last two decades, it most definitely will not have that intended effect. After all, why belong to a church of infidels? It could just as easily be a sex club or a den of iniquity.

Moreover, if the church stands for what is presently fashionable, unaffected by some transcendent standard of appropriate behavior, then its motto is ultimately dependent on the winds of change. This, in effect, isn't even relativism, it is nihilism, or the belief that one must explode the belief of today for a new one tomorrow. Alas, some homosexuals desirous of social legitimacy may join such a church, but for anyone else this is a church in name only, relieved of a moral compass and eviscerated of natural law.

Curiously, the *Newsweek* writers contend that "the Presbyterians have at least had the courage to grapple with the changes in the nation's sexual habits." What can these writers possibly mean? In what sense is a prescriptive manual challenging normative and moral behavior "grappling with changes in the nation's sexual habits"? Unless these authors believe that legitimizing sin is healthy for the nation or, the corollary, that sin itself is relative, this statement hasn't any meaning.

That a mainline Protestant church would even entertain such a committee report demonstrates how far down the slippery slope of moral degradation some churches have gone. No matter how this manual is dressed up, it still bespeaks religious debasement—a debasement with its roots in the spread of a democratic ethos in the middle of the nineteenth century. Until this Great Awakening, Protestants from a Calvinist tradition argued that salvation was limited to those who found a sign of election. Good deeds were considered to be manifest signs of a good person, a soul predestined to heaven. By doctrine, entrance was limited. Therefore, members of a Congregationalist community would try to act in a manner that indicated salvation.

This tradition was vitiated by what some scholars have called the Emersonian revolution. The spirit behind the reform movement a century and a half ago was the introduction of the egalitarian idea that all people are eligible for salvation, that they are endowed with a power of epiphany that permits the discovery of one's place in the afterlife. Moral law, the covenant on which Congregationalists relied to find signs of election, was rapidly replaced by an antinomian view that suggested that faith is the only requisite for salvation.

According to this view, anyone finding the spiritual component in his soul is eligible to be God's "resting place." This egalitarian spirit changed the religious landscape in the nation, but the effect was not restricted to religion. After all, if salvation is distributed democratically through a spiritual awakening, then there isn't any need to behave in a manner consistent with the elect in the church. With the ascendancy of an antinomian spirit, power was to be found in the individual; even the minister was to be removed from his role of interpreter of God's will.

This period was most certainly not what twentieth-century social analysts would describe as an age of narcissism, yet an individualism formerly reined in by the church's covenant was now unshackled by any moral duty. The dictates of spiritual conversion depended on an emotional frenzy, an evangelical soul-searching. Moreover, the very constraints in behavior Congregationalism demanded were unleashed by the Unitarian belief in personal revelation. For many, this shift in religious attitude represented a concomitant shift in behavior. Salvation lost its elusiveness.

To a rather remarkable degree the twentieth century is a continuation of this antinomian tradition except that in the modern era, belief in the afterlife has waned. What remains is the egalitarian belief in secular salvation, a salvation eviscerated of religious meaning, and based on the idea of personal fulfillment and satisfaction. The democratic ideal that within each of us is the power to find satisfaction is a relatively modern notion evolving from the Great Awakening and refined by the substitution of Mammon for God and of instant gratification for the afterlife.

In suggesting that there is a heaven on earth, modern man engages in a heresy widely condemned a century earlier. Yet it is the natural and inevitable consequence of antinomianism. A charge card is the modern equivalent of a church, offering rewards more tangible than salvation. The ability to consume is also provided to almost anyone. All one has to do is apply; no soul-searching is required.

There is something to be said for this materialist soteriology since it is the final expression of the nexus between capitalism and religion. However, it is a materialism reliant on its own ends shorn of morality and bereft of communal restraints.

Atomized man is an extension of Emerson's belief that the soul's content can be made palpable through inspiration. No longer does a covenant with God unite a community behind a common purpose. Now there is nothing between mankind and the great abyss. We are alone in the universe with only our dreams of seeking heavenly blessing here and now. As a consequence, there is the much-discussed alienation and an unwillingness to put off for tomorrow what one wants today. Yet the struggle for meaning, for an orthodoxy in the face of superficial pursuits, is a relentless feature of modernity.

Curiously, the answer to what ails us is found in the restoration of belief in an afterlife in which the desire to be fit for heavenly salvation is the basis of human endeavor. Instead, a materialist culture seeks salvation through psychoanalysis, self-awareness, and the grotesque search for self. Those who have achieved affluence ask *why*, and those who pursue it ask *when*. Yet inevitably all ask the question found in the Old Testament, "After satisfaction, what?" And the answers aren't to be found. This void is what serious philosophers consider the current malaise. It isn't just that materialism is bad or that self-fulfillment is an inappropriate goal, it is that when the things one craves are obtained and one pursues a new course of study or a quest for the fashionable, an emptiness remains, an emptiness borne of rejecting the quest for salvation in the kingdom of God.

Love and Marriage

A similar dissatisfaction was evident in the continuing story of the birds and bees in the '90s—and at times all-out war between the sexes did break out, often at a very young age. In the '90s, Lolita—in our case, Amy Fisher—lost her youthful innocence and opened fire.

Other students—those who at least "saw" someone their own age—found themselves lacking an institution going back several generations: dating. We are paying the price for losing a vital social institution. I'm not referring to television's *The Dating Game*. Nor am I suggesting that necking in the third balcony of a movie theater inoculated young adults against divorce. What I am suggesting is that the institution of courtship established a set of customs and familiarity with members of the opposite sex and eased the path to marriage.

Dating was an experience in which young men were obliged to audition in front of a girl's parents. Many dates involved public activity—sporting events, school dances—where social skills were cultivated.

Moments of privacy led to romantic and physical experimentation, but since this dating institution reached its apogee before the era of the Pill, there was a penalty for "going too far," just as there was a stigma for being "fast." Women

learned that there was a delicate line between being cool and being overly friendly. And men learned the difference between being subtle and being blunt.
Although dating had more to do with enjoyment than matrimony, the institution
encouraged learning about a variety of people. Even "going steady" meant going
together for a sustained, but terminal, period.

As the nation was transformed into a mass-consumption society, dating
taught young men how to budget an allowance so that they could take a young
woman to a movie and a pizza place and still have money left for carfare home.
Dating also taught people to understand their feelings. The difference among a
"crush," a "heartache," and "love" was an invaluable lesson to learn.

When it came time to choose Mr. Right or Miss Right, it was an easier choice
than in the socially progressive present. In the dating age, it was received wisdom
that you didn't marry your first sweetheart. You were not to rush into marriage,
because a variety of controlled experiences was more likely to lead to marital
success than whirlwind romances could.

New customs, specifically premarital cohabitation, undermined the dating
institution. Parents found it difficult to contend with the claim that if sexual satisfaction and compatibility were requisites for marital success, young people
should live together before marriage. This argument swept the nation like a
prairie fire, leaving dating in ashes on the cultural landscape. However, few
people asked whether premarital cohabitation actually ensured marital success.
Had they inquired, the evidence would have suggested the opposite of the conventional wisdom: Individuals who lived together without the advantage of a
license were *less* likely to have successful marriages than couples who did not.

Unfortunately in the era of the Pill and the AIDS scare, dating of the traditional variety won't be disinterred; neither is there any confidence in cohabitation,
since this arrangement doesn't offer the commitment many young people seek.

The liberal answer to this problem has been predictable—"education" and
"classes." Forget reading, writing, and arithmetic—our students may not be able
to spell, but they are receiving "marriage preparation" (at least in Florida since
1998) as a high school graduation requirement. Here is yet another example of an
intractable social problem—the soaring divorce rate—being installed in the
school for remediation. But just as sex education didn't reduce illegitimacy and
drug education did not reduce drug use, marriage education will not reduce
divorce.

The boy-meets-girl story was thoroughly confused throughout the '90s.
Young people did not know how to meet or how to sustain a relationship. When
I suggested to my daughter that a young man interested in seeing her should call
for a date, she looked at me quizzically and said, "You *are* old-fashioned." Indeed
I am.

Perhaps the world won't return to crinolines under dresses and young men
who say "good evening, Sir" to their girlfriend's father. Perhaps school dances are
passé and young people don't engage in "submarine watching." Perhaps inno-

cence is dead and seventeen-young-olds don't blush. But on balance, after all we've learned in the past fifty years, the institution of marriage might be healthier if we could only recapture the dating practice of bygone years.

Not Perfect? Who's to Blame?

Two threads stitch together many of America's moral problems—the national obsession with "perfection" and a failure to take personal responsibility for the fact that nothing ever is perfect.

Human perfectibility is America's real obsession. To some extent, this is understandable. Affluence is higher than ever. If you haven't achieved perfection, you might be able to buy it.

But the search for perfection has become a neurotic pursuit of the unattainable. From politics to liposuction, hucksters promise what cannot be delivered to a public increasingly convinced that it can defy the limits of nature. When a pol starts a speech with "Not one American should have to . . . " (fill in the blank: "live in marginal housing," "go to bed hungry," "be denied medical care," "reside in a crime-riddled community," etc.), what he's really selling is perfectibility.

But unless human nature is altered or wealth dematerialized—remote possibilities at best—crime and the other ills of life will not disappear, and some of us will have to live with them. But in a world searching for perfection, such modesty is in short supply.

Those hawking eternal youth and physical perfection pretend that aging and personal idiosyncrasies are unnecessary if you buy their ointments, massages, herbal cures, face-lifts, tummy tucks, liposuction, hair weaves, transplants, breast enhancement, breast reduction, tooth whiteners, enzymes, hormone additives, vitamins, weight-loss pills, etc. The psyche is presumably just as manipulable: magazine ads offer to help you improve your memory, reduce stress, increase your sexual appetite, relax, enlarge your vocabulary, get a zest for life, and have the perfect orgasm. Of course, some of these products do deliver on their promises, but none can restore youth or create perfection.

Perfectibility has taken root because people have rejected imperfectibility, the belief that some conditions are imposed by nature or Providence and are immutable. The fifth-century Pelagians asserted that all people are essentially good and can be perfected, opposing the belief in Original Sin, or imperfectibility. Today, Pelagianism is thoroughly ascendant in the West, where people commonly strive to defy mortality and create heaven on earth, deriding the transcendent as mere superstitions to be discarded like used tissues. Thus these personal makeovers are not entirely frivolous: They are the manifestations, the rituals, in fact, of a powerful religion.

Each day this cult finds new adherents even though its sacraments fail to deliver as promised. After all the waxing, cleansing, psychologizing, and herbalizing, all the panaceas and shortcuts to nirvana, life does not change substantially. Good and evil still exist. Truth endures. Beauty is admired. Bad behavior sometimes leads to bad ends. The perfectionists cannot change the fundamentals of human life.

The final judgment is not based on how youthful or pretty you are but how pure your soul is. Perfecting the soul is the one thing for which the hucksters do not have an easy solution.

But still Americans want to blame someone else for their problems. No longer will anyone assume responsibility for his actions; this is the era of pointing a finger at someone else. Feminists, for example, tell us that the oppression males have imposed on them keeps them from getting ahead, and young white men contend that they can't find a job in a market where women, blacks, Hispanics, and other designated minorities are given preferential treatment.

Black radicals blame whites for the deplorable condition of the inner cities, and many whites suggest that a cycle of welfare dependency has destroyed the work ethic. Farmers point the finger of blame at Washington, and the Congress suggests that farmers should learn how to get by without subventions. Labor is angry at management, and management talks about breaking the union stranglehold.

Wherever one turns, such views are externalized. The willingness to take responsibility for one's actions has been eviscerated before the onslaught of the blame psychology. So pervasive is this belief that one cannot run for public office without blaming an opponent for whatever ails the community. It is no longer possible to suggest that no one is to blame for some particular problem, or say that a confluence of events accounts for unfortunate circumstances, or simply to utter, "I made a mistake."

"I'm OK; you're OK," as a naive worldview of the '60s and '70s, has been transmogrified into "I'm not OK, and you're to blame." "It's your fault" is now the calling card of a generation weaned on the belief that "if only everyone were like me, we'd have no problems."

The blame game will end only when everyone has it and everyone is culpable. Mea culpas will appear routinely—a condition close to the present reality. The era of blame, like most fashions, will evanesce, to be followed by an age of guilt.

Chapter Eight

Cultural Fall-Deep

Four Wrongheaded Ideas of the Past Decade Stand Out

At the start of the new millennium, a review of the '90s is in order. Many widely embraced lessons from this decade are either wrongheaded, pernicious, or both. While each day warfare is poised to erupt, a substantial portion of the public is falsely persuaded that peace is at hand. While free markets have created unprecedented affluence worldwide, ideologists refuse to consider their beneficent effect. Truth, despite all the current claims to the contrary, is immutable, objective, and beyond personal whim. But this is a dark age. The door has been shut on the past.

The first lesson is that the end of the Cold War awarded the United States a peace dividend. Presumably, we have the luxury of spending less on defense than before. Not only that, but the conditions that warranted constant vigilance in the past have faded from public consciousness. The cliché "peace through strength," the hallmark of American defense strategy from World War II to the end of the Cold War, has been replaced by peace through negotiation. National interests, it is argued, are mitigated by shared assumptions—a homogenization of national interests into common ones. As a consequence, military preparedness is deemed less important now than at any point in the last half-century.

Second, the belief in free markets as the arbiter of social problems has waned. The '90s will be remembered as the decade that challenged unfettered markets. From Europe to Asia there is denunciation of the "Anglo-Saxon model of capitalism," a deprecatory interpretation of American and British market capitalism. Emerging as yet another "third way" is the belief in an active government to moderate the suffering of those left behind by their inability to compete in that marketplace. While the free market had its inning in the '80s, it is now under harsh scrutiny by many Western leaders who abhor economic stratification, conspicuous wealth, and relative poverty, believing that government intervention can and should work to reduce these conditions.

Third, moral assertions—even commonsensical attributions of right and wrong—have been relegated to the realm of relativism, seen as preachments without foundation. Invariably, anyone who dares to make a moral commentary receives the rejoinder "Who is he to tell me what's wrong?" The legitimacy of moral argumentation, buttressed by religious belief and normative judgment, has been undermined by a sophistry that converts all arguments into whatever one wants them to mean.

Political leaders replaced the politics of production—of results—with a politics of feelings. We went from "Ask what you can do for your country," to "I feel your pain." As the '60s generation came to power, "I" became the center of all things, and judgment itself was increasingly superseded by narcissism.

These chickens have come home to roost with a vengeance. The Starr Report, for example, told Americans as much about their culture as about the president's conduct. It is instructive that the president's apologists argued that private behavior was not as important as his public role, and that any critique of his actions should be evaluated against a backdrop of American Puritanism. This position is understandable, however, only if one scorns bourgeois values and ignores the symbolic leadership of the president. Only a polymorphously perverse culture built on lies and double-talk could argue about whether oral sex is sex. Only a massive breakdown of bourgeois social constraints could make possible a widespread public acceptance of deception.

Fourth, truth itself is under assault. The '90s have generated an attitude of "optic truth," where truth is in the eye of the beholder. With truth a casualty of perception, anything goes. The opposite of truth isn't lies, but merely a different perception. In a world without truth, you have your opinion and I have mine and they are equally valid.

Evidence over the past fifty years shows that the characteristics that have separated the United States from other nations—optimism, merit, and virtue—have declined. Wrongheaded ideas have emerged during this period of decline.

Perhaps the overriding American trait for most of the nation's history was optimism, which translated into a faith in the future. The belief that children will live better than their parents was, until recently, an article of national confidence. That belief, however, is in retreat. Polls show that diminished expectations are on the horizon.

Americans appear to be in the grip of a shrinking self-image. Happiness is not seeking more, but rather retaining what one has been able to achieve. While there are certainly economic factors involved, such as the high inflation of the '70s, the emerging attitudes have as much to do with a belief system as economic reality. For example, consumer expectations continue to decline even when the economy is in recovery.

The second distinguishing American characteristic was a belief in merit. This nation was predicated on the belief that parents' backgrounds were irrelevant to their children's eventual stations in life. The Founding Fathers relied on a model of individual achievement. It wasn't a perfect model—what is?—but it served to launch the careers of many distinguished Americans who came from humble beginnings and who, if raised in Europe, never would have been granted the opportunities found here. Despite the relative success of this meritocracy, a governmental desire to redress real and perceived wrongs of the past has reversed the national ethos, relying instead on ascription as a source of career mobility.

Affirmative action, in its many forms, is the clearest manifestation of this trend. Now one's patrimony, determined by sex, race, and ethnicity, helps determine how societal rewards will be dispensed. A black female from a wealthy family has a better chance of receiving a university scholarship than a white male from a poor family, even if the male has a higher grade point average and better SAT scores.

The third distinguishing characteristic of this nation was virtue. As Adam Smith noted, freedom in the marketplace or liberty in the political arena can easily be thwarted by a citizenry unrestrained by virtuous behavior. At the moment, self-imposed virtue is evanescing. The elite—once representing behavior to be emulated—regards virtue as an anachronism. Students spend more time learning how to use condoms than how to solve a mathematics problem. Fourteen-year-olds are enabled to have children out of wedlock by welfare agencies that serve as ersatz spouses. Environmentalists, wedded to pantheistic worship, are willing to sacrifice property rights, which the Founders considered an essential feature of the Constitution. The disappearance of virtue has resulted in an ever-expansive role for government, as Edmund Burke predicted. And as government expands to fill the void once occupied by virtuous behavior, there is little guidance in moral instruction, and growing emphasis on interests.

Are we, therefore, spinning out of control? Not yet. The forces I've described are moving ahead incrementally. But it is fair to say the United States is not the nation it was. It might no longer be the beacon of light that lit a path for others to follow.

The Twenty-first Century Will Continue to See a Struggle between Tribalists and Universalists

During the twenty-first century, neither the tribalists nor the universalists will disappear. Tribalists, who are descendants of moribund Marxism, represent one side of the philosophical divide. The ethnic war in the Balkans and the civil war in Rwanda are a few of the dozens of tribal conflicts in global wars. On the other hand, the universalists are represented by youthful computer hackers who do not recognize geographic boundaries; in the world of electric wizardry, Arab and Jew, Japanese and Korean, and Moslem and Christian are homogenized. Advanced technology doesn't recognize tribes.

It is clear that neither side in the equation will disappear. Tribalists will assert their gains, and universalists will search for common ground. At some point, however, there will have to be some give-and-take so that ethnicity is not the only way to define humanity, and humanity is not a homogenized construct of automations all looking and acting like one another.

While these categories have vague meaning on a macrosocial level, they have significant implications on the microsocietal level. Take, for example, the issue of the school curriculum. The tribalists are competing for space and emphasis with one another. In the "colorful mosaic," the now-standard metaphor for the nation, every ethnic group is at war for attention. By contrast, the universalists are suggesting that ethnicity should be subordinate to common human qualities. After all, the relationships between father and son and between mother and daughter transcend race and ethnicity.

As the tribalist tries to narrow his focus, driving a wedge among groups, the universalist is above the fray. While there is clearly justification for ethnocentrism, particularly the sheer delight that emerges from diversity, there is a point at which ethnic competition reduces all cultural differences to a cauldron of ethnic conflict. For example, which ethnic groups deserve special status in affirmative action policy, and why should they be so designated? The answer to this question invites conflict.

Universalists, by contrast, claim with ample justification that narrowly focused learning deprives all students of their common heritage, dividing mankind along a fault line. *Antigone* is not simply a tale about an anguished Greek woman; it is a story rich in conflict between filial piety and governmental allegiance. *Hamlet* is not a play about a Danish king, but instead a remorseless search for revenge against a backdrop of plotting and human frailty. Presumably, either of these story lines could be transferred to another culture and another time. For tribalists who insist that all culture is reduced to ethnicity, it is worth recalling that Kurosawa's *Ran* was a reworking of *King Lear* for a Japanese landscape.

At the moment, however, a compromise is not on the horizon. The heat of conflict has blinded those on either side of the divide from the resolution that is desperately needed.

The Cultural Wars of the '90s

Americans in the new millennium will continue to take sides in the cultural war that has been waged over the past decades. On either side of the divide are traditionalists who are eager to restore principles of the past and latitudinarians who seek to extend the boundaries of normative behavior. It is a war of attrition, and latitudinarians have won notable victories in recent times.

The Supreme Court decision on abortion acknowledged the power of the latitudinarians and has ensconced the *Roe v. Wade* decision as the law of the land. Condoms are now routinely distributed in urban schools as a response to the AIDS crisis, often over the objection of parents.

Traditionalists have fought back vigorously. But the media panjandrums are part of the latitudinarian clique and give scant attention to the other side, now routinely categorized as "religious primitives." After all, defenders of traditional concepts of morality and religion are deemed retrograde—part of another America that is out of touch with present realities.

Causing further fissures among traditionalists are the ostriches who contend that such social issues should remain in the bedroom. The "ostriches" are right, of course, except that they haven't bothered to notice that very little in the bedroom isn't also on the streets. In an era in which people let it all hang out, much is displayed that should be hidden. I suspect that most traditionalists would not worry about the extremes of social behavior if they were private matters between consenting adults. Once the streets are an extension of the bedroom, however, traditionalists are obliged to respond.

Latitudinarians often appear as though they are on the defensive despite obvious victories. They are convinced that any victory can be revised—and they are right. They are also firmly committed to a revolutionary posture that is designed to shatter the bourgeois ethos, even though most of the faithful are card-carrying members of the bourgeoisie. Like the student from the '60s who said, "You don't know what hell is like till you live in Scarsdale," the latitudinarians—most of whom are progeny of the '60s—want to eliminate the Scarsdales in the nation. They are equally adamant in keeping any semblance of religion out of public life. For the *Big Chill* generation, religion is society's evil, and the Catholic Church is the enemy incarnate. If religion cannot be diminished, it most certainly must be separated from the acts of government.

This civil war is no less fierce than the Civil War of the nineteenth century. Both represent moral struggle: slavery in the nineteenth century and abortion in the twentieth. Compromise, such as the Missouri Compromise in the nineteenth century and parental notification bills now, is proposed by politicians who hope to avoid a day of reckoning. There is indeed the possibility—hopefully a remote possibility—that the very fabric of the nation will be torn by the competing interests on each side of the cultural divide. In the abortion struggle, as in the Civil War, there aren't any victors. Battlefield victories for the latitudinarians only deepen traditionalists' resolve. Neither side will surrender, and meanwhile the bleeding saps the strength of the body politic.

Ending Endism Allows Hope to Reemerge and Salvationists to Overcome Nihilists

The end of the century is a period-mark providing closure to the "endisms" that were forecast during earlier decades. And there were many. George Steiner discussed the end of the humanities. Francis Fukuyama proposed the end of history. A number of articles were written suggesting the end of the novel. Some feminists were fond of the end of gender. Norman Mailer proposed the end of rationality. Many critics suggested the end of the arts had arrived. Daniel Bell discussed the end of ideology. Paul Hogan announced the end of science. And even I, inured to and repulsed by endism, wrote an article titled "Death of the University."

Clearly all things come to an end; death is merely the last stop in creation. There is, of course, little doubt that many institutions are decaying morally and physically. To some degree this is manifest in the public distrust of government, the courts, mass media, and educational institutions. The spiritual divide in the culture separates the salvationists from the nihilists; those who believe in redemption and those who assume all is lost. But on one matter there is consensus: Something is wrong.

Part of what is wrong is the malaise engendered by the belief that the Apocalypse is near. The society seems to be in the grip of millenarian dementia. Postmodernism contributes to this condition with its intellectual anarchy, an aversion to hierarchy, categories, and objectivity. In their swim against the tide, postmodernists ultimately commit philosophical suicide on the shoals of rationality. Along the way, however, they spread various toxins that promote endism scenarios.

Of course, the ends prognosticated never materialize. History evolves inexorably; some boys will be boys and most girls will be girls; rationality can still be uncovered amid the cultural mist; the arts survive, albeit by the skin of an occasional canvas; the humanities are in retreat but still nourished by the past; novels are sometimes written, although most are manufactured; and the university lives, even though a case for its continuation is increasingly difficult to make.

The argument behind my belief that endism should end is Schumpeterian "creative destruction"; some institutions must step aside so that others can emerge. This isn't endism, although it may sound as if it is, but rather the intrinsic seeds of emergence within social decay.

Pitirim Sorokin in *Crisis of the Age* said it best when he maintained that within sensate culture are the conditions, even evidence, of ideational and idealistic culture. Atheists, after all, have *faith* in God's nonexistence. Hard rock occasionally lapses into momentary melodic sweetness. Pathetically vacuous Hollywood films such as *Braveheart* drift miraculously into uplifting visions of courage. Spiraling divorce and illegitimacy rates lead to calls for family unity. Violent crime awakens a need for religious guidance.

The end doesn't end because decay is part of a cycle of rebirth and emergence. That endism should characterize so much of contemporary culture is a statement about cultural depreciation, a vitiation of standards in a sea of barbaric sensations and atavistic savagery. Like the cross that weakens the devil's grip, hope is the salve that soothes the blistering culture.

In the cycle of regeneration, hope should be sought in the scattered ashes of decay. Postmodernist absurdity should be scrutinized with rational dispassion. Demeaning language should be flailed with elegant riposte. Crass art should be held to a standard of the masters. Relativism should be tamed with the search for truth. Inertia should be scoured with determination. And endism should meet its match in renaissance.

It is not enough to say the end is at hand, to struthious-like bury one's head in the sand to avoid the cultural devastation. The salvation of the future is found in the cultural nuggets of the present. And they exist if one looks hard for them. In this search is renewal.

In a metaphorical description of the former Soviet Union, Alexander Solzhenitsyn argued that communism poured cement over the entire society. Yet one day a crack emerged in the cement monolith, and yet another day a tiny green plant emerged from the crack. As the plant grew it split the cement, widening the crack and demonstrating the vulnerability of the monolith.

It is incumbent on those inoculated from nihilism to search for the tiny plants in the cultural monolith. That is where hope begins and the myth of endism ends.

A Rich and Comfortable Millennium Awaits Us

An old chestnut holds that "he who lives by the crystal ball relies on a diet of crushed glass." Alas, from Nostradamus to the women who read tea leaves, from mystics to skeptics, the future has been a source of fascination and despair. What makes predictions particularly problematic at this time is the acceleration of change, the pace of technological evolution. As the poet Paul Valéry once noted, "the future isn't what it used to be." Each December 31, "experts" are asked to describe the year ahead with reference to the Dow Jones average, which team will win the World Series, and what the unemployment rate will be. Of course it's all a game; no one is held accountable and if you guess often enough, at some point you'll hit the target. Even a stopped clock has the right time twice a day.

While a surprise-free scenario of the future is not possible, digging deep into the past can yield useful clues about what is to come. This reality should be a source of hope for those fearing the worst as we begin a new millennium. For example, those who understand free markets are aware that people can adapt rapidly to circumstances seemingly beyond their immediate control. There is far more flexibility, fungibility, and adaptability on earth than many in the intellectual community often assume. Neo-Malthusians, for example, continually paint a dreary picture based on the planet's "carrying capacity," in which population outpaces food production, technology is overpriced for most consumers, the world's population rises beyond sustainability, and pollution results in cataclysmic environmental changes.

Most of these dire predictions ignore commonsensical precepts such as Justice Learned Hand's "Every accident is in search of a rescue," the old saying that "necessity is the mother of invention," and the obvious fact that people are not lemmings—in the face of disaster, we don't band together and jump off a cliff. History proves this point conclusively. The Black Plague of the fourteenth century decimated a quarter of the European population, but it also ushered in an inventive era of labor-saving devices. Six hundred years later, humanity's survival instinct has still not atrophied, current journalistic comments to the contrary notwithstanding. Yet it would be a mistake to underestimate the influence of neo-Malthusian scenarios, especially in the year 2000. Straight-line analyses and J-shaped curves, after all, invariably lead to doom. (The former describes negative trends that are assumed to continue indefinitely, and the latter refers to positive trends that reach plateaus and halt progress.) As a wit once noted, when a society comes to a fork in its historical road, it can go to the left and face devastation and disaster or go to the right and face horror and death. Needless to say, this black humor isn't history.

Technology is exploding at an exponential rate, forcing a reconsideration of economic and social arrangements. A world of instant communication is upon us. Long-held beliefs are continually called into question as morally neutral technologies have increasing influence on our lives. As a consequence, citizens are thrust into the breach, having to decide complicated issues such as the ethics of cloning and the legitimacy of research involving human stem cells that can grow into any part of the body. This is an era of widespread "creative destruction," in Joseph Schumpeter's famous phrase, on the societal level with old institutions dying or fading away so that new ones can be born. It is not easy, living in such a windstorm of accelerated change. Then again, what is the alternative?

Although society cannot put the genie of scientific advancement back in the bottle, people can harness economic and technological forces to serve many ends. Whether one likes it or not, we are in an age of dramatic innovation, as advances in biotechnology, microelectronics, and telecommunications affirm. Neo-Malthusians are right in asserting that we cannot turn back progress, but they are wrong in believing that technological change must bring increasingly negative consequences. The market is still a reflection of free will in action.

Technological wonders, of course, do not automatically bring contentment, just as material well-being has often led to spiritual malaise. But in the end, most people would agree that wealth is better than poverty and an improvement in the standard of living is better than the status quo. The very foundation of economic success, however, is often at the mercy of a spiritually broken culture that undermines the comforts of technological advance. The wealthy Wall Street broker who for the first time can afford recreational drugs may soon find both his job and wealth jeopardized by his cultural choice.

Of course there is much that can go wrong and much that will go wrong. But the trend lines are clear: instead of a Hobbesian world that is poor, nasty, brutish, and short, we are entering a new age that is rich, comfortable, and secure. Even cautious estimates of world economic growth suggest that wealth will continue to increase worldwide. In 1900, per capita world gross economic product was $500, in 2000 it will be $5,000, and by 2100 it should be around $30,000.

People will live longer and materially better lives than they have in the past. With the defeat of Nazism and communism, the twin pillars of destruction in the twentieth century, the next century is unlikely to yield as many casualties in war as the one we have just come through. The growth rate of the world's population will decline, as Nicholas Eberstadt has pointed out in the pages of the *Wall Street Journal,* and the cost of food and minerals will continue to decrease as Julian Simon has proven likely in his book *The Ultimate Resource* (1980). Life expectancy worldwide will continue to increase, from thirty-five in 1900 to sixty-five in 2000 to eighty in 2100. In the West, centenarians will be the fastest-growing group in the population.

For the world's youngsters, the emerging era represents unprecedented freedom. A relatively low birthrate translates into better employment opportunities as fewer new hires enter the workforce to chase the available jobs. Those who can master the new means of communication will, of course, have a distinct advantage in the job market. The phrase "knowledge is power" will never have been more true. Employment will be constrained only by skill. The more skill one demonstrates, the higher the wage and the greater the job flexibility. Already emerging is "lifestyle employment" in which highly skilled employees determine when, where, and how they work.

In other developments, high-definition television with increased bandwidth sufficient to transmit more than a television image is on the near horizon. The marriage of computers and television screens will make entertainment programming a matter of individual choice and will alter irrevocably our idea of reality. Computers will not only change entertainment; they will change schools as well. Although schools will continue to have a social function, most of the skills and information required for participation in the labor force will be computer-based. As a consequence, for-profit institutions will probably emerge to cope with issues unaddressed by government-funded schools, and software manufacturers will fill the knowledge gap with carefully targeted programs.

Computers will be given away, as telephones are now, to users who buy services from software providers. The precedent for the giveaway of communication instruments has already been set and the incidence is likely to expand. Banks will move to cyberspace, and transactions moving resources from one place to another will be conducted electronically. It is already apparent that money transfers are increasingly electronic and stock purchases are being done without a paper trail. Although it may take a somewhat longer period to reach fruition, it is likely that paper money may disappear entirely and be replaced by its digitized equivalent. Cars equipped with sensors that enable them to avoid obstacles and run on "smart highways" without the benefit of a driver will become available. Scientists have already developed new carbon products that are stronger than steel and more pliable than aluminum, which will reduce construction costs and accelerate construction timetables. I have been told that an airstrip for a 727 can be created in under a half-hour, using the latest generation of carbon products.

Advances in medicine will have far-reaching effects. New drugs being developed will deal with every inherited disease unearthed by genome mapping. Muscular dystrophy and Lou Gehrig's disease, to cite two examples, will be memories of a distant past. In a generation, osteoporosis, Alzheimer's disease, and heart disease, among others, will be controlled or eliminated. Blindness will be cured with computer chips so small that they cannot be seen with the human eye. Limb growth will be prompted through genetic stimulation, and most cancers will be controlled or cured by miracle drugs.

Moreover, this affluence will not be restricted to the West. The conditions that led to the generation of wealth in one area are, in an era of instant communication, reproducible in other regions. Economic booms, in fact, wait on the other side of busts. The Russian economy, bad as it is, may be at or near its nadir. However primitive and mafia-controlled nascent capitalism is in the former Soviet Union, there is an emerging consensus for order and a belief that without the rule of law economic development will be thwarted continually.

The Asian economic crisis, to cite another example, might lay the foundation for a greater good—a stronger world economy—but the transition has been rough. The Asian financial pneumonia brought on a mild North American cold— one not widely acknowledged here because of still-low unemployment and the buoyant stock market. Devaluation of Asian currencies has increased U.S. consumption of imports and decreased the earnings of many American companies. World productivity, however, is poised to increase once Asia's financial problems have been overcome, which may be imminent. In ways not yet widely understood, the American economic miracle of the last half-century foreshadows the takeoff of the global economy. Although the Asian economy has presented some stubborn problems, one of the lessons emerging from the turmoil is that managed economies do not work well over the long term. The inevitable liberalization of the Japanese economy, which will bring a greater reliance on the free market for capital investment, should create a boom in the next century that will percolate throughout Asia.

Yet these conditions, however welcome they may be, fall somewhat short of nirvana. In a materialist society, spiritual deprivation seems often to accompany affluence. The search for meaning in the sensate culture of tomorrow will be more intense than it is now. Already one sees youthful explorers riding a spiritual express to destinations unknown, in their quest for answers to unanswerable questions. Expansive choices and the extension of personal autonomy will not lead inexorably to contentment. In a world of atomized individuals, the idea of a community will take on new meaning. The meeting place of the future may be an electronic chat room, and it is not yet clear how that will alter human exchanges. Nor is the government well-suited to the job of moral regeneration. President Clinton had a great run with the buoyant economic environment, but his presidential legacy is in jeopardy because of reckless, immoral acts, and public confidence in the government's moral probity is very low. That leaves civil society as the main hope for cultural regeneration.

Thus, although there is much debate about a possible remoralization of society, it is increasingly obvious that faith-based organizations will be given much of the responsibility for bringing this about. The reason is clear: These organizations have been considerably more successful in ameliorating problems such as drug abuse and illegitimacy than have government institutions.

These widespread changes in our economic, political, and social arrangements are in the main a reflection of affluence. It is difficult to guess, much less know, whether people will be more satisfied with their lives than at present—satisfaction is a relative and contextual condition. Almost every positive change has within it a negative. For example, a declining birthrate will put pressure on wage taxes for the relatively small number of workers supporting the ballooning retiree population. When stock prices reached historic peaks, it was evident that they would eventually come down. But after that, they will rise again, and affluence will ultimately be greater and more widespread than before. The middle-class person fifty years from now will probably have three times the buying capacity one does today.

During a dark period it is difficult to see the light ahead, but markets, like the people whose decisions affect them, are adaptable. Still there is much to be hopeful about, even if predictions of gloom dominate the evening news. It is not that I am a Pollyannaish optimist, but rather, as Herman Kahn once noted, "In a world of manic pessimism, my realism seems like manic optimism." Despite Franz Kafka's assertion, "There is always hope, but not for us," I believe that there is always hope as long as there is faith. Faith in the future is ultimately the harbinger of change. If you believe that you can alter the course of history, that belief can go a long way toward achieving the goal. Despite the claims of professional doomsayers, whatever challenges await the next generation can be conquered. But it helps to be able to count on human intelligence, innovation, and confidence.

I am hopeful because the world of ideas and information transfer we have entered promises to create and distribute wealth like no other period in human history. There will be shocks along the way. But instead of a photograph of the market, imagine a montage compiled over decades. People make bets on the future, based on present conditions that will influence the outcome. The investor, for example, who leaves his investment in stocks is betting—based on performance—that the return on stocks will be better than that on fixed instruments. That decision will affect both his future and the future of the investment market. To some degree, everyone engages in prediction based on present knowledge. A car driver assumes that the road ahead is paved. Those taking a journey are bound to make this assumption. Thinking about the future is much the same exercise, one separated by years but joined by assumptions about the road ahead.

Women's New Dress Style Conveys Mixed Sex Cues

One day, while walking along Madison Avenue in New York City—the center of vogue fashion—I observed a very attractive woman with loosely flowing hair wearing a feminine lace dress. By any standard she appeared the quintessence of femininity and pulchritude. In many ways her look transcended the moment; it was universal. She might have been a Tintoretto canvas or a Calvin Klein television ad.

Then, in what was a jarring experience, I happened to look down, all the way down to her feet. This glance brought me back to reality. It also brought me back to the present, to a time of tastelessness. There on her feet were combat boots. Yes, the same kind of combat boots that John Wayne wore in *Iwo Jima,* the kind that adorned army recruits from World War II to the present, the kind now routinely worn by urban hikers presumably in search of utilitarian shoes.

Lest I create the wrong impression, there is nothing wrong with the boots themselves. Nor, I must point out, is there anything wrong with women of any age wearing them. What is wrong is the aesthetic contradiction between a feminine dress and masculine boots, between the appearance of elegance and utilitarianism. Combat boots are not worn for fighting or hiking; they are a statement: Women are as rugged as men or perhaps footwear is androgynous. Whatever the explanation, combat boots on a feminine frame are jarring to my sensibility. I don't like them as a statement of either fashion or the times.

Surely, this too will pass and not soon enough to please me. But I wonder what this contradiction suggests of sexual cues. How does a young man respond to a woman who wears combat boots with an elegant dress? My suspicion is that young men are confused. The signals they receive are mixed: she's alluring and she is prepared to stomp on me. Attraction and repulsion are in the same subject. Is it any wonder men are increasingly unsure of the way to engage a woman in conversation?

Courtship, a word in virtual disuse, suffers from the same confusion. On the one hand, many women expect gentility, but on the other hand, those combat boots suggest a "me Tarzan, you Jane" approach to relationships. Do you hold a door for a woman or do you have a woman slam a door in your face?

What the aesthetic sensibility of the moment displays is a feminist logic that has put women—and men to some degree—in the awkward position of being feminine and masculine at the same time. Women are asked to express a biological and natural self and a cultural and imposed self. They must be vulnerable and tough, attractive and unappealing.

Fashion is thereby a gallimaufry of competing cultural interests resulting in the competition of opposites. The avatars of fashion are those unsure of their sexuality. Vanguardists treat the present as merely a catalyst for the next wave of fashion, all the while in thralldom to the confusion wrought by this androgynous era. Models of fashion could be little girls or little boys; their bodies, aside from the obvious, are very similar—slim and formless. By contrast, the woman who caught my eye on Madison Avenue was quite feminine, up to a point. It was *her* calculated decision to stay feminine up to a point. She is the modern woman uneasy being entirely feminine; obviously compelled to make a statement that she is more than a stereotypical female.

While this issue has its trivial side, it is suggestive of a society that has lost its way. Women cannot be women and men cannot be men. The natural is to be shunned for some "higher" principle of cultural alteration. Sexual cues are misleading; the factors that promote the perpetuation of the species are submerged or confused.

Where this will lead is impossible to say. Pitirim Sorokin argued that a sensate society will implode by virtue of its sensuous extremes inviting the dawn of a new age based on ideational or idealistic considerations. Perhaps what I observe is countercyclical. Maybe I should merely take pleasure in the dress as the wave of the future rather than emphasize the statement in the combat boots. After all, the same attractive female who inspired my concatenations might have been wearing jeans a decade ago. But I am troubled, troubled by the mixed aesthetic message and troubled by cues that leave males in perpetual bewilderment. Perhaps what I need are blinders that shield me from what is coarse and degrading. Or maybe I shouldn't be walking on Madison Avenue.

Seeking Easy Solutions to Complex Issues May Be Natural but It Is Empirically Frustrating

H. L. Mencken once wrote that "every complicated question has a simple solution . . . which is usually wrong." That admonition, however, hasn't deterred theorists from reducing all of life's complicated questions to simple solutions. If the computer—to cite one illustration—has value, it is in reducing life's complications to simplifications. How else can one keep from drowning in the information glut? Yet, ironically, the instrument for simplification tends to aggravate the condition it was designed to alleviate.

As one travels the information autobahn searching for answers to life's knotty problems, there are detours and turnoffs everywhere one looks. Much of the "information" is unreliable and, even when reliable, hard to distinguish from the theoretical and unproven. In the end, the information highway as metaphor retreats before the babble of democratic participation. In a medium where everyone participates, the good and the bad compete on equal terms.

Similarly, all political discourse has been reduced to the thirty-second sound bite. Someone pointed out to me at the time that Clinton sounded better than Dole during the 1996 campaign because the former knew what to do with his thirty seconds. However, is leadership a reflection of a thirty-second commercial? Has politics been reduced to sound and fury meaning nothing at all? Alas, *Sesame Street,* that "paragon" of children's programming, has reduced learning to one-minute commercials for the letters of the alphabet. A generation has been nurtured on impatience and instant rewards.

The idea of delayed gratification is as alien to contemporary America as courtship. Popular magazines from *Reader's Digest* to *Harper's Bazaar* reduce life's tangled questions about love, sex, contentment, and success to ten easy lessons. "Find the right mate," "Be all you can be," by following the guidelines in bold letters. It's a simplification love-fest. What would Romeo or Don Juan and Cleopatra or Isolde make of these formulaic responses to love, passion, and fulfillment? The answers tax the imagination.

Journalists trained in the school of "I am at the center of every story" recount events with the simple "what if" assertion: What if the politicians had pursued strategy X instead of strategy Y? What if, indeed! Only the simplification theorists believe history can be rewritten. Instead of explication, journalism is in thralldom to imagination—yet another symptom of the simplification game. Simplifying has been combined with utopianism, and the political Left has been joined by the Right. The Left is still enthralled with perfectionism and has been joined by contemporary conservatism, which insists that tax cuts, enterprise zones, and deregulation will usher in a golden age.

Neither liberal nor conservative employs the language of complexity. Neither is harnessed by the humility that solutions do not exist for every issue. Keep in mind that the simplification theorists rarely talk about modest improvement: These are secular salvationists seeking heaven on earth. They will not be deterred by imponderables and unknowns. There aren't any mysteries for the simplifiers. Since everything can be known, a formula must exist for revelation. Psychologists have answers for every worry, therapists have an elixir for every problem, and technocrats are building a highway to the future where risk is eliminated and feeling good commonplace.

Yet if these formulas exist, if simplification is within our grasp, if we can be all we want to be, why is malaise ubiquitous, why are so many Americans dissatisfied with their lot in life? The answer is simple (no pun intended). Life is not subject to simplification. Seeking easy solutions is natural but empirically frustrating. The more we know, the more we realize we don't know. Formulaic solutions are fool's gold, bright and shiny but not the real stuff. Genuine learning of any discipline, for example, does not have a simple shortcut. It requires hard work and patience. Love requires compromise and dedication. Finding out about contentment is a life's work. The computer autobahn gets you to a destination only if you know where you're going. Simplification theory may be a national addiction: It has all the characteristics of Chinese food—great taste, but not very filling.

Though Weakened, There Is No Substitute for the American Family

The typical family on American TV is a repository of solace and contentment. There's no knot in the social web that it can't untangle. If Johnny has a drug problem or Mary is having a child out of wedlock, the family is there to offer succor and understanding. Of course, some real families do just that, but many don't. Even at their best, real families are less than ideal. Parents are unreasonable, children incorrigible, girls moody, boys sloppy, and pets uncooperative. Life is not a picnic, notwithstanding TV accounts to the contrary. Winston Churchill used to say democracies were the worst form of government except for all the others. Much of the same can be said of the family. It is the worst form of social organization except for all the others.

Even if the family is not always functional, it would be a mistake to argue, as many do, that the family isn't an essential social structure. To replace the family with a kibbutz-like environment is fine in theory. But in reality, it would leave children searching for the attachment of parents. To replace parents with childcare supervisors is a hit-or-miss proposition at best. Who will care for a child more than a parent? While that question may seem rhetorical, much evidence suggests the opposite. Many parents are so self-absorbed that they have neither time nor interest in their own children. Some parents are so deranged they wish to torture and, in some instances, kill their children.

The age of *Father Knows Best,* alas, is gone. Now father is torn by the need to be a provider, a counselor, a guide, an authority—even as his wife searches for independence and his children claim he hasn't any understanding of contemporary culture. Moms don't get off lightly either. For most kids, mom nags incessantly and is invariably intractable.

Entering the contemporary family mix is something called the alternative family. While the term has many meanings, it has three distinct contemporary attributions: homosexual parents, single women who choose to raise a family without the presence of a male, and single women who, as a result of divorce, are obliged to raise a family on their own. Clearly, the presence of these three families has increased during the '90s and has intensified the pressure on the nuclear family.

If Heather has two mommies, where is dad? If single women can have children without male assistance, should a child assume his father is in a petri dish? If divorce severs or reduces the ties to a father, is there a price to be paid in the aberrational behavior of teenagers? Each of those conditions threatens the traditional idea of the family, albeit solutions are not readily apparent. And a society as permissive and narcissistic as America's cannot put the genie back in the bottle.

It is better for a child to receive love and care under those conditions, even if the relationship isn't ideal. Then again, once any model of the family is countenanced, the traditional family is vitiated. In the end, we must make do. The ideal family doesn't exist, even with the maudlin assertions about its importance. And some family is probably better than no family.

The good news is that as family members age, nostalgia mitigates past unpleasantness. Photos are laughed at, memories of the past are always less grim than the way originally perceived. I won't offer three cheers for the family, but I will offer two, because home is the place where a crying child can find a hospitable shoulder, where kids find Band-Aids for scraped knees, where husbands and wives can share dreams, and where one can sometimes find solace for the pressures of life. The family will survive current attacks, technological wonder, and even treacly commentary, not because it always works, but because there really isn't any substitute.

Assaults on the Family, Especially Children, Come from Many Sides

In the continuing search for perfection, a wealthy, infertile couple has offered $50,000 for the eggs of a tall, smart, athletic woman. According to a representative of the couple, the search has been reduced to ninety candidates. More than three hundred women responded to the ad the couple ran in the student newspapers of several elite private universities: "Intelligent, Athletic Egg Donor Needed for Loving Family. You must be at least five feet, ten inches, have a 1400-plus SAT score, and possess no major family medical issues." After sifting through the applications, the prospective parents selected twenty candidates from Yale, thirty from Harvard, forty from Princeton, and fifteen from Stanford. The $50,000 payment is about ten times that offered to egg donors by fertility registries. Predictably, a family spokesman said, "This is not about money. This couple wants a baby, and if you were in their place and you wanted a child that would be six feet, three inches, and have blond hair, you would choose the appropriate donor."

But what the family spokesman neglected to point out is that tall, intelligent women also carry the recessive genes that result in five-foot, eight-inch males who score 900 on the SAT. Even in the Brave New World of today, one cannot ensure biological perfection. Moreover, consider the irony of insinuating a eugenics model into elite student newspapers where the prevailing opinion undoubtedly holds that one's environment has a greater effect than genetics. It boggles the imagination. Has the search for perfectibility overtaken liberal orthodoxy? Or are the prospective donors caught up in the quest for a fast buck? Now that in vitro fertilization is widely used and human genetic mapping near completion, are we reaching the point in human evolution where reproduction becomes a technical achievement devoid of love and sexual contact? Will sperm cells and eggs go on sale with prices based on desirable characteristics, and is a master race of carefully bred children on the near horizon?

Maybe not. The human genome system can be and will be manipulated, but creating the perfect person with the desired height and IQ may defy parental aspirations. Even more curious is the flawed view that an ideal person can be created like a clay figure.

The one easily anticipated result of eugenically based breeding is surprise. Many of the characteristics considered desirable may be linked to undesirable ones. For example, blondes are more vulnerable to skin cancer than brunettes. Also, important characteristics may not be attributable to one's genetic makeup. Is there a genetic tendency for compassion or understanding? Do superficial traits such as height and SAT scores reveal anything about character, integrity, decency, and perseverance? Naturally, every parent wants a smart child, but intelligence is only partially a function of genetic endowment. On the basis of the screening done for egg donors, should one conclude that Harvard students are brighter than Yale students and Princeton students are brighter than Harvard students? Can one be sure—including the wealthy parents seeking the ideal egg donor—that the "best" candidate will be found at an elite college?

Many years ago the noted British thinker and novelist C. P. Snow told me that during World War II an attempt was made to determine the person with the highest IQ, for encryption duties at a special division of British Intelligence. After the exams were evaluated, it was discovered that the person with the highest score was the building's janitor, who was neither equipped for the job nor inclined to take it on. IQ is a necessary condition of general intelligence, but it is not sufficient in itself to determine general intelligence, much less intellectual competence. Similarly, height is an advantage if you want to play basketball or go into politics, but it is a distinct disadvantage in warfare and airplane travel. Some medical problems are certainly inherited, but it is difficult to know when genetic proclivities will skip a generation.

Life usually smiles at the best-laid plans of human designers. I would love to know what will happen to the expensive, carefully selected egg twenty years from now. Will he be attending Harvard? Will she be the starting center on the female Princeton basketball team? Or will he be a janitor happy with his work but inexplicably disinclined to fulfill his parents' dreams?

Republicans' Lost Vision Hits Them Hard at the Polls

The 1998 U.S. elections were an unmitigated disaster for the Republican Party, which did much worse than expected. Republicans registered a net loss of seats midway through a Democratic president's term in office. It was a stunning reversal of historical perspective and denied Republicans their anticipated filibuster-proof majority. And this disappointing result occurred against a backdrop of an immense advantage in campaign funds and a scandal that was rocking the Clinton presidency.

Republicans found that opposition to Clinton did not give them any kind of agenda. Instead of focusing on Bill Clinton's impeachment, Republicans should have focused on their own agenda. In 1994, House Speaker Newt Gingrich nationalized local elections through the "Contract with America." The party's obsession with Clinton's alleged perjury and with obstruction of justice charges had the effect of localizing national elections. To the dismay of many Republicans, the party did not provide reasons to vote for the GOP. In fact, after the budget deal in which Republican leaders conceded to higher spending horizons for the president, the difference between the two major political parties on fiscal issues became blurred. Similarly, the highway bill, which Republicans generally embraced, is among the nation's most scandalous boondoggles. When Republicans become big spenders, voters are likely to say, "If spending is what we get, then a vote for the Democrats is a vote for the genuine article."

Republicans must return to the "vision thing," a statement of core principles that distinguishes Republicans from Democrats. It is also worthwhile to assess why an extraordinary opportunity to refashion the policy front after overwhelming success in 1994 was frittered away. While Gingrich and company assumed that the Monica Lewinsky matter would bring out core Republican voters, exit polls indicated that only 6 percent of the electorate turned out to express an opinion on this issue. That means the other 94 percent was not given a reason to vote for Republicans, an extraordinary miscalculation.

For several years, rank-and-file Republicans have been asking what happened to the party impulse that called for limited government, spending decreases, tax relief, and the restoration of military preparedness. The best that the conservative journal *Human Events* could say about these midterm elections was "vote Republican anyway." The anyway revealed a great deal about Republican sentiments. Gingrich and Senate Majority Leader Trent Lott tried valiantly to put a positive spin on the result. But many of their fellow members were restless, believing—quite appropriately—that the leaders must assume responsibility for the disappointing performance. Gingrich's resignation was the first manifestation of this. Voters were generally pleased with the state of the economy, and this belief accounted for the support of incumbents at all levels. For most Americans, the scandal surrounding the White House was a nonissue.

If Republicans learned anything from the election, they should have remembered that they must have a policy agenda about which Americans care. As I see it, this agenda should include an education plan that embraces competition and a dramatic alteration in standards for graduation and promotion. This policy view should be framed as a '90s' "Sputnik Crisis" based on the proposition that the standard of living we have enjoyed is now imperiled by a woefully inadequate educational system.

Second, the party must emphasize tax cuts and a sensible flat tax that serves as a rallying cry for economic growth. Since neither Lott nor Gingrich fought vigorously for tax cuts in the 1998 budget deal, this argument may be hard to make.

Nevertheless, it is a Republican principle that cannot be abandoned without adversely affecting core GOP voters. Last, Republicans should repudiate arbitrary regulations and mandates that militate against business activity, trade, and job creation. If Republicans want to be the party of opportunity, they should target, argue against, and reform government acts that stultify business development.

Taken together, these issues form the basis of the Republican agenda, one that takes aim at Democratic sacred cows. It is also a response to the complacency that afflicts the party. Unless leaders can provide a reason for Republican voters to go to the polls, the midterm election may foreshadow many electoral failures ahead.

Political Corruption Is Rampant As the State and Nation Are Held Up to the Highest Bidder

"Pay for play" is an expression etched into political practice. What it means is that government officials offer favors, legislation, and approvals to those who are willing to pay the going price for them. This practice hasn't any relationship to partisanship; as the following illustrations indicate Republicans and Democrats use the precedent for their own advantage. There are, of course, the occasional demurrals when in an act of high dudgeon someone blows the whistle, but more often than not both parties have maintained an attitude of modus vivendi.

The real loser in this political equation is the public, who rarely appreciate the extent to which integrity and national interest are being sacrificed. For example, it was recently reported that the president of Loral Space Company contributed more than $2 million to the Democratic Party. While President Clinton and Loral chief Bernard Schwartz both vigorously denied any relationship between the contribution and a presidential waiver allowing Loral to send a satellite into space on a Chinese rocket, the approval was very suspicious.

After all, Clinton granted the waiver despite a warning from the Department of Justice that his action would hinder a criminal probe into whether Loral gave sensitive technology to Beijing that could be used to improve missile accuracy. As Representative Dana Rohrabacher noted, "It seems . . . a coldly calculated decision to fix those problems (flight guidance system in Chinese rockets) with no consideration of the national security implications to the United States." Moreover, this technology transfer occurred despite repeated warnings from former secretary of state Warren Christopher, Defense Department officials, and members of the Justice Department. At the time, at least a dozen Chinese Intercontinental Ballistic Missiles (ICBMs) were targeted at the United States very likely employing a sophisticated guidance system sold by an American company after the Clinton administration insisted on a presidential waiver for this technology. Talk about selling the rope used to hang oneself.

On another front, revelations from a *Wall Street Journal* report led to an investigation of bond underwriters for the New York State takeover of the Long Island Lighting Company. Initially, underwriters sold $3.5 billion bonds—the largest municipal bond issue in the nation's history—and the Long Island Power Authority planned to sell another $3.5 billion worth of bonds in the ensuing months. What the *Journal* reported was the pattern of political donations and the hiring of well-connected people in the underwriting decision process. Four underwriters with the opportunity to make hundreds of millions on the deal—Bear Stearns & Co., Lehman Brothers, Morgan Stanley, and Dean Witter and Salomon Smith Barney—contributed enormous sums to the New York State Republican Party and hired almost anyone Governor George Pataki or Senator Al D'Amato recommended. Senator D'Amato's son, for example, was a broker at Bear Stearns. While the Power Authority planned to use savings from the tax-exempt bonds to reduce Long Island's extremely high electricity bills, the state takeover will create a government monopoly that in time is likely to increase rates, notwithstanding claims to the contrary.

However, the overriding issue is the soft money contributions made to the state party by the same underwriters who will profit handsomely from the deal. Even though limits now exist on donations to candidates, investment banks can circumvent the rules by contributing unlimited sums directly to the state parties. Here again, Governor Pataki and the investment banking house vigorously denied any wrongdoing. But does any sensible person consider the hundreds of thousands contributed to the state Republican Party an act of political charity that does not connote a quid pro quo?

Clearly such practices have been going on for many years and both parties have a stake in their continuation. Nonetheless, the public should take notice lest the state and the nation be held up for sale to the highest bidder. This corruption goes to the very core of politics; it inspired campaign-finance reform and public cynicism. It raises the issue of statesmanship and the dangers of a free market unrestrained by the national interest and the public welfare. Most important, the pay-for-play practices tell us about elected officials whose decisions are influenced by money and whose aspirations for public office will allow any contributions, however corrupt, to continue unabated.

The Dilemma of Generation X

Members of Generation X have grown up in affluence but are finding great discomfort in the world. They have witnessed colossal political events with the dismantling of the Berlin Wall and the dissolution of the former Soviet Union. Yet despite this progress, Generation X lives deeply fearful of the future and its place in it.

The members of Generation X do not represent a mass movement. They are, however, disgruntled spokesmen of a generation that believes that Americans are eroding the economic foundation stone of the nation with massive debt and short-term economic programs. Servicing debt at the moment costs more than what local, state, and federal governments combined spend on education. Each year a substantial percentage of the U.S. tax revenue will go to pay only interest on the national debt.

These generational voices question how they can assist the poor, attend to the environment, or create families with the Damoclean sword of massive debt poised over their heads? It could be argued that the future of this generation has already been mortgaged in order to attend to present concerns.

Neither liberal nor conservative, the voice of Generation X is apprehensive—appropriately so. For too long, government has permitted a form of generational exploitation in which a spending spree by the elderly was paid for by debt imposed on children and grandchildren. Like the somewhat manufactured generation gap in the '60s and '70s, a new gap of real dimensions may be emerging. But, instead of ideological differences about lifestyle, bread-and-butter issues may characterize the fault line.

It is neither new nor surprising that those in their twenties will harbor resentment against those in their forties. Those in a takeoff phase of their lives invariably resent those already established. What is somewhat unique about Generation X, however, is that it points with scorn to the so-called accomplishments of its predecessors and asks, "How could you have done this to us?" Alas, they are correct. A libertine attitude toward drugs, immediate gratification, lax education requirements, and corrupt politics have led inexorably to the failures of the moment. Those in their twenties are now asked to clean up the mess of a psychedelic generation which thought the Eden express had no stops.

In a way Woodstock—the baby boomers' shrine—is a metaphor for contemporary woe. As Robert Lukefahr, one of the ardent voices of Generation X, points out, few of those who attended the bacchanalia purchased tickets; most simply crashed the gate as if it were some sort of birthright. Three days later the Yasgur farm was trashed, and happy boomers began their departure, leaving their mess behind for others to clean.

As it turns out, the cleaners are members of Generation X, now confronting the detritus of spiraling divorce, illegitimacy, AIDS, and drug addiction. So much for the Woodstock shrine. Jonathan Karl and Douglas Kennedy, two impressive spokesmen for the Third Millennium, a politically diverse group of activists in Generation X, wrote, "Our generation stares down the barrel of a $4.2 trillion debt that threatens to destroy our future." That gun is also escalating from a revolver to a howitzer as the years pass.

In the conclusion of the Third Millennium Manifesto, the authors maintain: "By reaffirming individual responsibility—responsibility for our own actions and responsibilities to our communities—we will rise to meet the great challenges ahead. Our generation—the generation that will come to power in the third millennium—simply has no choice."

The Workplace of the New Millennium Accommodates Generation X's Changing Values

The days when American workers were happy to hold nine-to-five jobs and looked forward to their weekends are fast disappearing. An increasingly tight labor market, particularly in areas that require special skills, allows employees to set the conditions of their employment. Members of Generation X tend to prefer jobs that are consistent with their "lifestyle."

The *Wall Street Journal* profiled a software engineer, who earns a six-figure salary, but who jealously guards his personal freedom as the most important dimension of his employment. And so no one at his company cares if he flies a plane during the day or goes river rafting. In the present market for programmers, he can quit his job tomorrow and find a dozen jobs the following day. As a consequence, his employer respects his lifestyle decisions as long as the job gets done.

Many people whose skills are desired are willing to exchange salary and stock options for free time. Even with storm clouds over the global market, high-tech employment is booming. A feverish demand for talent is redefining ordinary notions of the workday and a career path. Needless to say, there is a price for freedom: During those weeks with a deadline looming, a sixty-hour workweek may be in the offing. But this is regarded as an appropriate tradeoff for lifestyle avatars. Many in this Generation X crowd work relentlessly so that they can later go on vacation for the rest of their lives. It is interesting to hear twenty-year-olds talk of retirement in their forties.

Clearly these examples are aberrational at the moment, but not for long. Demographic data indicate that long-term labor shortages are in store for us. Employees, especially those with special skills, will be in a uniquely advantaged position, provided there is no economic depression. The stereotypical example of an employee's begging his boss for a raise has a distinctly anachronistic ring to it. Many employees will be in the proverbial driver's seat. There are already signs that many women enjoy lifestyle employment that encourages mom to be at Johnny's soccer games and other assorted activities. This condition is not merely a function of feminist lobbying, but also of a tight labor market that depends on female employment.

Turn the clock ahead to between 2015 and 2020, a time when the bulk of the baby boomers retire, there is likely to be a desperate search for employees to sustain industries and services and to maintain a national standard of living. The combination of an aging population and a low birthrate (already less than replacement level) suggests a premium for productive employees. It is not exaggerated to contend that, around the year 2020, the sky will be the limit for those in their twenties who possess marketable skills. Those prospective employees will be part of a large army of lifestyle workers who can be found hang gliding, skiing, or scuba diving as easily as at a computer station.

The dawning of the new age of employment is almost here. I only wish my father and those of his generation were around to see it. These people, conditioned by the Great Depression, considered themselves lucky to have a job. Too bad they were born at the wrong historical moment. For those soon to be born, history is on their side. Lifestyle employment is beckoning, and it will subsume play into work. The dream of a workers' paradise in the not too distant future isn't so far-fetched at all.

A Lean, Mean Population Will Convulse American Culture

During the '90s, the Food and Drug Administration (FDA) approved a product promising to reduce, if not even eliminate, obesity. This drug, which has properties similar to Prozac, works by releasing serotonin, a brain enzyme that produces the satisfaction that accompanies ice cream consumption. Presumably, a person can take the drug and gain the satisfaction without lifting a spoon to the ice cream.

Some snacks such as potato chips are now made with a fat substitute that reduces both calories and the dreaded cholesterol. Americans can sit back and enjoy the Super Bowl with nonfattening snacks and reduced-calorie beer.

On one level, these technological breakthroughs are noteworthy, since obesity, far more than starvation, is a national scourge. It is a contributor to high blood pressure, heart disease, diabetes, and lethargy. For people who are always dieting without success, pharmaceutical breakthroughs are heaven-sent. Although the ads for the serotonin product probably advertised more than they could deliver—a 20 percent loss in body weight was the estimate—this was still welcome news for about a third of the nation's population.

What this means for the culture is something else again. The desire to be thin, to fit some abstract model of beauty, is on its face absurd. It goes beyond health consciousness and enters the realm of social expectations. In fact, it is interesting to ask what our society would be like without overweight people. For one thing, people would no longer be named Fats Waller or Fats Domino or Chubby Checker. Comic strip characters won't be called Haystack Calhoun. Of course, most people still won't resemble the women Tom Wolfe calls "X rays." And men won't all look like Sylvester Stallone. But conditions will be different. The Dallas Cowboys' offensive line, which averages 320 pounds per lineman, won't be consuming these fat substitutes, unless, of course, their wives and girlfriends prefer the svelte look to million-dollar salaries. Words that have a long and lofty history will go out of common use. *Pudgy, round-bottom, fat-stuff* will disappear from our vocabularies. Kids will have to insult one another in less superficial language.

This change in the culture will also affect the American economy. Clothing manufacturers, to cite one example, that specialize in oversized products from suits to T-shirts will be obliged to get out of the XX-large business. Beds and chairs for the very large will be obliged to cease production. And, of course, if you can gain the pleasure of cheesecake without the cake, what happens to the bakers? Sumo wrestlers would lose their exalted status in Japan. Weight Watchers would go the way of Earth shoes. Television talk-show hosts would be hard-pressed to find a theme as captivating as being overweight. Baseball players won't have to pay a fine for entering spring training twenty pounds over a pre-scribed limit. Much lamented "love handles" will disappear. The waddle will no longer characterize a walking style. And the slog—a slow jog—will no longer characterize a running style.

Yes, a revolution is in the offing. Not only will American business be lean and mean, the American people will be lean and mean. Jolly is out, hard is in. Double chins will be relegated to the dustbin of history. Liposuction doctors will be looking for new business. The fad of health clubs—once called gyms—will pass. After all, you don't have to pay for overeating with perspiration—a few pills will do.

Will we be better off in this new age? Well, some erstwhile fatties will reach nirvana; businesses that cater to those who are overweight will most likely be in Chapter 11 and the culture will be in confusion. Jazz musicians depend on a chubby to blow the trumpet, linemen need potbellies, the contemporary Rubens is left with small pickings for his modeling corps. One can only guess what will happen to the garment trade without half sizes. The FDA does not know what it has wrought. America will look back at 1997 as the year of cultural convulsion. Instead of a nation of all shapes and sizes, this will be the land of only Jack Sprats. His poor wife will have filed for divorce and become a long lost memory.

Today's Humanitarians Are Old Socialists in a New Guise

While much of the world embraces the free-market system for its economy and democratic reforms for its polity, and while most scholars of formerly totalitarian states contend that socialism is dead, leviathan lives in a rival philosophy of communitarian beliefs that calls for environmental regulations and social welfare programs.

Former Marxists and self-styled socialists in this nation and elsewhere have couched their former ideology in a humanitarian banner that calls for a save-the-earth program and a social edifice for any problem the well-healed imagination of do-gooders can conjure. This view of national affairs conspicuously shuns the socialist tag, yet in practice it relies on a large state bureaucracy of regulators and high taxes to sustain its agenda.

Proposals to ban most pesticides which have been shown to have caused cancer in rodent tests, regardless of the tolerances now allowed by the FDA and the Environmental Protection Agency, can cost consumers billions of dollars in higher food prices alone. Other humanitarian reforms, such as those proposed for national health care, would run into additional billions.

What these illustrations indicate is that while the Left may concede that socialism in Eastern Europe is dead or dying, the program of the Left has not undergone substantive change. What has changed is the language. Contemporary socialists call themselves humanitarians. They do not refer to historical inevitability since it would appear as if recent history is not on their side. Instead, these people speak of social needs, human despair, and environmental contamination—conditions that unquestionably call for remediation. For the neosocialist, the remediation inevitably takes on the form of government intervention. Rarely do these government interventionists ask why they propose this instrument for reform when government institutions have demonstrated their ineffectiveness from New York City to Moscow. Could these reformers embrace the Marxist bromide that the unvarnished idea in all its splendor hasn't really been tried?

The durability of socialism in all its guises cannot be fully appreciated. Most socialists of old have become the new humanists. Rather than accept defeat in the war of ideas, they admit defeat and continue their crusade. The dogma of the past has been replaced by an open-mindedness that relies on the contemporary social psychology of looking out for one's fellow man. After all, it is the free-market types who lack sensitivity and warmth, these avatars of humanitarianism contend. (Recall that Senator Pat Moynihan said the classic oxymoron is "a compassionate conservative.") The neosocialist argues as if he has dominion over social welfare; ergo those ideas that may benefit mankind but are reliant on human initiative, not government, are relegated to a category of inhumane options. While it is comforting to believe the endpoint of history has been reached, this is an opinion shared only by a handful of neoconservatives. It could as easily be maintained that the socialist has merely changed his colors, not his goal.

Chapter Nine

Cultural Fall-Deeper

The Race Card Trumps All Others

The verdict to acquit O. J. Simpson of the murder of his ex-wife Nicole and her friend Ronald Goldman was a sad moment in American judicial history, for both blacks and whites. Despite all the denials by jurors in the O. J. Simpson case that race was a factor in their decision, there is the lingering impression that the "race card" was indeed decisive in the outcome. When Johnny Cochran, Simpson's lead attorney, raised the gruesome specter of race in his strategy to convert this murder trial into a race trial, he told the jurors in effect that, even if Simpson was guilty, they should acquit him to compensate for the racial injustices of the past. Why else would he compare racist detective Mark Fuhrman to Adolph Hitler? Even defense attorney Robert Shapiro claimed to be "deeply offended" by the Hitler analogy.

Fred Goldman, Ronald Goldman's father, said, "This Prosecution team did not lose today. I deeply believe this country lost today." Alas, that is true in ways even Mr. Goldman may not realize. With the decision to acquit in the face of overwhelming evidence of guilt, with a decision reached in merely four hours, it was apparent that this jury (composed of nine blacks, two Hispanics, and one white) would not entertain any verdict other than acquittal. What this suggests for the nation is that our idea of America as an exceptional land, a place where efforts have been made to transform race questions into matters of economic mobility, is a myth. America is now like Bosnia or Malaysia, where the composition of the jury presages the outcome of a trial.

Assume for a moment that the defendant in the O.J. Simpson case were white and the victims blacks, with every other consideration in the case exactly the same. Is there anyone who seriously doubts that there would have been a different verdict? The Simpson case made it clear that race would thereafter be the overarching consideration in criminal cases, whether reflecting an attempt to balance the scales of history or antecedents of mistreatment by rogue cops. Even Johnny Cochran had to admit that "race plays a part in everything in America." Of course, he is at least part of the reason for that claim, notwithstanding his public denials about the use of the "race card."

The O. J. Simpson case is, in my judgment, the culmination of racialist perceptions. From the Brown decision in 1954 to the black-power movement in the late '60s, the nation attempted, however imperfectly, to integrate blacks and whites. Theories such as Kenneth Clark's that "separate but equal is inherently unequal" were in ascendancy. Gradually, however, separatists on both sides of the racial divide changed the character of the debate. Their view that integration can't work, that blacks can never be accepted in a predominantly white society, came to prevail.

It would seem that the politics of division replaced the politics of unity. Electoral victories are based on putting together a coalition of racial and ethnic groups. National considerations, as a consequence, have been subordinated to clannish concerns. As the Simpson trial revealed, race trumps all other matters in the social calculus. While politicians in the United States routinely criticized South Africa's policy of apartheid, on a level almost unimaginable three decades ago, apartheid has been Americanized with black acquiescence. Racial separation is very much in the air.

The disparate responses of white and black audiences to the jury's decision in the Simpson case displayed the enormous racial gap that still exists in the nation. No serious person can regard this result with equanimity. It is not the first time that racial solidarity transcended evidence, as the second Rodney King and Lemrick Nelson trials would suggest. One could also cite the Beckwith trial, as an example of white racism trumping evidence. But the Simpson trial was the so-called "trial of the century." It wasn't only Simpson on trial; the American judicial system was on trial. Television coverage magnified every condition in the case; this was a global event.

Under the magnifying glass, the American system did not fare well. The distinctive characteristics of fairness and a review of evidence before reaching judgment were not evident. How could a jury review 50,000 pages of testimony in four hours? Obviously it couldn't and didn't. The word is now out: Race counts before evidence. America is now riven with division and on the road to Pretoria. What a sad moment in our history; and what a lamentable position for both blacks and whites!

The Double Standard on Race Crimes Must End

Fairness eluded the O. J. Simpson verdict. It also escapes multiculturalists, who have arrived at the perverse conclusion that only "people of color" can be targets of racism. No matter how consumed with hate "people of color" may be, they are always the victims and are protected from racist accusations by virtue of their skin pigmentation.

This ruse has been going on for some time, and media panjandrums have been complicit in it. On March 21, 1997, in Chicago, a youthful black named Lenard Clark was wantonly beaten by three white teenagers with baseball bats. The incident received national coverage, including several editorials in leading newspapers, and was cited by President Clinton as evidence of racism in our society. He referred to the Clark incident in calling for a national dialogue on race.

An outcry from black leaders across the country was duly recorded. In my judgment, their outrage was justified and appropriate.

However, one month earlier (on February 7) in Chicago, a writing teacher at the Sumner Elementary School in West Towndale was bludgeoned with a hammer by a fourteen-year-old man-child almost six feet tall and 170 pounds, because the teacher threatened to suspend the young man for flashing gang signs and performing other disruptive behavior during class. According to an account in the *Chicago Tribune* (July 22, 1997), the assailant came up behind the female teacher, and "She heard him say the words 'white bitch' and saw a flash." That flash was a steel hammer that traveled in an arc toward her head, fracturing her eye socket and shattering her cheekbone. The plastic surgeon described the fractured jaw as resembling "the broken pieces of a jigsaw puzzle." Moreover, the youngsters in the class were told what this angry assailant was likely to do, and not one warned their teacher about a possible assault.

This reprehensible incident was reported in only one newspaper. It was not a national story. Neither black nor white leaders expressed their indignation. President Clinton did not mention it in any speech. It was simply another terrible, but largely ignored, event.

What emerges from these two incidents roughly one month apart in the same city is that a double standard is at work. It strikes me as the essence of hypocrisy to contend that a white attack on a black person deserves national, indeed, presidential attention while a black attack on whites should be virtually ignored. To argue, as some in the press do, that designated-victim status entitles the bearer to hold grudges and act on those impulses, is to countenance racism for some and not others.

What goes on here? Racism should be condemned in all its forms, whether it comes from Khalid Abdel Muhammed, a Louis Farrakhan disciple, or from the KKK. It is instructive that the rantings of anti-Semites on American campuses have attracted acolytes and apologists. Janet Hadda, head of the Jewish Studies program at UCLA, explained away a vulgar exercise in anti-Semitism by black students: "You're dealing with something they [blacks] use to organize their view of themselves and the world. It's not simply a matter of hating—*it's a belief struc-ture,*" (my emphasis). Can anyone imagine the rationalization of KKK activity as a group's way to organize a view of itself—"a belief system"?

If this nation is to come to grips with racism, as President Clinton has requested, then racism must be considered in all its manifestations. *Racism* is an ugly word mitigated by frequent and false use. It is also a word deracinated if skin pigmentation inoculates some people from the charge even when their behavior warrants the attribution. Members of the press corps should be held accountable for this double standard. If a person is attacked and he is white or black or Oriental or Jewish or Hispanic or of any category of race, religion, or ethnicity, that should be noted without regard to designated-victim status. A crime is a crime, no matter who commits it. It cannot be explained away as a function of his-torical wrongs. Once we go down the route of explaining away or emphasizing some crimes because of the skin pigmentation of the victim, then we are indeed two nations torn asunder by a preoccupation with race.

Celebrities Take on "Good Causes"

So far down the slippery slope of adopt-a-cause have Americans gone that one can-not be a public personality without advocating some cause. Ed Asner searched for the quintessential poet-revolutionary somewhere in Latin America. Bob Barker crusaded to prevent people from wearing fur coats. Sting discovered the Brazilian rain forests.

Marlon Brando and Jane Fonda were among the celebrities who appeared at the side of Robert Satiacum, a leader of Washington State's Pulp Indians, as he led the campaign for Indian fishing rights in the Pacific Northwest in the '60s and '70s. Although Satiacum had fled the United States while on trial for trafficking in contraband cigarettes, arson, and the attempted murder of a rival leader and was later convicted for molesting a ten-year-old girl, he lived at a time when sen-sible judgment was suspended by celebrities looking for a cause. Febrile political manifestos took center stage, and since Native Americans by definition were good guys, simply being an Indian at this period made Satiacum a candidate for beautification. How could any member of an oppressed group act irresponsibly? One's history and skin color were sufficient qualifications for sainthood. His crimes were relegated to the category of minor peccadilloes from an "essential-ly" decent man. He was even afforded political refugee status, a decision that was later reversed by an appellate court.

Celebrities like Brando and Fonda gravitated to self-appointed oppressed groups. It is hardly coincidental that Jane Fonda found the North Vietnamese a victimized group as well. Hollywood is still enamored of causes, particularly those groups that are on the need-to-be-supported list. In most instances,

Hollywood's judgment in these matters is poor. Satiacum was a well-known rabble-rouser and lawbreaker by the time Brando and Fonda flocked to his side.

There are Hollywood personalities against chlorofluorocarbons and Hollywood personalities against incinerating garbage. There are corpulent residents of Beverly Hills sending food to Ethiopia and telling poor people not to eat meat. There are staged protests at McDonald's and demonstrations in front of the White House.

The homeless class have been manipulated with the often fraudulent argument that they simply cannot afford housing—a claim that ignores the extraordinary representation of drug addicts and the mentally ill in this population—and the manipulation of these people by celebrities is the most base form of exploitation.

There aren't any limits for religious fanatics of secular causes. They are the new Holy Rollers, having denounced religion only to find salvation in political causes. Unfortunately, those too weak to defend themselves are targets of succor and those who resist will be targets of rancor. In the era of causes, anyone will be manipulated to achieve the ends of the good society as seen through the prism of modern-day celebrity.

The Erosion of Common Sense in Public Opinion

The loss of common sense among the public leaves Americans vulnerable to demagoguery. The '90s were an Orwellian era in which truth and lies were equally effective on a population unable to tell the difference. This is worrisome in a culture that historically has had the rare ability to make the right decision when it has been demanded of them. Whether it was Franklin Delano Roosevelt's forgotten Americans or Richard Nixon's silent majority, Americans have invariably been described as possessing unusual common sense. French statesman and author Alexis de Tocqueville claimed that this was the real strength of this nation.

In the late '90s, however, public opinion polls overtly challenged this belief.

Revelations about the contributions of fund-raiser Johnny Chung to the Democratic National Committee, for example, provided incontrovertible evidence that the Chinese military had attempted to influence our presidential election. Moreover, one of President Clinton's largest contributors was allowed to sell a sophisticated missile guidance system to the Chinese government despite protestations from defense experts. It is understandable that the American people would give the president the benefit of the doubt in the Monica Lewinksy affair, but complacency about acts that are possibly treasonous and certainly threaten our security is incomprehensible. Maybe the full story hadn't yet been digested. Perhaps there were so many flagrant violations of propriety that one more indiscretion didn't seem to make a difference. But my suspicion is that common sense may no longer be as prevalent in the body politic.

Let me cite other examples.

It was reported that the outrageous behavior of guests on *The Jerry Springer Show* is staged for the television cameras. Recognizing that only the most extreme language and bizarre antics are shown, and recognizing as well that these acts aren't authentic, one might assume that a sensible public wouldn't be interested in this form of "entertainment." That assumption, of course, was wrong. Despite the revelations, Springer's show continued to be the highest-rated afternoon program in the country.

It also appears that a "significant" number of Americans believed that they were kidnapped by aliens and taken to a spaceship, according to one report. In fact, Harvard professor John Mack has written seriously about these claims. Now these were probably innocent delusional accounts brought about in no small part by suggestions in Hollywood films. Yet the fact that some people (I am not sure what is meant by a significant number) believe these accounts and that a Harvard professor wrote about them demonstrates an obvious departure from common sense.

It may well be that Americans have been able to indulge their fantasies and hedonistic tastes and ignore political realities in the '90s and thereafter because affluence has shielded them from quotidian concerns. In a society where needs are largely satisfied, exotic "wants" emerge. Television programming pushes the envelope of acceptable behavior and language to new and once-hidden areas of moral turpitude. Political excesses are unchallenged largely because of cynicism about all politicians and a growing belief that they are irrelevant anyway.

The real casualty in these public opinions is common sense itself. Public attitudes can no longer be relied on. A combination of complacency, a search for new thrills, and a taste for the bizarre has brought the nation to a place it has not been before. This is the American Oz, a land of manufactured pleasures and political leadership without a conscience. It is a place where no one wants to look behind the curtain. There is the fear that much of what we have been told about our own lives and this polity is fraudulent. For the most part, we prefer to avert our gaze.

It is not that virtue, loyalty, goodwill, and honor have disappeared. Rather, with the public's diminished power of discernment, it is hard to find unadorned sentiment amid the false and superficial claims. This may still be an exceptional nation, but it is less exceptional than it once was, since common sense became increasingly less evident in public opinion.

Marxist Scholars Look for an Escape Hatch As Communism Falls

To paraphrase Calvin Coolidge, the business of American Marxists following the fall of communism in Eastern Europe was to stay in business. Marxist scholars ensconced on American campuses shared a desire to survive. After all, what could happen to a discipline that had been thoroughly discredited by observation and empirical evidence? Could the alchemists rightly demand a place for themselves in science departments? Could the discoverer of the nonexistent element phlogiston demand a chair in the chemistry department?

The Marxist scholar Ralph Milibrand, in an article published in the *New Left Review,* contended that Marxism had "nothing to do with it"; that is to say, the fall of communism and Marxist theory were unrelated. Communist states may have toppled, but then they must not have been rooted in Marxist theory. The "has-nothing-to-do-with-it" argument absolves Marxists of intellectual responsibility and any complicity with the political nightmares their ideology implemented.

The Marxist rescue operation went into full swing, with intellectual heavy-weights throwing their best punches at conservative critics. While the Marxist intellectuals called for absolution for so-called communist states, the former leaders of these nations roiled the waters by maintaining that they had indeed acted in accord with Marxist dogma. Alas, it isn't easy to determine who were the real Marxists. Was it the theoretician on an American campus or the political leader acting in Marx's name and relying on his theory?

Many Marxist scholars avoided this embarrassing question by suggesting that neither Western democracy nor communism holds the key to future social emancipation. This is the intellectual trump card for Marxists: moral equivalence. In Edward Herman and Noam Chomsky's book *Manufacturing Consent,* the authors contend that "in countries where the levers of power are in the hands of a state bureaucracy, the monopolistic control over the media, often supplemented by official censorship, makes it clear that the media serves the end of a dominant elite." Of course, that dominant elite could be either a Soviet *nomenklatura* or the American bourgeoisie.

While equivalence and imbalance have appeared in communist literature for years, the Marxist rationalizations during this period were particularly grating. While communist leaders denounced their despotic former regimes, American Marxists offered apologies. The most significant rescue operation involved absolving Marxism from the sins of communism. It has been customary for Marxist intellectuals to argue that the modifications introduced into Marx's theory by Lenin vitiated the shape of communism. It follows that if Marx was blameless, his disciples remain equally so.

Most of these Marxist intellectual rantings occurred at a time when communism was beyond salvation. That explains why these intellectuals were often critical of communism but never Marxism. In fact, most Marxists believe that the master's theory is well equipped to analyze the flaws in capitalism as well as the flaws in communism. The authoritarian rigidity of communism, they claim, is detached from Marxism, for the intellectuals contend that the theory at its core entails the subordination of the state to the society.

Yet no matter how clever the absolution, Marxism remains inextricably tied to the failure of communist states. These experiments in human nature followed a line of argument taken directly from the master's ideas. To deny that reality is to deny Marx. That is precisely what the Marxists cannot do. As a consequence, they engage every circumlocution their clever minds can concoct. In the long term, however, this cannot work. Those who were ravaged under Marxist rule will never again allow the theory to be translated into a social organism, no matter in what benign form the theory is presented. It is one thing for American academics eager to justify their positions to legitimate Marxist theory; it is quite another to live under a Marxist regime that violates the dictates of human nature.

Some scholars have gone even further and sought to absolve communist horrors, such as those visited on the citizens of the Soviet Union. Richard Thurston, a history professor at Miami University of Ohio, offered an explanation for the American apologists of the former Soviet Union. In response to a Library of Congress exhibit on the Soviet Union, Thurston wrote: "The exhibition's brochure highlighted only the repressive nature of the Soviet regime, ignoring its positive (though flawed) accomplishments." Thurston went on to suggest that the exhibitors had a responsibility to present a balanced picture. Instead, he contended, the exhibit related "almost solely to state repression and violence, ranging from 'Repression and Terror' and 'Secret Police' to 'Deportations.'" According to Professor Thurston, there was an astonishing gap, since nothing was shown on "the growth of education, upward social mobility, increased availability of medical care, urbanization, or anything else that might be considered positive." Presumably these features of Soviet life would have provided a textured and somewhat less monochromatic view of Soviet life. Yet it is in precisely this "balanced" analysis that the truth gets twisted; it is in suggesting that evil means had an occasional desirable end that the picture of Soviet communism becomes blurred.

Surely if the Soviet Union is depicted in a balanced way, so too should other totalitarian regimes. Nazism should be seen against a backdrop of an orderly society with industrial production increasing dramatically. Maoism should be evaluated on the basis of declining Chinese birthrates. In fact, there is virtually no rationalization to be spared in the interest of balance. Professor Thurston asks epigrammatically, if Soviet repression was so widespread "why, for example, did so much popular zeal exist for the Soviet effort in World War II? Why, decades after Stalin's death, did numerous Soviet citizens continue to speak favorably of him?" If these are baffling questions to Thurston, he should also ask why some Germans continue to speak favorably of Adolf Hitler and why there was general support for the German invasion of the Soviet Union in 1941. That some people may support, indeed benefit, from repression does not in any way mitigate its horror. That documents may exist rationalizing Soviet repression is hardly surprising. The entire Soviet government's information apparatus was designed to rationalize repression.

In fact, when Professor Thurston writes, "It is no longer evident that terror, in the sense of mass violence imposed on society by the state, was the key to Soviet life at any time, with the possible exception of the period of collectivization," his true apologist stripe appears. No longer evident to whom? Most former

Soviet leaders now readily admit that the state imposed mass violence on those in the Soviet Union for its entire history. That Thurston cannot accept this fact is yet another painful example of the extent to which American scholars of the Soviet empire have been compromised in their effort to create a balanced picture. Thurston notes, "Of course we should pay considerable attention to forced labor camps and prisons, the horrors of collectivization, and other grotesque crimes against humanity that occurred under Soviet rule." But, he says—and here is the rub—it is misleading to rely on this theme as a depiction of the period from 1917 to 1985. Misleading?

That the Cold War should end with American scholars defending the former Soviet Union is the clearest testimony that their commitment was unmoved by evidence, that "balance" was a delusion of superficial pedagogy. The one overriding theme in Soviet history was its repression at every level of life and in every sector of the culture. To deny this conclusion or moderate its effect is to be complicit in concealing the crimes of the past. And that is precisely what Thurston and his ilk did. They fostered new crimes by concealing or explaining away old ones.

The 1996 Campaign Was Most Notable for Being Bereft of Political Discourse

While few presidential candidates in the past had the ability to discuss issues against a backdrop of fundamental political concerns, there was nonetheless an implicit awareness that philosophy formed practical politics. However, the political discussion of the 1996 campaign was little more than the assemblage of fragments from the past without meaning or depth. Several factors accounted for this. Television coverage compressed all conversation into sound bites. The two presidential debates were characterized by candidates addressing as many topics as possible. Hence the need for shorthand responses. It defies imagining to consider the Lincoln-Douglas debates taking place in the television age.

Another issue is the dumbing down of debates to accommodate audiences unresponsive to sophisticated argumentation. Arthur Finkelstein, Al D'Amato's Svengali, ran several successful U.S. Senate campaigns organized around the puerile suggestion that D'Amato's opponents were liberal. Presumably, a "liberal" designation disqualifies a candidate for public office. Why this should be so, of course, isn't explained. Candidates rely on compassion and quips and avoid erudition.

It is obvious that a "man of the people" persona must be cultivated. How else can one explain President Clinton's saxophone rendition of "Heartbreak Hotel"? This treacly attempt at the common touch makes it impossible to consider universal themes such as Pelagianism and original sin or perfectibility and imperfectibility. The Aristotelian question of politics—how ought we organize ourselves to live together?—is lost amid the welter of overheated clichés.

In an effort to produce a victory, pollsters attempt to formulate a constituency map. The topography is based on appeals to "soccer moms," the elderly, baby boomers, Generation X, etc. Every group gets something, as the campaign engages in a seduction of various constituencies in an effort to produce a margin of victory. Therefore, themes are reduced to promises, and there is something for everyone.

Campaigns are run to win elections; they are largely unrelated to governance. As one state chairman indicated to me, "Ideas are fine, but my only interest is in winning." Policy positions are first and foremost instruments for electability. Is it any wonder the public has grown cynical about campaign promises? Dumbing down may be the handmaiden of campaigns, but the public intuitively recognizes the fraudulence of grand campaign promises.

A brave new world of images and coiffed hairstyles and hollow speeches characterize politics. Don't be shrill, don't be contentious, don't sound learned, don't ignore the admonitions handlers offer candidates. The result is blandness, a Hollywoodization of politics in which tinsel covers more tinsel. Candidates don't have souls; in fact, if they did, the pundits would reject them. These are hollow men on a mission of deception.

Investigation teams are the campaign henchmen. It is their job to dig up dirt or find a quotation which, taken out of context, will embarrass the opponent. I can vividly recall a reporter asking me, during a statewide campaign, if I was an idealogue. Amused by the question, I replied, "I am an idealogue in the tradition of Lincoln, Solzhenitsyn, and Reagan." This comment appeared in a television ad paid for by my opponent, but the last half of the sentence had been dropped. I appeared on camera saying, "I am an idealogue. . . ." In fact, the strategy works. Newspaper editorials described me as hopelessly rigid. The 1996 presidential campaign used a quote Bob Dole had made about Medicare twenty years ago. Here again, a statement was taken out of context to convey a false impression, in this case that Dole was opposed to Medicare for elderly citizens.

So debased are political campaigns that it is no exaggeration to claim that American political discourse came to an end in the '90s. Politics today is nothing more than the competition over ads and images. The candidates no longer run for office; they have become puppets to be handled, manipulated, coached, coaxed, and restrained. Independent political thought unfettered by pundits has been relegated to the dustbin of history. Where this will end is anyone's guess, but it stands to reason that a democratic republic cannot withstand this challenge to its essence. The end of political discourse may foreshadow the end of our system of government as we have known it.

Children Are Forced into the "Small Adults" Role of Yesteryear

When I was a youngster living on Coney Island, I was fascinated by the signs advertising the sideshow at Luna Park. Appearing were the man with a forty-foot beard, a woman with three breasts, and the original Tom Thumb. Although I beseeched my parents to take me through the sideshow portals, my overtures were invariably greeted with the reply, "That show is not for children." Today, the sideshow sometimes appears on local television at 3:30 in the afternoon, timed to attract children returning from school. Guests on *The Jerry Springer Show,* syndicated by Universal Television, are invited to discuss every perversity the mind can conjure.

In fact, television producers are hard at work destroying childhood. When I was told, "That show is not for children, " I understood that there were adult secrets that should not penetrate the innocent barriers of childhood. There was a clear and inviolate shield. Some conditions were appropriate for kids, and some weren't. Although childhood is largely an invention of the twentieth century, it has (at least until recently) served bourgeois society very effectively. Mom and dad determined the value system of their children, acculturating them in the appropriate ways of the world.

In the distant past, the sixteenth to nineteenth centuries, children were simply small adults, exposed to all the secrets of adulthood at an early age and expected to embrace adult responsibilities such as full-time employment. The line between a small adult and a mature adult was blurred. But now, to an astonishing degree, the youngest Americans are revisiting that distant past. Television, the Internet, films, and popular magazines reveal all the secrets of adulthood to children at a very early age, despite the best-laid plans of parents. The remarkable condition of contemporary children is their relative sophistication. If a child merely listens to the communications din, he is exposed to oral sex, philandering, ménage à trois, and homosexual practices.

The sideshow of Luna Park in my distant past is literally child's play today. As a consequence, childhood is rapidly evanescing. The language of children is coarse and devoid of innocence. Young girls dress in a manner that is intentionally coquettish. The styles at retail shops like The Gap and The Limited are the same for adults and children. Children hear and see everything, including things that were once the preserve of adults only. Parents rarely say to children, "That comment isn't for your ears."

Although President Clinton glibly refers to the need for an information autobahn on which students are linked to the World Wide Web, pornography dominates this system and is as accessible to youths as adults. Meanwhile, the U.S. film rating system, designed to differentiate age-appropriate films from adult films, has pushed the envelope of taste to new extremes. The "R" of several years ago is now "PG-13," supposedly appropriate for the youngest teenagers. Kids also act like adults in the marketplace. In our affluent society, kids have their own financial resources. They don't have to ask dad for a five-spot (or is it now a ten-spot?). Marketers, recognizing this trend, appeal directly to youthful consumers.

It is also the case that the age of the first sexual encounter gets younger each year, according to recent polls. Virginity after fifteen is the exception rather than the rule, and college freshmen are very often chastised if still virginal. Monica Lewinsky became the pinup girl for a generation: a child of divorce and youthful sexual encounters. Alas, it is hard to protect youths from pedophiles when so many children act like adults well before their time. The disappearance of childhood has been accompanied by the disappearance of innocence. Children are now expected to fend for themselves, to make sense out of a world of arcane adult secrets that are no longer encrypted. The code of adults has been exposed by prime-time television and, try as they may, parents cannot shield their children from the onslaught of popular culture.

It is difficult being a child of modernity. Technology has brought us back to the sixteenth century. Children are increasingly treated like small adults and in every crevice of the culture are confronted by sophisticated themes rarely considered by children in most of the twentieth century. From a personal perspective, I prefer the childhood of innocence, when a child accepted the admonition, "That isn't for you." Perhaps I did miss something in the Luna Park sideshow, but it was nothing my tender sensibility really needed.

Some Contemporary Children's Books Lack an Appropriate Moral Basis

Once upon a time, children's books told tales of heroes and villains. They invariably presented a Manichean world in which good triumphed over evil. Children might be scared, but they were assured that the forces of light could easily be distinguished from the forces of evil. Well, that scenario of yesteryear has been replaced by a very different condition today.

The 1994 Newberry medal for the "best" children's book was awarded to Lois Lowry for *The Giver.* This is a tale about a hypothetical community in which issues of suicide, euthanasia, and mental telepathy are emphasized. Characters in this novel reside in a controlled community with narrowly defined roles as birthmothers, caretakers, nurturers, laborers, givers, etc. The government determines how many children will be allowed in each family. In the House of the Old, leaders decide when a person is to be released (read: put to death). At the Ceremony of Release there is a toast, and a goodbye speech given by the person to be "released." Upon the birth of twins, only one is permitted to survive. Invariably, the smaller twin is "released" through a lethal injection. On one occasion in the book, a twelve-year-old objects to the practice, but he is mollified by a Giver who points out that her daughter asked to be released ten years earlier and was given a syringe with which to inject herself.

In one California town, several parents complained about the use of this book in an elementary school. But when they complained about this literature as insensitive to the value of life, these parents were told that "public education may not be the best choice for them." I am sympathetic to the complainants.

What conceivable benefit can there be for youngsters in a book of this kind? Are ten-year-olds prepared to make judgments about euthanasia?

Now that Ms. Lowry has a prizewinning book, she will be given another contract and her book will be accorded a special place in school libraries. The question that remains, however, is the role of philosophical relativism in children's literature. What once inspired, now enflames. What once was the axial standard for moral behavior—tales of *Horatio Alger, Toodle,* and *The Little Engine That Could*—has been converted into amorality. After all, contend teachers and librarians, in this complicated world do we have a right to tell children how to conduct themselves?

My reply is, you have a right and an *obligation* to do so. Teachers have an obligation to select books that provide a moral basis for good behavior. Homer is a better guide for the future than Ms. Lowry, no matter what the rationalizers contend. Virtue must be cultivated. The good must defend itself not merely against the bad but against the indifferent, the complacent, and the relative.

If the myths in our culture are derived from merely the pragmatic, then "anything goes" will be the lyric for social discourse. Children cannot be expected to make philosophical judgments without a grounding in what is right and what is wrong, what is good and what is bad. To assume, as contemporary pedagogues do, that students can arrive at sensible judgments from the exchange of opinion about controversial issues is wrongheaded. Critical-mindedness does not occur in a vacuum. Students must have a knowledge of morality if they are to make moral decisions.

Unfortunately, the democratic idea that the free exchange of opinion will inevitably yield truth is betrayed by a different reality. The free exchange of *intelligent* opinion may lead inexorably to truth, but *only* if the opinions have value. In our era we have debased this notion with a belief in the equality of all opinions and a reliance on the pedagogical idea that any controversial notion can be the subject of class discussion. Is it any wonder that Johnny can't read, Mary can't add, and neither can distinguish between right and wrong?

Television News Presentations Destroy Historical Perspective

I often have the impression that the public suffers from historical amnesia. The issues of yesterday have been dumped in the dustbin of the past. News images stretch across our television sets only to be discarded moments later. The crisis of the moment becomes a distant memory in a few weeks.

Whatever happened to the Three Mile Island crisis, an event fraught with potential doomsday scenarios? Whatever happened to the word *meltdown,* which once entered our consciousness as a fearsome prediction? Whatever happened to the North Korean crisis? Weren't Kim Il Sung and then his son Kim Il Jong prepared to launch nuclear weapons against their southern neighbor? Weren't we told that if Saddam Hussein remained in power the Middle East will be destabilized? Isn't he still Iraq's leader?

Weren't there dire predictions of Armageddon ten years ago? Didn't we hear of threats to the world's food supply? Weren't there predictions of a Greenhouse Effect with millions of worldwide casualties? Whatever happened to acid rain? Why have these thoughts drifted from our consciousness?

It may well be that there is a continuing competition for our attention. Events are packaged. Half the celebrities on the cover of *Time* magazine in the last twenty years are probably unknown to us now. An incident is usually described as a "crisis." A matter that is sometimes ordinary must be given panache to convert it into a news story.

Each night, stories are shoehorned into the half-hour evening news. Invariably, producers will say upon entering a studio, "What's happening?" Suppose nothing of note is happening; then it is up to the producer to find a "lead." It must be interesting (read: sensational). It must pack a punch; it must keep an audience riveted to the screen. Nuance must be removed, lest confusion reign. Words like *crisis* are so overused in an effort to attract an audience that "an important issue," a "crucial matter," and a "crisis" are all melted down in the cauldron of news programming. What emerges are story lines whose seriousness is impossible to determine. Moreover, what is reported is what is known. That which is unknown, quite obviously, is not reported. Most significant, what is not reported is, from an existential point of view, nonexistent. Therefore, we know only what television news directors tell us, and they tell us only what is likely to attract an audience.

As a consequence, every story is earth-shattering. It isn't possible to engage in refinements. If someone decides to run for president, it's a story, and if someone decides not to run, it's a story. Every theory about world affairs that has Cassandra-like qualities is given a headline. It is only a slight exaggeration to contend that the fall of the Soviet empire is, from the standpoint of television news, not so different from a weather report, a film review, or a story about the dangers of Alar, an insecticide used on apples. Some of the most dramatic stories of the last few decades were bogus: the "meltdown" at the Three Mile Island nuclear facility; the Paris peace talks to "end" the war in Vietnam; Gorbachev's desire for "socialism with a human face"; the "great depression" of 1987 after a precipitous slide in the stock market. Yet there are rarely public corrections, because the news is like a stream whose water flows without cessation. There isn't time or inclination for reflection. The public is battered from side to side, panicked about food that shouldn't be eaten, water that cannot be consumed, air that you shouldn't breathe, and sun rays that mustn't touch your skin. If one takes news stories seriously, it's time to move into a fully air-conditioned, fully climate-controlled box.

For kids, the news is nightmare time. My eight-year-old asks, after catching a glimpse of the news, "Daddy, is the world coming to an end?" How can one believe anything else? Chiliastic scenarios sell. The mundane or even the uplifting does not attract audiences. Consider the enormous popularity of the O. J. Simpson trial—a case of murder, sex, drugs, beatings, and perversity, all set in Beverly Hills. It's as if Aaron Spelling had produced the event as prime-time programming.

Hype destroys perspective. Only what we see this moment, counts. History, to quote James Joyce, is a nightmare from which we cannot awaken. Yet television news is for sleepwalkers. It is to history what a shooting star is to eternity. In the aggregate, news has an effect: It numbs our sensibility, destroying the power of discernment. The information explosion is the enemy of judgment. How can one decide on anything when there is so much to know?

The next result, I suspect, is that the public's power of discernment will be arrested. There is virtually no way to determine the importance of current events. Television news failed to present an equivalent of VJ Day after the fall of the Soviet Union. There was no celebration of our victory, in fact there wasn't even any recognition of our achievements. Trivia dominated and still does. There are merely reports, never-ending reports, until the news is like chatter without respite. One report is attached to the next, and the boundaries between stories are lost in the fog of continual reportage. Perhaps one day, when histories are written, we will appreciate the magnitude of the moment. But for now, we are deprived of any glory, lacking any perspective.

Teachers, relying on a pedagogy of openness, might say to their students, "What should we do about the consumption of fossil fuels?" It is a question pregnant with possibilities, but in the absence of knowledge and context, the teacher would be as well disposed to ask what we should do about extraterrestrials or ghosts. Lacking historical perspective and knowledge of economic theory, any answer will do. In fact, in assessing the news, any answer will do.

Is the present merely the beginning of the deluge? Any answer will do. Is the image of the day a crisis about which I should be alarmed? Any answer will do. This, in a nutshell, is the disease of presentism. At the moment, it has no known cure.

The Government Health Gestapo Switches from Cigarettes to Burgers

The '90s demonstrated vividly that the American government is willing to go almost to any length to protect Americans from the consequences of their own decisions. It is increasingly apparent that the same elite—in conjunction with government officials—that have demanded $516 billion from the tobacco industry will now be turning their attention to other business targets.

The *Wall Street Journal* has nominated Big Booze as the next target. But I'm persuaded that the next target will be a food industry that is allegedly inattentive to cholesterol levels and fat contents. Never mind that Americans eat better, more nutritious foods than ever before. Big Mac and the Whopper will replace Joe Camel. Already, a spokesman for the Yale University Center for Eating and Weight Disorders has said of America's eating patterns, "We have to start thinking about this in a more militant way." The Food Police are mobilizing.

The offensive is predictable: A causal link will be established between the consumption of Whoppers and heart disease. Health officials will testify that this linkage imperils the health of Americans. Plaintiffs' attorneys will jump into the controversy with a class-action suit arguing that hamburgers shorten life expectancy. Young witnesses will contend that the advertisements for burgers are irresistible and the taste makes them addictive. Attorneys general will demand just compensation for increased health costs. Finally, Congress will demand a deal that will pay for Washington's next spending splurge.

The case against Big Tobacco set the stage for the case against fast food. McDonald's beware. The argument, however foolish, will appear to hold water, because obesity is a national scourge. Oprah Winfrey will likely devote a program to the notion that what you eat can kill you. Some Naderite group will consider putting "skull and crossbones" stickers on McDonald's and Burger King windows. Of course, what will clinch the case is that burgers—it will be noted—are "killing" our children. The food police, like the tobacco gestapo, will be shameless.

The president will appear on television after jogging and say, "I've finally broken the burger habit. From now on I'll eat tofu rice cakes. They taste good, and they're good for you." McDonald's, Burger King, Wendy's, and others will fight back, but they will be overrun by the healthy-food juggernaut. The newly imposed taxes on burgers will be equivalent to the former price of a hamburger. This move, a prominent legislator will say, will curb the consumption of these "terrible" products.

What all this will mean, of course, is that a black market for Big Macs will emerge on Indian reservations, where the consumption tax does not apply. Eighteen-year-olds will be found dead on the highway after speeding to reservations in an effort to buy the now-very-rare Big Mac. Once the anti-burger campaign is in full swing, a university study will undoubtedly demonstrate "conclusively" that the consumption of hamburgers does shorten lives . . . by two days and seven hours. Nonetheless, the president will be compelled to say that any shortening of life is a matter about which we as a people should remain vigilant. Even the president's supporters will chortle at this whopper.

Cars that had "Save the Forest" bumper stickers will have bumper stickers that say, "We nailed the Whopper, Pizza Hut is in our sights." Tennis pros will publicly rip McDonald's emblems from their gear, to convince food guardians that such "despicable" sponsors will not be embraced. Eating "properly" will soon take on a moralistic tone. "What you eat is not only good for you, it's good for your country." The tidal wave of public opinion will be unstoppable. Children will ask their parents what it was like when you could go to McDonald's for hamburgers and fries. Such freedom will be a distant memory.

Of course, the cancer and heart disease rates won't change. People won't live longer. Health costs won't go down. Moralists for a healthier America will feel better about the state of public health, but after hamburgers pass from the scene, it will be hard to recall why the campaign started in the first place. Does anyone remember cyclamates? Welcome to the brave new world where the public health gestapo is on the march for new targets in its ever-expanding extortion racket.

Liberals Have Freedom to Criticize Some Issues for Which Conservatives Would Be Flogged

New Age critics have finally come to their senses about American social conditions and now proclaim that one need not be "a right-wing crazy" to promote . . . (fill in the blank). The Op-Ed page of the *New York Times* regularly runs liberal apologias for conservative opinions. Self-proclaimed liberals say that sex education doesn't work, or push abstinence. They now recognize that two-parent families are better than one-parent families.

In fact, a liberal can get away with criticism for which a conservative would be verbally flogged. It is now possible for liberals such as Nat Hentoff to criticize abortion from a left-wing perspective. For years, conservatives argued that the era of self-fulfillment and narcissism was having a deleterious effect on the family, and saying that the nation would pay dearly for such self-indulgence. Such criticism was usually described as a narrow-minded attack on feminism. Thirty years after feminism began its radical assault on the family and the damage could be assessed, however, the family was rediscovered by many of the selfsame feminists. Who would have thought that the same editorialists who dismissed the family as a nonutilitarian social construct would eventually embrace it as the answer to anomie?

This is not another version of "what goes around, comes around." The conservative view of society hasn't changed. In fact, sensible people—whatever they call themselves—understand that social experimentation comes with a cost. Yet that point doesn't mean very much unless it is cast as liberal apostasy—from the person who went through the experiment, even promoted it, only to discover that moment of illumination, that epiphany. Most sensible people greet such revelations with a justifiable ho-hum response: "Oh you mean it finally dawned on you that teenagers who have children out of wedlock increase their chances of living in lifelong poverty. How clever of you!"

But since liberals' apostasy is now ritualized in the newspapers of record, I propose that conservatives act as if they too had lost their way. They should contend that after trying drugs, divorcing, ignoring their kids, growing long hair, quitting their jobs, indulging sexual cravings, seeking liberation through therapy, searching for the real self, rejecting their parents . . . the epiphany came when they hit bottom. There, looking up from the social pit, came the realization that there are no substitutes for the family, morality, common sense, altruism, hard work, and traditional principles.

For the most part, the liberals who have conceded that they were wrong have only partially come to their senses. We usually see only narrowly selected understandings. A New York City liberal might decide that there are too many homeless people on the streets of her neighborhood, for instance. Or a parent who once thought it appropriate to say "anything goes as long as you use condoms," now finds that her advice may have been misguided.

Let all of these liberals speak at once. Let them be anthologized in a book that examines their partial admissions. And then let them have the credit for a Victorian counterrevolution. Let them set right what they have torn asunder.

The Statue of Liberty Is a National, Not International, Treasure

Multiculturalists and devotees of spiritual groups support the placement of a brass plaque of a poem by Sri Chinmoy, the leader of a spiritual group, on the base of the Statue of Liberty. The plaque is the latest of the Sri Chinmoy's Peace Blossom poems devoted to spiritual peace and self-transcendence. That a guru, a native of Bangladesh, preaches tranquility and hope is not unusual. What is unusual is that the U.S. Park Service deemed it appropriate to have Chinmoy's poem grace the Statue of Liberty.

Plaques are few at the statue. There is a marker from the Masons to honor their role in building the statue, another designating the statue a National Corrosion Restoration Site, and one from the Association of Civil Engineers. In the museum at the statue's base is a bronze rendering of Emma Lazarus's "New Colossus," which includes the memorable line, "Give me your tired, your poor, your huddled masses, yearning to breathe free." Clearly, the Sri Chinmoy goals of international peace and friendship are on the surface unobjectionable. Some might contend that the poem evokes a '60s mantra of peace, love, truth, and beauty, but that is beside the point.

Diane Dayson, superintendent of the Statue of Liberty and the person who made the decision about the plaque, said at the installation ceremony, "With this initiative, the Statue of Liberty now belongs not only to America, but to the whole world. What better symbol than 'Lady Liberty' to lead us all to the light of peace and harmony!"

Not so fast! The Statue of Liberty may be a gift from France to cement a relationship between the two nations, but the statue does not belong to the world in either a figurative or a literal sense. Many nations in the world do not share our view of liberty, and many are not devoted to the goals of peace and harmony. Most significant, wresting the statue from the unique traditions of the United States and internationalizing her drives yet another nail in the coffin of our distinctive heritage.

Multiculturalists view the United States as a geographic entity without a national ethos and historical tradition. The United States is considered one of many nations, no more distinctive or prominent than others and certainly not exceptional in any way other than economic abundance. This is not to suggest that either Chinmoy or Dayson shares that view. But what the Peace Blossom plaque does suggest is that an idiosyncratically American monument can be internationalized by the people entrusted with preserving our national treasures.

This condition is not lost on some Americans, who have managed to withstand a reeducation in generalized peace, harmony, brotherhood, and goodness. On reading the Chinmoy plaque, a visitor from Ohio said, "This is too much fluff. You can't read through it. And it doesn't really encompass the meaning of the statue." Indeed it does not. For most Americans, the statue is a symbol for people who came from every corner of the globe to find hope and opportunity in the United States. Clearly, immigrants always seek hope and opportunity whatever their destination, but rarely have dreams been realized as they have been in this nation. Hence, the distinctiveness of America, where the dream and the reality converge.

To transform that vision into an abstract spiritual family of all people seeking peace is at once sciolistic and pernicious. The Statue of Liberty is a national treasure, not an international one. The dream it embodies is an American dream. The statue doesn't belong to the whole world any more than the Grand Canyon does. Can you imagine the French response at "internationalizing" the Eiffel Tower?

Although the Statue of Liberty conveys a message many Americans would like others to imbibe, most people realize that only this nation has transformed that message into reality. To make an esoteric spiritual argument is to debase, however inadvertently, the heritage of this nation. And to monumentalize the Chinmoy plaque was a slap in the face of those immigrants who looked to the Statue of Liberty as the distinctive face of American culture.

Bizarre Fashion Reflects Postmodernist Culture

The world of deconstruction, with its characteristics of cultural nihilism, has afflicted fashion. Where once couturiers made dresses to enhance a woman's appearance, now designers have "deconstructed" clothes to make women look like bag ladies.

In 1992, European collections showed the "impoverished" look. Holes and tears were made in the clothes to create the illusion of destitution. It is hardly original for the wealthy to spend thousands of dollars to look poor, but these dresses, representing the latest in deconstructionist fashion, took dressing down to a new low. "Unfinished" fashion, with pants crying out for cuffs or a hem, or torn jackets with threads hanging down, represented a cultural wasteland in which aesthetic quality had retreated before nihilism. The down-on-your-luck look was not restricted only to holes, linings, and tatters; it also included wrinkles, introduced in rumpled dresses.

This fashion was characterized by destruction, a desire emboldened by a culture that excoriated beauty and apotheosized ugliness and disfigurement. These fashion cultists were the children of Nietzsche entering a netherworld of self-involvement and destructive behavior. Fortunately, sensible women didn't buy these dresses, which were quickly consigned to the ash heap of history. However, the effect these designers have on the culture is underestimated at one's peril. It is the tastemakers that receive attention, not the designers of traditional, easy-to-wear, comfortable, and attractive clothes.

Another bizarre fashion trend of the '90s was to wear pants so low on the hip that one's underwear was revealed. This style was born when rap singers decided to imitate prison inmates, who wear trousers on their hips because they aren't issued belts or suspenders.

The low-hip look eliminated the waistline and produced a walk that resembled a shuffle. In some respects, the new pants look defied gravity—which might explain why its adherents walked as if hurtling a hula hoop around their waist. To have your pants fall down, in the street parlance of the time, is to be street-smart. Presumably, wearing one's pants on the hip leads to some sort of identification with one's brothers in prison. The look forces the pants to bunch at the ankle. To assure this bunching, high-top, unlaced sneakers are required. Not any sneaker, of course. The sneaker of choice was Nike, the one Michael Jordan advertised. Finally, the '90s look was not complete unless one wore a baseball cap backward. It was as if a whole generation of kids were training to be catchers, who wear their caps backward in order to accommodate a mask.

That wearing a cap backward and letting one's pants fall down were thought of as cool is testimony that any silly idea can translate into a fashion trend. This fashion trend, however, was designed as a political statement. The antisocial, the criminal, and the sociopath were the models for youths who transcended proletarian identification and jeans for the world of inmates. Being street-smart meant being street-tough, and tough translated into an imitation of rap singers who thumb their nose at the establishment and give the finger to authority. Many fashions have been ugly and occasionally ridiculous, but few were more bizarre than deliberately having your pants fall down. In some respects, even Rudi Gernreich's topless look was more aesthetically credible than a fashion statement resembling a pratfall.

The fashion world's effort to push the envelope to ever-greater extremes reached its apogee with "grunge." Grunge is the name of a Seattle-spawned style that emanated from an apparent desire to identify with the homeless. It was the '90s version of '70s thrift-shop chic, consisting of baggy, ripped clothes, plaid shirts that weren't tucked into pants, goofy knit hats, bell bottoms, and army boots or heavy Doc Martin shoes. Designers Marc Jacobs, Anna Sui, and

Christian Frances Roth engaged in their own versions of sloppy attire for a price well in excess of the Salvation Army model.

Grunge, popularized by Seattle rock groups, was not restricted to clothes; it involved an entire look. If you wanted real grungy hair, you simply didn't wash it. If you should shower as a result of mom's urging, there was no need to despair. Rusk Radical Hair Creme turned squeaky-clean hair into credible, lived-in hair. But why, in heaven's name, would anyone want to be grungy? Clearly, grunge is yet another in a long line of ephemeral fashions that have challenged bourgeois culture and conventional dress. What it presupposed was that the rebellious children of the middle class needed to find another way to irritate their parents. That children might accept this nonsense is understandable. But grunge challenged the very essence of fashion when rags were worn by the rich who could afford any design.

In my misguided bourgeois state, I once thought it odd that the homeless population should parade around urban streets collecting rags from garbage cans and piling them into shopping carts. Now I realize that they were recycling designer clothes. They were in the vanguard of grunge. They weren't in the back of the trend line; they were leading it. Privileged Americans can now experience homelessness without living on the streets. Filth, sloppiness, and rags are their statement. Parents can't tell kids to wash behind their ears. That dirt is a fashion statement. Teachers must not declaim sloppy attire. It is fashion. How dare Miss Brooks tell her pupils that they must wear clean, white shirts to school? Doesn't she know that stained, torn plaid is in? Even upscale New York area department stores such as Bloomingdale's featured grunge, and I wouldn't have been surprised if Bloomingdale's proprietors started inviting the homeless waifs lying outside the store to parade through its fashion aisles.

Here is re-tread culture with a vengeance. The rags of yesteryear are the fashion statements of today. Where this will lead is hard to imagine. I've heard tell that tailors working with imaginary thread have produced a suit fit for a king. These fellows charged a high price, but the fabric is light as air and easily recyclable. Their work has been featured in Europe, so one can surmise that it will reach these shores shortly. In fact, Madonna often wears their clothes to events where photographers are present. Yes, be the first on your block to wear Will of the Wisp fashions. It may not be much, but it sure beats grunge.

Rap Music Is an Assault on American Culture

Writing in the *Boston Review,* Mark Zanger noted that rap music was "a grassroots poetic movement, massively popular, with sporadic moments of the best popular poetry since Dylan." Here, in unvarnished form, is the misguided view of a proponent of popular culture. It is indeed true that rap is popular, and it is arguably appropriate to suggest that this so-called art form has emerged from the grassroots. But to call it the best poetry since Dylan is absurd, unless, of course, Zanger is making that claim to unmask the banality behind Dylan. I think not.

Mr. Zanger went on to suggest that "rap is the first truly postmodern popular art integrating new technology with neo-primitive content." According to Zanger, rap brings black male folk culture "out for public examination"; it is an art form that gets us "out of the intellectual doldrums." To some degree, Zanger wants to be to rap what Richard Poirier was to the Beatles. He is the intellectual decoder; the person who recognizes the cultural contribution even as others decry rap as ugly and degrading. Lest one forget Norman Mailer's defense of graffiti, there are always intellectuals about to tell us that the marginal is interesting and the degrading has redeeming qualities.

In fact, rap is primitive. It reflects a crude language of the streets that is brutal and obscene. Although some critics contend that the music reflects an urban reality, it is a reality solely devoted to the feral and unethical. The working poor who raise their children with a sense of decency and moral concern don't relate to a "poetry" of violence, hate, and obscenity. It is hard to conceive of decent people who would sanction popular rap lyrics that include the most blatant of obscenities. Those words, by the way, are mild compared with the promotion of rape, abuse of women, and race hatred found in underground rap records, which rapidly moved aboveground. In fact, there is scarcely a human indignity this so-called art doesn't countenance. Yet there are critics like Zanger who contend that rap is merely a cultural expression of adolescence and is therefore a barometer of youthful exuberance. If this is true, we are almost certainly on the way to complete degradation. However, the claim is probably grotesque.

Most adolescents don't share the expressed immorality in much of this music. And most teenagers don't listen to rap, notwithstanding its extraordinary appeal. The music appears to be most successful with inner-city youths lacking a moral compass. In their case, rap reinforces a sense of anomie engendered by the ghetto environment. The obvious question is why critics, who presumably should know better, embrace an art of debasement. Although critics have exalted Genet, Artaud, de Sade, and every manner of perversion in the past, there has rarely been a time when a popular art form has sunk so far into the abyss of cultural backwardness. I would contend that some rock critics have found in rap what they have always sought: a way to offend bourgeois sentiments with virtual impunity.

Rap is without pretense. It doesn't couch the horror of its message in verbal symbols like conventional rock; it is raw, unadulterated belligerence. It entails sledgehammer logic. If rap can be called poetry, then tabloid journalism is tantamount to classic literature. It seems to me that the first step in understanding art is describing it accurately. Rap isn't postmodern, because postmodern is a solecism whose meaning is available only to its purveyors. Rap isn't poetry, because all that rhymes isn't poetic. Rap cannot take us out of the intellectual doldrums, because its deafening sounds deracinate thoughtful responses. All the exaggerated claims made in rap's name won't retrieve this music from cultural detritus. The critics who sing its praises suffer from the misguided belief that whatever offends middle-class sensibilities by definition is art. However, any sensible person who can tolerate these sounds long enough to listen for a while will quickly realize that rap is primarily an assault on the culture.

Epilogue

In my opinion, this book doesn't require a conclusion. My musings over a couple of hundred pages offer, one hopes, some insights into the '90s. Yet there are points that I would like the reader to consider.

If the Victorians could reclaim a culture from the clutches of debasement, are there strategies that could be employed to do the same thing now? Perhaps there is an Antonio Gramsci of traditionalism capable of marching through and capturing the cultural institutions of the moment. Perhaps, as well, institutions engaged in "best practices" can pool their resources in order to have a deep and lasting cultural impact.

Why hasn't the hypocrisy of the '60s and '70s radicals received a full airing in the '90s when the results of their efforts have been so apparent? Is that the fault of a media architecture beholden to radicalism, or is it due to the failure of traditionalists who haven't made their arguments effectively, or is it a function of an inexorable Gresham's law of culture in which the bad drives the good out of circulation?

The disparity between a high-octane economy and a moribund culture continues to confound. Obviously, there are positive things to be said about entrepreneurship, initiative, trust, the rule of law, and the free market. Yet one wonders if cultural decay won't at some point bring on the decline of industriousness and the other conditions that foster economic growth. This is an issue at the heart of the '90s culture, yet there aren't many examples from the past from which to make predictions.

Clearly, a society can absorb some degree of hedonism without severely hindering economic gains. But what degree of such erosion is acceptable? No one really knows. Some analysts, such as Francis Fukuyama, contend that we have already reached the logical basement for cultural decay, and that upticks consistent with history and nature will occur. Is this view Pollyannaish or realistic?

Again, it is hard to say.

When the Oscars were conferred for the films of 1999, homosexuality, trans-sexualism, and abortion were celebrated in the films that were honored and in the awards given. Wherever one stands on these matters, celebration seems odd, to say the least. Admittedly, Hollywood is but one barometer of cultural taste, but the level of degradation the film industry promotes is beyond the ken of the average person and may indeed be an unadorned expression of nihilism. Can such an attitude last in an industry dependent on popular taste?

Here, too, the jury is out, albeit the proposition that audiences will tire of the perverse and the bizarre is plausible, if not yet apparent. Implicit in this position is the notion that the children of baby boomers and their children will rebel against the attitudes of their parents and grandparents. After all, a quite small proportion of the population can have a profound effect on cultural trends, as the '60s and '70s generation attests.

Now that I've raised the questions, let me offer several predictions. The course of history is obviously unpredictable, yet if the past is any guide, several conditions might be considered. If wealth is dispersed, as it assuredly will be—probably six times greater in 2100 than it is now—the search for meaning will be even more intense and more of a national concern than was ever the case before. Religious revivalism, what might well be a fourth Great Awakening, is a realistic possibility. In the face of queries that secularism cannot address, spirituality flourishes. The last great religious movement in America was the nineteenth-century Mormon emergence. Perhaps this century will have yet a new religion.

Last, even advanced sensate cultures like ours have within them ideational and idealistic elements. Country music, *Star Wars*, the History Channel, and sports untrammeled by narcissism and money are examples—rare as they may be—of a potential cultural resurgence. It is incumbent on those who care about this matter to emphasize what is uplifting, to remain a refuge for a culture that promotes life-affirming principles. This is the mission for the newly emerging counterculture of this decade.

Admittedly for traditionalists the cultural metamorphosis of the '90s was discouraging. But culture is not static; it can be refreshed. From that observation springs faith, and faith, after all, is always the harbinger of change. As Justice Felix Frankfurter noted, "The ultimate foundation of a free society is the binding tie of cohesive sentiment. Such a sentiment is fostered by all these agencies of the mind and spirit which may serve to gather up the traditions of a people, transmit them from generation to generation, and thereby create the continuity of a treasured common life which constitutes a civilization."

The decade of denial recklessly damaged that treasured common life, but it can still be reclaimed. Just as the '60s generation sundered the binding ties of cohesive sentiment while enjoying their positions of power in the '90s, new generations await the opportunity to restore society's foundations. America's seemingly boundless capacity for change may soon be our saving grace.

About the Author

Herbert I. London is the John M. Olin University Professor of Humanities at New York University. A graduate of Columbia University (B.A.) and New York University (Ph.D.), Mr. London has served as a senior fellow of the Hudson Institute for more than thirty years and as a member of its Board of Trustees since 1974. He became president of Hudson Institute on September 1, 1997.

He currently serves on the Board of Directors of the National Chamber Foundations, the Board of Trustees for Merrill Lynch Assets Management, and the Rose Hulman University Board of Trustees.

Mr. London ran as a Republican Party candidate for mayor of New York City in 1989, the Conservative Party candidate for governor of New York in 1990, and the Republican Party candidate for New York State comptroller in 1994.

A noted social critic, Mr. London has published articles in major newspapers and journals nationwide, including *Commentary*, *National Review*, the *Wall Street Journal*, the *New York Times*, the *Washington Times*, the *Los Angeles Times*, *Investor's Business Daily*, *Encounter*, and *Forbes*.

He is the author of thirteen books, including *Myths That Rule America* (with Al Weeks), which inspired an NBC Television series of the same title; *Why Are They Lying to Our Children?*; *Military Doctrine and the American Character'* *Armageddon in the Classroom*; *From the Empire State to the Vampire State: New York in a Downward Transition* (with Ed Rubenstein); and as editor of *A Strategy for Victory without War*.